D1527062

LEARNING FOR LIFE

LEARNING FOR LIFE

Moral Education
Theory and Practice

Edited by
Andrew Garrod

Foreword by James R. Rest

Westport, Connecticut
London

370.1140973
L43

Library of Congress Cataloging-in-Publication Data

Learning for life : moral education theory and practice / edited by
Andrew Garrod ; foreword by James R. Rest.
    p.   cm.
    Includes bibliographical references and index.
    ISBN 0-275-94045-4 (alk. paper)
    1. Moral education—United States—History. I. Garrod, Andrew,
1937–
LC311.L43 1992
370.11'4'0973–dc20   91-46756

British Library Cataloguing in Publication Data is available.

Library of Congress Catalog Card Number: 91-46756
ISBN 0-275-94045-4

First published in 1992

Praeger Publishers, 88 Post Road West, Westport, CT 06881
An imprint of Greenwood Publishing Group, Inc.

Printed in the United States of America

The paper used in this book complies with the
Permanent Paper Standard issued by the National
Information Standards Organization (Z39.48–1984).

10 9 8 7 6 5 4 3 2 1

Copyright Acknowledgments

The author and publisher are grateful to the following for allowing use of their
material:

Excerpts from Association for Values Education and Research (AVER), *Prisons:
Teacher's Manual*, Values Reasoning Series. Toronto: Ontario Institute for
Studies in Education, 1978. Reprinted with permission.

Excerpts from Joseph Adelson, "The Political Imagination of the Young
Adolescent," reprinted by permission of *Daedalus*, Journal of the American
Academy of Arts and Sciences, from the issue entitled, "Twelve to Sixteen: Early
Adolescence," Fall 1971.

Excerpts from Erik J. Erikson, *Growth and Crises of the Healthy Personality*.
Reprinted from *Identity and the Life Cycle*, selected papers, published by
Psychological Issues 1, #1, (1959), with the permission of W. W. Norton & Co.,
Inc., Copyright by International University Press Inc.

This book is dedicated to the memories

of

Ann Breslin

Jeremy Vincent

and

Lawrence Kohlberg

Contents

Foreword

James R. Rest

Moral education in U.S. public schools has long been a lively topic. From the early discussions of public schooling in the United States (schooling that would be compulsory and supported by taxes), through the philosophies of education promulgated especially by John Dewey and Émile Durkheim, to current laments about the lack of morals of U.S. youth (which cite increases in vandalism in schools, teen pregnancy, delinquency, and drug abuse), moral education has been seen as a vital part of schooling. Moral education takes place whether or not there is a deliberate and formal curriculum in moral education. The inevitable influence of teachers and schooling upon the values of students has been described as the hidden curriculum, mediated by the moral atmosphere of the school. In addition to these unavoidable influences, throughout the history of U.S. public education there has been a great variety of deliberate and formal curriculum programs in moral education, sometimes allied with religious education, sometimes following from the general humanitarian traditions of Western civilization, and sometimes in the service of frankly partisan and parochial ideological indoctrination.

About 20 years ago, Lawrence Kohlberg initiated a new approach to moral education. One novel aspect was the attempt to cast the products and the process of moral education into psychological constructs that could be measured and tracked throughout actual people in programs and that would enable empirical evaluation, exploration, and experimentation. In other words, Kohlberg attempted to bring the methodology of social science into the educator's art. Educators have long had interesting and reasonable ideas for the goals of moral education, the conditions under which teachers might attempt to influence the moral development of their students, and ideas for curriculum materials and classroom activities; but Kohlberg's innovation was to attempt to conceptualize the features of these activities and processes in psychological and sociological terms amenable to empirical research.

Another new aspect of Kohlberg's approach was his attempt to deal with the problem of indoctrination. The problem of indoctrination arises not only as an abstract concern of educational theory. According to most theorists, education should empower the student by enabling the student to see options and by providing effective strategies for making choices; it is not the role of education to foreclose options and train or otherwise mindlessly condition the student to behave in certain ways chosen by the teachers. So, in abstract educational theory, indoctrination is wrong. Moreover, about 20 years ago, the pluralistic nature of U.S. society was becoming clearer, and political forces were challenging educators who attempted to foist their values upon their students. The Supreme Court, in a series of court cases, interpreted the separation of church and state amendments to the Constitution to mean that teachers in compulsory, tax-supported public schools must not engage in indoctrination of any religious or partisan ideology. Kohlberg's approach to this problem was to emphasize the activities of teachers that empowered students to make informed choices of their own in moral education — in contrast to activities of teachers that might foreclose choice making or impoverish the process of deliberation. Later, Kohlberg emphasized that the teacher's role was not simply that of process facilitator (a value-neutral agent who was there merely to facilitate deliberation) but was also to advocate a vision of an ideal "just community." In other words, the teacher was to portray a possibility that might not otherwise be imagined by the students. But the advocacy was to be through persuasion and appeals to the students' idealism, not through coercion.

Implicit throughout Kohlberg's work was the conviction that moral education was extremely important. Public schooling is the main hope that society has to offset the powerful centrifugal forces that divide our society into different classes, races, religions, and social groups. Public schooling is one of the few chances that society has to prepare people for socially responsible and ennobling lives. While it is true that churches, families, psychotherapists, and other private institutions are important influences in many people's lives, nevertheless more and more of the burden for more and more U.S. youth is falling upon public schools. Moral education must be effective. Kohlberg was really the first to undertake regular, systematic, formal evaluation of his moral education programs. Previous to Kohlberg, evaluation was hit-or-miss if done at all. Taking moral education seriously meant gathering systematic information on the impact of the process — having a bunch of good ideas to start with was not good enough. The educator's job was not complete by making a good case for a program but he or she also had to demonstrate the program's effects. With such information, the educator, hopefully, would learn from the program, come to understand which activities are effective with whom, and could then redesign a more powerful program the next time.

This book shows that much has happened in moral education in the past 20 years. We are now far beyond the phase where mere possibilities and approaches were sketched out. These chapters report a large array of programs that have been ongoing for years. The rich and diverse initial ideas actually have been tried out and there are experiences and track records to report. Moral education is now deliberately attempted in the context of history and English classes, in sports, and in student participation in school governance. As one reads these accounts, the complexities and opportunities are spelled out. The chapters contain the richness of many specific curricular adaptations. The chapters provide specific reactions of students and quotes from group discussions that come from the many years of experience that these authors provide. The chapters contain analyses of evaluation data generated by the many projects.

In these chapters, one sees another sign that moral education is moving along. This is the concern of educators interested in moral education for interfacing with other people and groups also having a stake in public schools. The chapters discuss interfacing with families, with parent groups and school administrators, with the politics of school boards, with rival public-pressure groups, with the nation's secretary of education, and with Supreme Court rulings.

A third sign of the evolution of moral education over the past 20 years is that conceptualization of the main constructs and variables involved in moral education have become more complicated and inclusive beyond the original set of ideas. The work led by Kohlberg himself on the just community has produced a more complicated picture of moral education, and attention to new variables and new analyses of the process of moral education are called for. Other chapters in the book call attention to other variables besides moral judgment and state that moral development is more than concepts of justice. Several chapters propose ways of integrating Kohlberg's key variables with the ideas coming from other traditions. Beyond the conceptualization of the basic process of moral development itself are concepts about the other roles of teaching, working in the school setting, and working with other professionals.

This book should be of value to those who regard moral education as a very important enterprise and who want an update of the experiences and current thinking of many of those working in the field.

Acknowledgments

I am much indebted to the following individuals who provided editorial comment and other assistance in the preparation of this book: Jay Davis, Katherine Fennel, Ann Huebner, Margo Shearman, Felicity Callard, and Vanessa Callard.

I am also grateful to the Presidential Venture Fund of Dartmouth College for providing generous financial support for a conference that was the stimulus for this book.

I give special thanks to A. Keith Willacy for editorial assistance and for preparing the book for publication. Gregory Norman is also thanked; he masterfully coordinated the conference at Dartmouth College for which many of these chapters were written.

Introduction

Andrew Garrod

There is a growing consensus in society that schools and even colleges need to address the issue of moral education, despite arguments over the philosophy and psychology that should guide it and the practice that should characterize it. The familiar litany of juvenile crime, drugs, adolescent pregnancy, the school drop-out rate, and questionable ethics in high places has led to a rekindling of debate. In a period of perceived declining standards, what exactly should educational institutions do about ethical guidance for our youth? How can institutions choose values acceptable to a pluralistic society from among sometimes competing demands from different groups?

The determination to enhance morality, build character, and strengthen ethical standards in the young has found expression in three theoretical models of moral education — values clarification, cognitive development, and character education — that differ radically in their assumptions, methods, and interest in measuring the success of programs derived from the models. These three models have each had a period of ascendancy in the United States in the last 30 years. Values clarification, linked with the names of Rath, Harmin, and Simon and dominant in the 1960s takes as its starting point the philosophy that values are personal things. Given the plurality in our culture of religious, moral, political, and ideological perspectives, values must be a matter of personal concern, reflection, and choice, not of indoctrination or subjugation of the individual to the group in the values domain (Chazan 1985). Through clarifying questions, the teacher must help the students look at alternative values and understand and cherish the values they do choose. Although the model does not appear to be informed by an organic theory and is criticized for its relativism, it is accessible and has been popular with teachers and students.

The cognitive development model was influential in the later 1960s and in the 1970s; it is associated primarily with Lawrence Kohlberg and his colleagues and focuses on moral reasoning. The newly resurgent character education model is currently linked with Ryan, Wynne, and Bennett and stresses the inculcation of a core set of traits and behaviors. These are the two models of moral education that are currently the most influential (Nucci 1989). Both camps are concerned with the moral malaise in our society and put primary emphasis on the role of schools; each sees the role of the teacher as an advocate in one form or another. Both appeal to the same moral ideals and see the role of public schooling as introducing students to conventional norms. Both emphasize moral achievement, which is seen by character education as a set of moral imperatives and by developmentalists as a set of moral procedural imperatives. Both, too, aim to produce full and productive citizens in a democratic society.

Although the development and the character education approaches share common concerns about disturbing trends in contemporary society, there is ultimately no easy resolution between these two camps because their methods are, in large measure, mutually exclusive. Character education focuses on teaching what is right and wrong and emphasizes the moral achievements of the society and culture as a seedbed for moral education. Exposure to elevating role models is viewed as essential, as is the selection of wholesome curriculum materials to transmit culturally approved values to the young. Learners who will absorb these values are viewed as blank slates, essentially passive; they acquire virtue through instruction, social rewards, and punishments. Indoctrination is seen as a legitimate means of transmitting moral values and traditions to the young. An example of the character education approach is Boston University's Center for the Advancement of Ethics and Character that emphasizes, in its moral teaching, core values (respect, integrity, courage, and empathy) and in its didactic teaching, the common philosophical roots of U.S. culture.

Developmental moral education focuses on how to decide what is right and wrong and emphasizes the moral principles that have been established to guide one's moral deliberations in action. It portrays moral education as a process to be developed rather than as truths to be inculcated and views moral knowledge not as transmitted by the culture but as actively constructed by each individual through interaction with the social world. The developmental model characterizes the teacher as an advocate for his or her position, but this advocacy must fall short of indoctrination (Garrod and Howard 1990).

While acknowledging the strength of the character education school, we are presenting a book whose contents are entirely reflective of the developmental mode. Much of this book originated in the conference "Old Challenges/New Directions in Moral Education: What Parents, Teachers, and Colleges Can Do" held at Dartmouth College, New Hampshire, in 1988. A year after the tragic death of Lawrence Kohlberg, it seemed appropriate for scholars, researchers, and educators aligned with the developmental school to take stock of past thinking and programs and to explore future lines of research and practice that held promise. The conference included recent work in philosophy related to the practice of moral education, theoretical discussions, curriculum presentations, and reports of psychological intervention studies from the elementary school through the college level. Two central foci of the conference were the burgeoning research on moral orientation and girls' development indebted to the theorizing of Carol Gilligan and reports on democratic schools at elementary, junior, and senior high school levels. Research and writing that fell into three interrelated categories — the process of knowing and the connection to moral issues, the process of reasoning about moral choices, and the process of teaching and how particular interventions may aid moral development — have been collected elsewhere (Garrod in press).

The philosophy and theoretical papers and those strongly grounded in curriculum, pedagogy, and democratic schooling have been collected here. Covering a diverse range of topics, this volume's chapters are connected by their singular focus on, and concern with, issues that are central to moral education. Whether addressing different theories of moral education (Part I), different attempts to implement some of these theories into practice (Part II), or the renewed interest in democratic schools (Part III), the authors collected here represent the cutting edge of the moral education debate.

PART I: THEORETICAL ORIENTATIONS

Broad in scope, Part I offers an overview of theoretical perspectives on moral education. Its four chapters include a synthesis of current thoughts about moral education, an investigation of educational policy option, an exploration of the conflicts parents and children face when the parents want to educate for the child's own good or growth, and an explanation of the moral orientations of justice and care in the context of the classroom.

Barry Chazan argues the commonly held opinion that the discussion of moral education in the academic community has been characterized by great diversity and great confusion. In Chapter 1, "The State of Moral Education Theory," Chazan presents an overview of current thought about moral education. His specific objective is to delineate the major questions, issues, and directions of the topic. Organizing his discussion around three major questions he asks:

What questions has contemporary moral education theory addressed, and what are some of the answers it has proposed? What are the questions that have been neglected or have been inadequately dealt with by contemporary approaches to moral education? and, finally, What are some of the directions that moral education could take in the coming years and decades? A number of the issues raised by Chazan, such as the goals of moral education and how values can be taught, are addressed in depth in subsequent chapters of this book.

In Chapter 2, "Moral Character Education in the United States: Beyond Socialization versus Development," John Snarey and Thomas Pavkov discuss the recent interest in moral character education as an educational policy option to address a perceived decline of morality in U.S. society. They critique two divergent approaches toward moral character education: the socialization approach, which extends the perspective of Émile Durkheim, and the developmental approach, which extends the perspective of Jean Piaget. Traditionally, Durkheimian and Piagetian perspectives have been regarded as standing in opposition to one another. Analysis of current expressions of both views, however, indicates that they also share areas of agreement regarding moral character education. The chapter outlines this common ground and proposes basic guidelines with which to approach moral character education, suggesting that the classroom be used to teach values anchored in the universal principle of justice as exhibited in our nation's classic documents, especially the U.S. Constitution.

Perhaps the most influential movement in moral development and education in recent years is the feminist critique of existing theories and theorists for inadequately representing the moral reasoning and development of women. Carol Gilligan's psychological research and theorizing on caring as a different moral voice and Nel Noddings' exploration of the ethic of care are widely recognized and cited in psychological, educational, and philosophical journals and forums. In her chapter, "Shaping an Acceptable Child," Noddings offers a powerful philosophical and educational argument for caring as a foundation for moral reasoning and education. In her contribution to this volume, Noddings advocates maternal thinking as a basis for both the moral treatment of children and their moral education. This maternal thinking is not limited to mothers or women, Noddings asserts, but arises out of direct care-taking activities. The maternal perspective is characterized by creating and maintaining relationships through caring. Noddings argues that environments should be created to encourage autonomy and empathy in children. For Noddings, educating acceptable children means preparing them to be acceptable in an inner circle of close familial relationships and to be acceptable in wider circles of relationships with friends, colleagues, members of a political community, and so forth. Part of the educational process is also preparing students to select and evaluate the groups from which to seek acceptance. In each, caring and relationships should form the basis of the decision. In Chapter 4, "Two Moral Orientations: How Teachers Think and Act in the Classroom," Kay Johnston brings together theories about moral development and problem solving with a theory about teacher education. Having established her belief in the role of teachers as moral craftspersons, she stresses that the knowledge of moral orientations can help perfect a teacher's craft. Indeed, she argues that successful teachers *must* be able to address an individual student's needs in the greater context of that student's moral orientation toward either the care or justice perspective. In this sense, the ability to react productively to different moral perspectives becomes a very effective strategy in the teacher's interactions with both individual students and the class as a whole. Drawing on her own research with junior high students, Johnston suggests ways in which teachers can develop this strategy.

PART II: MORAL EDUCATION IN PRACTICE

Focusing on the transition from theory into practice, Part II looks at several innovative approaches to the implementation of moral education theory. Chapter topics include the relationship between families and schools as forces in moral education, the use of literature to teach moral reasoning, an educational program that stimulates thought about moral decisions through its examination of the Holocaust, and a discussion of the potential value of competitive team sports in moral development.

In his chapter, "Schools and Families: Partners or Adversaries in Moral Education?" Thomas Lickona explores the reciprocal roles families and schools have as educators of the young. To be effective in their roles as moral educators, schools need the active support of families — support that is often not readily given. Parents are wary of moral lessons in schools that promote moral standards different from those of the home and are upset with activities that undermine respect for parents or invade the family's privacy. By looking at several case studies, Lickona demonstrates that these tensions can be avoided through careful planning and cooperation between sides, whether in the form of parent-teacher peer groups or weekly conferences on moral issues. He asserts not only that parallel forms of moral education can be carried out in both home and the school, but also that deliberate collaboration between schools and families will make significant contributions to the child's moral growth.

In Chapter 6, "Teaching Moral Reasoning in the Standard Curriculum," Robert Swartz focuses on moral education in the classroom. We see how history teacher Michelle Commeyras uses

U.S. literature to teach moral reasoning and decision making. For example, the ways in which dilemmas are faced by characters in *The Hessian* present the opportunity to teach decision-making skills such as considering options, ascertaining relevant facts, and weighing the significance of these facts. Swartz also discusses the difference between teaching moral principles and teaching moral reasoning — "teaching students what is right and wrong versus teaching good thinking about what is right and wrong." Here we see moral education presented from a thinking-skills approach, an approach designed to equip students in this morally complex world to make well-reasoned choices of their own.

In Chapter 7, "Facing History and Ourselves: A Synthesis of History and Ethics in Effective History Education," Margot Stern Strom, Martin Sleeper, and Mary Johnson describe the Facing History and Ourselves National Foundation, which is committed to helping teachers and administrators bring education about twentieth-century genocide, specifically the Holocaust, to students in their communities. The authors show how the program has developed a flexible, interdisciplinary unit appropriate for adolescents who are engaged in understanding human behavior, particularly around the themes of peer pressure, conformity, individual and group behavior, and the role of the individual in a complex society. The chapter explores in detail the goals and materials of the program, the responses of the students and teachers to it, and the reasons for its effectiveness.

In Chapter 8, "Athletic Development and Personal Growth," which explores the opportunities for moral development outside the classroom, Jeffrey Pratt Beedy offers a historical perspective of youth sports in the United States and reviews the ongoing debate as to the value of sports in encouraging personal growth in elementary children. Stressing that adults need to understand the ways children experience the social aspects of sports, Beedy highlights both the potential of social and moral development theories to meet this need and the crucial role that coaches must play. With coach-athlete interactions remarkably similar to those between teachers and students in the classroom, sports and group games can do much to facilitate the process of moral growth. At the very least, they can "encourage thinking, discussion, and interaction between people with different roles" — an encouragement that can help prepare children for an adult world that desperately needs thinking, discussion, and interaction.

PART III: MORAL EDUCATION AND DEMOCRACY

While the previous sections explored moral education theory and practice, Part III focuses on the role that schools can play in the development of democratic values and ways of thinking. Its four chapters describe what is generally known about the cognitive, sociomoral, and political development of adolescents; elucidate the just community approach to high school education; examine the possible role of democratic schooling as a solution to such democratic problems as small voter turn-out; and discuss the founding and maintenance of a democratic forum at the Heath School.

In "The Adolescent as a Citizen," Ralph Mosher argues that if we are to educate for democracy we must recognize that democratic understandings and competencies are inextricably linked to the broader cognitive, sociomoral, and political development of U.S. youth. Summarizing the findings of Piaget, Kohlberg, and Adelson, the author examines what we know generally about these developments in adolescents, especially as they bear on adolescents' abilities to think and act democratically.

Arguing that democratically governed schools promote the psychological development of both students and educators, Robert Howard and Robert Kenny examine the relationship between the governance of schools and moral reasoning in Chapter 10, "Education for Democracy: Promoting Citizenship and Critical Reasoning through School Governance." This chapter outlines the issues that any democratic school must address, such as representation, organization, and respecting the rights of minorities. The authors include descriptions of some of the solutions that have been created in existing democratic high schools.

In Chapter 11, "The Just Community Approach to Classroom Participation" (a chapter congruent theoretically with Chapter 10), Clark Power and Ann Higgins describe and elucidate the just community approach to high school education by focusing on the value of participation as a central moral concept. Where Howard and Kenny emphasize representative democratic governance, Power and Higgins examine direct democratically governed school-within-a-school programs. Examples from the Cambridge Cluster School are given that show that one result of valuing participation seems to be an increasingly serious attitude toward academic learning by the students. Examples that highlight the effects of valuing participation on students' self-esteem and social and interpersonal abilities are also given from the ongoing Bronx project. Finally, research results looking at changing attitudes toward attendance by the Bronx just community students and comparison group students in the two schools are presented and discussed as exemplifying the theoretical connection between the moral value of participation and positive but conventional student attitudes and behavior.

In her description of a democratic forum at the Heath School — a kindergarten through eighth grade school in Brookline, Massachusetts — Ethel Sadowsky shows that democratic schools are not confined to the high school level. Her chapter, entitled "Taking Part: Democracy in the Elementary School," discusses the reasons for starting the Heath Community Meeting and its initial links with the bicentennial of the Constitution. She highlights some of the issues encountered and resolved at the meeting and the "fit" of the Heath Community Meeting into the other structures of the school. The chapter concludes with an enumeration of the positive outcomes this experiment has had on community feelings and on the potential for helping children regard themselves as responsible and able thinkers and doers. Given the burgeoning turn to democracy worldwide, an assessment of the success of our own educational institutions in educating students for citizenship is a worthwhile one indeed.

REFERENCES

Chazan, B. 1985. *Contemporary approaches to moral education: Analyzing alternative theories.* New York: Teachers College Press.
Garrod, A., ed. In press. *Emerging themes in moral development.* New York: Teachers College Press.
Garrod, A., and R. Howard. 1990. Making moral youth: An essay review. *Harvard Educational Review* 60 (4):513–26.
Nucci, L., ed. 1989. *Moral development and character education: A dialogue.* Berkeley, Calif.: McCutchan Publishing Corp.

THEORETICAL PERSPECTIVES

1

The State of Moral Education Theory

Barry Chazan

While the last quarter century has not been the best of times morally
(Selma, Vietnam, Watergate, Soweto, the Texas book depository in
Dallas, the Lorraine Motel in Memphis, and countless other less
famous but no less painful human indecencies), it surely has been a
golden age for the study of moral education. In the past few decades
we have been witness to a multiplicity of books, articles, scholarly
papers, journals, conferences, academic chairs, and professional
organizations devoted to moral education. Whereas in the 1950s,
philosophers lamented the neglect of moral education,[1] in the
1980s, they apologized for writing yet another book or article on the
subject.[2]

One indication of the interest in morality on the contemporary
U.S. scene is the existence of a popular party game, A Question of
Scruples, which has joined Monopoly and Trivial Pursuit as a best-
seller in U.S. toy stores. A Question of Scruples enables you to spend
a pleasant evening with friends (while sipping a glass of beer or
wine) discussing adultery, cheating on income tax, and racial
prejudice — and then to vote about what is right or wrong. (And the
best part is that it's only a game, so you can do whatever you want
afterward!) In the 1980s, talking about morality became an interesting and entertaining activity.

The discussion of moral education in the academic world has
been characterized by both great diversity and great confusion. The
constant stream of articles and materials on the subject has led to
exciting debate and reflection; at the same time, it has frequently
generated uncertainty and even despair about the enterprise. Can we
make any sense out of the many words about moral education? Is it
possible to suggest guidelines and signposts for the good-willed yet
bewildered traveler along this road?

This chapter presents an overview of current thought about moral education, and its specific objective is to delineate the major questions, issues, and directions of that topic. We will focus on three organizing questions.

THE QUESTIONS

First, what questions has contemporary moral educational theory addressed, and what are some of the answers it has proposed? In responding to this question, we shall analyze and compare the kinds of philosophical and educational questions and answers of those who have reflected on the nature of moral education.

Second, what are the questions that have been neglected or inadequately dealt with by contemporary approaches to moral education? In this case, we shall point to several philosophical and educational issues that seem central to the discussion of moral education but have been inadequately examined by contemporary theories.

Third, what are some of the directions that moral education could take in the coming years and decades? In this part of the chapter, I will speculate on the kind of issues that may conceivably occupy practitioners, theoreticians, and policymakers in this sphere in the years ahead — that is, I will engage in some philosophical and educational crystal ball gazing.

WHAT ARE THE MAJOR SCHOOLS OF MORAL EDUCATION?

Many articles and books have been written about moral education in recent years.[3] Some of this literature has focused on analyzing specific philosophical and educational issues, such as the meaning of justice, how to teach about morality, and what constitutes indoctrination. Other thinkers have been concerned with developing comprehensive and systematic responses to a host of interlocking questions about morality and education. This sort of literature has been preoccupied with the creation of organic schools of thought about moral education that give an integrated set of answers to the great philosophical and educational questions of this domain.[4] In looking at the literature, I shall focus on six contemporary theories (some of which are represented in this volume) that I regard as major twentieth-century schools of moral education: Émile Durkheim's moral socialization, John Wilson's rational utilitarianism, values clarification, Lawrence Kohlberg's cognitive-developmental moral interactionism, John Dewey's moral pragmatism, and the "caring" school.

I shall also periodically refer to an aggregate of educational theorists (the "antimoral educationists") who, in the name of morality, have argued against the legitimacy of the very enterprise of moral education in schools.[5] This list does not embrace all types of contemporary thought on the subject;[6] however, it does encompass the broad range of issues that characterize the current agenda of moral education.

ISSUES IN MORAL EDUCATION

The Relationship Between the Individual and Society: Are Moral Issues Personal or Public?

A major concern of contemporary moral educational theory has been on the relationship between the individual and the group and specifically on the following two questions: What is the role of the collective in the moral sphere? and What is the nature of the relationship between group morality and autonomous moral being?

Three characteristic responses have been made to the question of the relationship between personal and social morality. The social theory regards morality as essentially a group phenomenon (the morality of a particular society),[7] and it conceives of the group as both the initial and the ultimate force in morality. Émile Durkheim is often considered the exemplary representative of this approach. To be moral in this view means to behave in accordance with the moral norms of one's particular social group (class, community, nation, or ethnic group). If the collective affirms the limitless pursuit of material gain, to be moral is to join the pursuit; if the group preaches chastity, being moral in that society means being chaste.

Proponents of this theory are not particularly concerned about the origins of group morality, which can be rooted in custom, law, social contract, or divine revelation. Wherever morality comes from, it is, according to this approach, ultimately about social behavior that is consistent with group moral norms.

The individualist school totally reverses the order suggested by the social theory; it proposes that the locus of control in morality be shifted from the group to the individual.[8] According to this approach (most vividly represented by the values-clarification school), societies are the enemies rather than the champions of morality because they impose moral norms on individuals and restrict their moral autonomy. This school presents some powerful and painful examples from the twentieth century to bolster its claim that, in the name of morality, societies have sometimes been great adversaries of morality.

The individualist theory argues that values are ultimately personal expressions rather than societal norms; they are, as the emotive school of ethics has suggested, deeply felt personal and individual exclamations. Although society does influence them, these expressions ultimately are "mine," and education's concern should be to foster individual moral valuing rather than to transmit a social code. Indeed, advocates of this school argue that in this day and age it is necessary to invest great energy in fighting against group mores and for the liberation of children from oppressive societal forces of imposition.

The third approach to the question of the relationship between the individual and the group (interactionism) rejects the utility of the individual-social dialectic for the analysis of morality and moral education, arguing that morality is the outcome of the organic relationship between individuals and social settings. According to this view, most prominently represented by Dewey and Kohlberg, the very nature of morality is found in the dialectic between the person and the social context. As Dewey puts it, "the human being is an individual because of and in relation with others."[9] And in Kohlberg's view, "morality is neither the internalization of established cultural values . . . nor the unfolding of spontaneous impulses and emotions; it is . . . the reciprocity between the individual and others in their social environment."[10]

The interactionists argue that morality is not a war between civilization and the individual as the first two theories imply, but rather the offspring of their creative interaction. Hence, the individualists argue that the concern of education should be the development of autonomous moral being; the social theorists suggest that this autonomy will occur via the crucible of group experience and education.

Reason in Ethics: Is Morality Rational?

There are three main approaches to the responses to the question of the rationality of morality: the noncognitivist, the neocognitivist, and the caring schools. The noncognitivist school in twentieth-century ethical thought has focused on the limitations of the relationship between reason and ethics.[11] According to this position, ethical issues have little to do with cognitive and rational thinking and are minimally affected by it. Although few major theories of education have overtly adopted noncognitivism as their credo, much of the practice of moral education in schools over the years seems to have focused on morality as doing good deeds and learning a bag of virtues rather than as a rational system of ideas and generalizations.[12] Thus the noncognitivist stance has frequently found expression in the practical work of moral education in schools.

The neocognitivists in ethics and education do not accept the noncognitivist approach, and their mission is to restore reason to its rightful role in ethics and moral education. The neocognitivist schools of moral education have been concerned with refuting the popular belief that moral issues are simply a matter of taste and style; rather, they contend that ethical issues should be approached rationally and that moral education in schools should be very closely related to cognitive development.

Such adherents of the neocognitivist view of moral education as Dewey, Wilson, and Kohlberg argue among themselves about the exact way reason functions in ethics. Dewey proposes a notion of moral reasoning based on his paradigm of scientific thinking. Wilson presents a multidimensional model of moral reasoning that combines philosophical thinking, practical reasoning, and a priori moral principles. Kohlberg's model of moral thinking is rooted in the notions of universalizability, prescriptivity, and impartiality. As much as they disagree among themselves about the nature of reason in ethics, these representatives of the neocognitivist approach argue even more vociferously with those in contemporary philosophy (the emotivists), psychology (Skinnerians), and education (the moral habits and training approach) who would significantly limit or deny the role of reason in ethics and moral education.

A third group in contemporary moral education has attempted to move beyond the neocognitivist position toward an expanded notion of the nature of the moral process. This approach says that there is some additional quality or trait beyond reason that is ultimately a central force in the moral point of view. Buber says that the ontological grounding for morality is to be found in the ideas of ethical caring and dialogic relation.[13] Gilligan has suggested that some people (especially women) approach moral issues in a way that differs from the exclusively rational models of the cognitivists or neocognitivists.[14] Noddings develops this idea further in terms of the trait of caring, which she postulates as a central element of moral life and education.[15] MacIntyre advises us to consider moral dimensions that go beyond a rational virtue, and Blum and others reintroduce the term altruism into the discussion of moral development.[16] These new voices have sometimes been characterized as critical of the neocognitivist position; in many instances, they are actually engaged in expanding and sophisticating a line of thinking initiated by the neocognitivists. The neocognitivists argued against the idea that morality is nonrational; the caring school agrees but suggests that there is more to morality than reasoning.

Moral Principles: What Is a Moral Principle? What Moral Principles Should Guide My Life?

The nature of moral principles and their role in the moral life is one of the great issues of ethics and moral education. There are three prominent conceptions of moral principles in contemporary moral educational theory.

The first position (represented by Kohlberg, Wilson, Dewey, and some religionists) affirms the centrality of moral principles to the moral sphere. According to this approach, morality encompasses the choice of a course of action that reflects some all-encompassing and generalizable value(s) or moral principle(s). Some versions of this approach (for example, certain approaches to religious moral education) assume that there are universal, divinely ordained moral principles that should be the content of moral education. Others (for instance, Kohlberg) agree that there are universal principles but argue that their origin is in reason, not in God. Still others (such as Dewey) suggest that moral principles are not universal and binding but that they can nevertheless serve as helpful historical or sociological guides for an individual's ultimate choices. The various members of the principled camp disagree over the origins and contents of moral principles; they are, however, united in their affirmation of the inherent centrality of principles to morality.

The second position (best represented by values clarification) shifts the focus of attention from moral principles to moral process, seeing morality as the individual's confrontation with specific situations without the aid of either a set of principles or a bag of virtues. It rejects moral principles as definitive determinants of moral choice and instead postulates the act of individual human will as the ultimate moral force. Some representatives of this position totally reject the role of moral principles in moral choice, arguing that they are arbitrary and other-directed. Others think that moral principles might, in some instances, be helpful signposts in the process of moral deliberation, but they regard such principles as suggestions or examples of past experiences and not as authoritative or binding imperatives. All those taking this position believe that the critical factor in moral decision making is not a bag of virtues but a well-developed sense of the procedures of confronting the moral problems and conflicts that we all face in our daily lives.

The third approach to the question of moral principles (best represented by Durkheim, although also evident in Kohlberg's stage 4 civic education and Wilson's premoral education)[17] regards moral deeds and habits, rather than moral principles or moral processes, as the essence of moral education. This approach de-emphasizes principles and re-emphasizes good deeds and habits. It shares the principled approach's belief in the centrality of consistency and universalizability in morality; it suggests, however, that these qualities are expressed and realized in the behavioral rather than in the reflective or cognitive domain.[18] According to this approach, the great principles of morality are in fact the common moral deeds and habits of everyday existence.

Moral Education and Moral Action: What Is the Connection between Knowing the Good and Doing the Good?

Philosophers, educators, and children throughout the ages have asked whether knowing the good is the same as — and will lead to — doing the good. Is there any connection between moral thinking and knowledge and moral deeds and action? This issue is of particular importance for educational practitioners, since much of their daily work is about the knowledge and deeds of children. The educator in the classroom is continually confronted with the dialectic between moral talk in texts and curricula and the actual lives of children in halls and lunchrooms.[19]

What position do contemporary theorists of moral education take concerning the moral knowledge–moral action question? It is generally assumed that much of contemporary theory on moral education (Wilson, values clarification, Kohlberg, Dewey, the antimoral educationists, the caring school) shifts the emphasis from the moral deed to moral thinking and deliberation. Values clarification focuses on the stimulation of a process of valuing rather than on specific values. Wilson is concerned with the internalization of a philosophical process of moral reflection rather than with the learning of specific moral principles. Kohlberg is concerned with looking beyond specific deeds to the mode of thinking implicit in them. In the caring school, you learn how to care rather than to care for specific people, values, or beliefs.

Unquestionably, much contemporary thinking in moral education argues that there has been an overemphasis on teaching specific habits and deeds in schools and an underemphasis on teaching a pattern of moral thinking. Many contemporary theories come to argue that there is some pattern of thinking that characterizes the moral perspective (the moral point of view) and that our ultimate concern in moral education should be to develop the moral way of thinking rather than specific moral habits or beliefs.

The concern with moral thinking and with valuing processes has sometimes been criticized by good-willed people who are dismayed by the (im)moral behaviors of children and adults today. These concerned people point to the degeneration of basic human behaviors in contemporary life — slovenly dress, poor manners, drugs, sexual license, and verbal and physical violence. We regularly hear parents, politicians, and concerned citizens urging schools to return to the good old moral virtues and behaviors. Indeed, some educational theorists — particularly Dewey and Kohlberg — have been accused of being knowing or unknowing agents in the moral degeneration of society by leading schools astray from their true moral mission.

Dewey, Kohlberg, and their colleagues defend themselves in two ways. First, they affirm the importance of moral education that promotes some basic decent behaviors. Dewey's little book, *Moral Principles in Education*, is a powerful statement in support of a notion of moral education as training in some basic moral virtues and actions.[20] On the occasion of the United States bicentennial in 1976, Kohlberg pleaded for a return to a stage 4 civic moral education, which would develop some good old civic virtues.[21] (Kohlberg's professional and personal involvement in Bronx high schools in the 1980s was very much oriented in this direction.) Wilson talks about some basic human codes of behavior that he regards as preconditions for the moral life.[22]

These three thinkers argue that they do not disregard basic moral behaviors; rather, they are making a more basic claim against the very distinction between moral knowledge and action. They propose a conceptual framework for analyzing the relationship between thinking and doing in the moral sphere that assumes that the patient and deliberate process of developing a reflective, moral personality is a better guarantee of moral behavior than is moral skills training. Thus several of the major schools of contemporary moral educational theory propose a route to moral deeds that winds its way through the corridor of moral thinking.

Durkheim's school of moral education gives primacy to moral deeds and habits and, according to many interpretations, places little emphasis on moral thinking. While it is true that Durkheim's approach to moral education is rooted in deeds, knowledge is not an irrelevant dimension of the Durkheimian conception of the moral life. Durkheim argues that moral deeds are not arbitrary but are linked to moral ideas and ideals. The moral way is a reflection and concretization of moral principles. Consequently, teaching morality in the Durkheimian perspective focuses on the social and natural sciences rather than the humanities, since the former enables young people to see morality as reasonable and systematic patterns of behavior and the latter leads them to regard morality as only emotion.[23] Thus the world of reflection also pervades the corridors of Durkheim's action-oriented school.

The major twentieth-century schools of moral education do not seem to reject the traditional commitment to the centrality of moral deeds to the moral sphere; they seek to balance the traditional focus with a greater emphasis on the process of moral reflection and valuing as part of the educational imperative.

Who Is the Morally Educated Person?
What Does It Mean to be Moral?

The fourth question of moral education theory focuses on the nature of being moral: Who is the morally educated person? and What are the qualities we expect such a person to have?

Many theorists have emphasized the multidimensional nature of the morally educated person. In this view, morality is understood as a complex property or set of properties rather than as a one-dimensional phenomenon, and the moral person is one who has mastered a set of diverse skills, abilities, and predispositions. The range of dimensions of the moral person includes rational, social, personal, affective, and behavioral qualities.

Several multidimensional models of the moral person have been suggested in the literature. Wilson talks about four categories of moral components that characterize the morally educated person: PHIL, EMP, GIG, and KRAT.[24] PHIL refers to a basic belief in the worth of others; EMP is the ability or skill to understand and relate to others; GIG is the process of contemplating moral issues in terms of facts and realities; and KRAT is the ability to contemplate and reflect on moral issues and to translate one's moral decisions into actions.

Durkheim claims that the morally educated person is characterized by three abilities: discipline (a sense of obligation and duty to ideals), society (actions consistent with the ideals and practices of a society), and autonomy (a choice and acceptance of the worth of these ideals).[25] These abilities combine behavioral, social, and reflective dimensions.

The valuing person, according to values clarification, is one who knows how to choose, prize, and act in the moral sphere. These three categories are subdivided into detailed lists of specific abilities that together are essential for the valuing process. A valuing person is one who is equipped to use these abilities in the daily confrontation with moral issues.

Kohlberg's morally educated person reflects on a moral problem that arises in a social setting, considers the various alternatives, arrives at a decision in terms of the most general principle of justice (rather than on the basis of custom, law, or whim), and translates this deliberation into a deed.

Dewey's morally educated person is reflective, is concerned and involved with the issue, is committed to social concerns and responsibilities, follows an operative set of moral habits and dispositions in his or her daily life, and lives on the basis of some consistent, reflective life pattern.[26]

Clearly there is no unanimity among these schools of moral education regarding the combinations and constellations of components that characterize the morally educated person; there is, however, surprising unanimity concerning the notion of a multidimensional model. Models of moral personality that define morality in terms of singular character traits or personality factors are seen as more dubious.

Teaching the Good (The Goals of Moral Education): What Are the Goals of Moral Education?

Although the questions we have dealt with up to now have been philosophical in nature, some of the most critical questions about moral educational theory are educational rather than philosophical in nature. The most prominent educational question concerns the goals of moral education. There have been three responses.

The first says that the goal of moral education is the transmission of a set of moral norms and practices to young people. According to this approach, our objective in moral education is to develop in the young a clearly defined set of moral behaviors that reflect agreed-upon values of the society (the good, a bag of virtues, the do's and don'ts, the Ten Commandments, the good boy and good girl morality, what one ought to do). Moral education is about the transmission and inculcation in its young of a society's moral values. This approach is extremely clear about what it wants to teach, what it proposes to achieve, and how success can be measured; indeed, it is probably the most clearly understood and popularly accepted notion of moral education in everyday life.

A second conception shifts the focus from the transmission of social norms and behaviors to the development of moral reflection and valuing. According to this approach, the essence of morality is not in specific contents or behaviors but in a procedure or process that one uses to confront moral problems. This process, denoted as the valuing process or the moral point of view, is constituted by a series of procedures that a person must develop. The goal of moral education becomes the development in the individual of the procedures or processes that constitute the moral point of view. Thus the second school differs from the first in two significant ways: it focuses more on moral process than on moral content and it focuses on the individual rather than on the collective.

As we have seen, there are several notions about the nature of the moral process, and various advocates of the second approach do not agree on the specific procedures that should be taught to children. Some suggest a very rational and philosophic emphasis (Wilson); others emphasize a more introspective and self-searching focus (values clarification); and still others see the moral process in transcendent and spiritual terms (Buber). A small group of proponents of the second approach (for example, Neil, Bereiter, and Ferrer) doubt that it can ever be effected in schools, because they believe that the contemporary structure of schooling is simply too authoritarian for such autonomy.

The first approach sees the goal of moral education as moral socialization, the second as moral process or autonomy. The third approach argues that it is both. According to the third school, the goal of moral education is to transmit certain social norms and to develop individual moral valuing. This school agrees that morality is defined by certain social norms and behaviors but maintains that it also encompasses individual reflection and choice. Thus theorists such as Dewey and Kohlberg suggest a two-pronged approach to moral education that sees moral socialization and moral reflection as complementary rather than contradictory. While the first two approaches assume an inherent conflict between moral socialization and moral autonomy, the third approach assumes a necessary and potentially harmonious relationship between them.

The Teacher: Who Is the Moral Teacher?

What kinds of traits, abilities, and personalities do we expect of teachers who will be asked to engage in moral education in schools? Three models of moral teaching have been suggested: the moral exemplar, the moral therapist, and the moral deliberator.

The moral exemplar approach regards the teacher as a representative and transmitter of the great values of a particular society. Moral teachers, in this view, should be the servants and priests of society, and they should transmit moral values through both their teaching and their personal behavior. Durkheim tells us that teachers of morality should be total personalities who are authoritative and passionate about their moral values and who aim at consistency in their words and deeds.[27] The mission of such a teacher transcends the prescribed curriculum, required texts, and the limitations of the school day; it is an all-encompassing commitment to the cause of shaping the character of the young.

The therapist or facilitator model removes the priestly mantle from teachers, defining their function instead as that of helping students to confront themselves and their own moral dilemmas. This model has been greatly influenced by the world of psychotherapy, and it suggests that the teacher should serve as a sort of educational therapist and catalyst for questions, self-analysis, and introspection. The educational task of the teacher in this approach (most clearly enunciated by values clarification) is to help a student develop skills in moral self-reflection and questioning but is not to inculcate a specific moral view. Just as the professor of mathematics is expected to teach certain mathematical skills but is not expected to be a triangle, so the moral teacher's task is to teach about morality but not to be an exemplary model of the good life.

The third model of the moral teacher, the moral deliberator, proposes a synthesis of the other two models. This model is uncomfortable with the notion of the moral teacher as an exemplar of moral goodness; at the same time, it hesitates to discard completely the teacher's priestly function. It is attracted by the reflective and introspective dimensions of the therapist model, but it believes the model goes too far in stripping the teacher of moral content. The moral deliberator model wants the teacher to be an exemplar, not of specific norms or deeds, but rather of the three key processes of the moral life: moral reflection, moral decision making, and moral passion. According to this model, the teacher's ultimate goal is to stimulate the processes of moral deliberation, moral judgment, and moral caring in children. This approach suggests, however, that such a goal can only be realized if the teacher is a model of moral personality in both the reflective and affective realms.

Dewey wants the moral teacher to be a reflective person who is also concerned with great human causes and social commitments. Wilson's teacher should be both a moral philosopher and a person with PHIL-concern for others. Kohlberg's teacher should be both Plato and Jesus. The moral deliberator school regards the moral teacher as a combination of the cool, modern therapist and the passionate person of faith.

Curriculum and Pedagogy in Moral Education:
How Do We Teach Moral Values?

The story of moral education is ultimately the saga of teachers and children in classrooms throughout the world. It is very much related to nitty-gritty matters of education — time, materials, texts, and teaching methods. Theories of moral education have been pressed by the world of practice to relate to these real issues, which for the teacher in the field are no less important than the larger theoretical issues.

Much of contemporary moral educational theory has taken seriously the practical questions of teaching values. This commitment to practice reflects the belief of many moral educational thinkers in the possibility of affecting morality through educational intervention.

This commitment can also be seen in the practical activities of many of the important theorists. For example, Durkheim's main academic appointments in France were in the area of pedagogy, and he spent much of his life lecturing to teachers. Dewey's professional life encompassed both the worlds of philosophy and schools of education, laboratory schools, and grass roots educational move-ments. Kohlberg was a central figure in the academic study of moral development and in practical programs of moral education — teachers' workshops, school intervention projects, and prison reform. Clearly, twentieth-century moral educational theory is committed to moving from the ivy-covered walls of theory to the cinder block walls of practice.

Three practical areas of schooling have generally concerned contemporary moral educational theory: curriculum and instruc-tional materials, school atmosphere, and the child.

Many curricula and instructional materials for moral education have been produced in recent decades, including textbooks, instructional units, films, videos, games, workbooks, and teachers' guides.[28] Many of these materials are closely identified with or purport to reflect a particular theory of moral education. The theories of Kohlberg and values clarification have proved to be the most prominent influences on practical educational materials.

At the same time, none of the major theories of moral education has produced either a comprehensive curriculum or a detailed program of basic themes, texts, concepts, and teaching practices for moral education. Durkheim does not establish a course of study for moral education. Followers of values clarification have collected and published many exercises that were developed in classrooms, but these are nonsystematic and random collections of teachers' experiences. Wilson published one pamphlet that showed how specific subject areas of the curriculum might be used to teach about the moral components,[29] but this was only an isolated example. Dewey and his disciples devoted substantial effort to the issue of translating curriculum theory into detailed educational practice, especially through the use of the laboratory school.[30] However, as the history of progressive education so vividly illustrates, the road from theory to practice is not a primrose path. Moreover, Dewey's enterprise was never exclusively concerned with moral education. The Kohlberg school has probably done the most extensive pedagogic work of any contemporary theory, encompassing hypothetical dilemmas, social studies units, model questions, and just community issues.[31] These efforts, however, have not resulted in the development of a comprehensive curricular blueprint for all subject areas and for all years of the school. In short, while contemporary moral educational theory has been very concerned with practice, it has been reluctant — or unable — to develop either the broad structure or the fine details of a comprehensive curriculum of moral education.

A second pedagogic concern of many contemporary theories has been with the role of noncurricular or extracurricular factors in moral education (the hidden or covert curriculum). John Wilson speaks with fervor about the great potential of the nonclassroom side of the British boarding school for affecting moral growth. Kohlberg highlights the importance of school atmosphere and community as forces in moral growth.[32] Ferrer and his disciples devote much effort to free-time activities, family events, and Sunday and holiday programs as part of the total educational planning of their schools.[33] Durkheim regards the dynamics of the class as a social group as one of the three critical arenas for moral education in schools.[34] Thus contemporary theory is sensitive to the totality of atmospheric forces that can affect the process of moral development.

The third practical concern is the role of the child as a force in the process of his or her own moral education. Wilson and Kohlberg emphasize the importance of the child's actual participation in the process of the moral dialectic through a series of moral deliberation exercises. Values clarification develops an extensive set of questions and exercises that encourage students to talk about and consider their own value concerns. Dewey proposes a set of educational experiences that begin with children's interests and eventually move to the presentation of desired modes of moral reflection. In short, most of our contemporary theories regard the participation of the child as a critical factor in the process of moral education.

Some approaches to moral education doubt the viability of schools to affect moral growth. Some of these theorists have argued that education is defined by the intention to impose a social ethic on the individual; hence schools are settings in which it is impossible to stimulate individual moral reflection and growth. Others have seen schooling, particularly in the United States, as a manipulative tool of a nonegalitarian capitalist ethic; hence the schools' very existence is, from the outset, immoral.[35] Still others contend that schools should teach only bodies of knowledge that are verifiable and objective, holding that, since morality is categorically not of this genre, it should not be a school concern.[36] Finally, there are those who contend that a growing mass of empirical evidence shows that schools play a minimal role in changing moral thinking or behaving, so schools should concentrate on what they do best, which is the transmission of knowledge and skills.[37]

Do not be put off by these theorists. They are not misanthropes or moral anarchists; they love morality and children very much — and you probably would be thrilled to have them teach your children! They simply do not have the great faith in schools that Durkheim, Dewey, and Kohlberg did.

THE NEGLECTED ISSUES OF MORAL EDUCATIONAL THEORY

We have considered eight themes that have been discussed extensively in the literature of contemporary moral education. There are several other important issues related to morality and education that have not received the same comprehensive treatment. We shall now look at five issues that I believe have not been adequately treated by contemporary moral education theory.

Community

The concept of community and its effect on personality and identity is a major contemporary issue. We are faced on all sides with the challenge, promise, and horror of the collective in our lives. Some have seen the vision of community as a promise of salvation; others have attacked it as the source of our discontent; and millions have perished because of its wild and barbaric excesses. The good, the bad, and the ugly of community have preoccupied artists, writers, musicians, philosophers, and politicians in the twentieth century.

Contemporary moral educational theory has been uneven in its treatment of this topic in general and in the role of moral community in the process of moral education specifically.[38] Both critics and supporters of community as a force in moral education have had trouble formulating a rich notion of moral community.

The individualistic schools of moral education have been skeptical about the role of community in moral development, and they ascribe little constructive value to community as a moral force. For them the concept of community is a problem to be dealt with rather than a value to be nurtured.

The interactionists regard community as an integral and organic component of their moral and educational theories, and for them the development of the moral sense is very much related to the idea of moral communities that nurture moral growth. They have, however, had difficulties in presenting comprehensive theories of moral community.

Kohlberg's just communities are constructs that often have to be created from nothing, and they frequently lack the rich symbolic, historic, and affective dimensions that are so important to the idea of community. Dewey's writings reflect an almost mystical attachment to the idea of community (particularly to a community reminiscent of an idyllic vision of rural American life), but Dewey had trouble with the realities of communities (for example, the church), in practice.

The concept of moral community is an important dimension of the thought of such philosophers as Durkheim and Buber. Buber talks about the idea of the kibbutz as a new-old society that functions as a caring moral community, and Durkheim refers to prechurch Christianity as an example of a rich system of symbols, rituals, and moral models. These two approaches see moral community as a positive moral force rooted in authentic social groupings with rich and organic historical legacies, traditions, and symbolic systems. These moral communities are not new or artificial constructs in schools, but organic social and cultural collectives.

In our age, we have seen the horror of immoral community; the promise of moral community still intrigues — yet it eludes our grasp.

The Contents and Texts of Education

The discussion of moral education encompasses many complex philosophical questions. However, elementary and secondary school teachers have classes to teach tomorrow morning, and they want to know, "What texts and contents should we use to do moral education?"

The question is important for two reasons. First, teachers ask it; therefore, it is something that concerns them, so it should be answered. Second, the question of what to teach in moral education reflects some important prior questions about the nature and meaning of good and the goals of moral education.

Many contemporary theorists are uncomfortable with the notion of the texts of moral education. The idea of moral texts has often been understood to imply a fixed set of sources that are used to preach a moral catechism and gospel, and this has been regarded as antithetical to the concern for moral reflection and autonomy. As a result, there has been a reluctance to produce "the textbook" on moral education.

In fact, contemporary theories have generated texts of moral education, some of which have even become classics. Heinz, Sharon, and Mr. Peterson, the protagonists of Kohlberg's moral dilemmas, are well known in school and university classrooms throughout the world. Values clarification's open-ended probe questions (How do you feel about that choice? What does it mean to you? What do you prize? What would you do?) have become standards of the questioning repertoires of teachers. Literary works about the experience of caring have been incorporated into English and literature curricula of schools. School-based projects in England and Canada have attempted to produce a systematic body of teaching materials for moral education.[39]

Some theorists have not proposed specific texts but rather have suggested subject areas or disciplines that they regard as the content of moral education. Thus Wilson believes that the study of philosophy will help students develop the necessary traits and abilities to engage in the moral process. Durkheim proposes science and history as the two most important curricular areas for moral education, since they are about "life in earnest" and they enable us to truly confront and understand reality. (Art is more damaging than helpful because it "makes us live in an imaginary environment; it detaches us from reality and from the concrete beings that comprise reality.")[40]

Nevertheless, there is a sense that the teachers' question remains unanswered and that contemporary theory has not given enough assistance to the practitioner concerned with the translation of theories into actual classroom teaching materials. Contemporary moral educational theory has not generated a significant corpus of texts and sources for the classroom that would reflect its theoretical insights (like, for example, the Paideia curriculum),[41] and in that sense, one wonders whether contemporary moral educational thought has not had more impact in academic journals and university lecture halls than in teachers' lesson plans and instructional programs.

The Notion of Moral Personality

One of the achievements of the moral education movement is that it has forced us to reconsider our assumptions about the nature of the moral person, and particularly, it has encouraged us to begin to think about the moral person as more than a creature of habits and behaviors.

However, contemporary theory has yet to develop a full and rich portrait of the notion of moral personality. Although many contemporary theories seem to propose multidimensional models of the moral person, ironically they also seem to perpetuate surprisingly one-sided and one-dimensional conceptions of moral development.

For example, despite Kohlberg's clear commitment to a comprehensive notion of cognitive-moral development, his educational practice seems to be richer in its treatment of moral judgment than in its dealing with moral passion or moral affect. Values clarification postulates the cognitive-affective-behavioral unity in the valuing sphere, but its practice seems to be mostly about inner feelings and choices. Noddings and Gilligan remind us of the importance of the commitment to others — to a moral personality — but they don't tell us how that connects with many other components of the moral person.

Contemporary theory has done both a service and a disservice to the notion of the moral person. It has critically disassembled conventional understandings of morality and has suggested the possibility that there are factors beyond actions or habits — for example, judgment, caring, passion, and even the spiritual factors — that are part of moral being. However, contemporary theory has not succeeded in putting Humpty Dumpty back together again — that is, it has not yet delineated the many complexities, interactions, and patterns that seem to characterize the dynamics of moral personality. The moral person is emerging as a complex organism whose development encompasses a host of human traits and abilities; contemporary theory has only begun to grasp the complexity of that idea.

Life-Long Moral Development

Much of the current discussion of moral education has focused on childhood and youth, and one of the great contributions of contemporary moral educational theory is its affirmation of the centrality of morality in the life and development of the young.

In emphasizing childhood, however, contemporary theory has frequently neglected the dynamics of moral development at other ages. Specifically, most contemporary theories have paid little attention to issues of morality and moral development in adults.

Indeed, it is ironic that approaches (such as those of Dewey, Kohlberg, and even Durkheim) that attempted to break out of overly limiting conceptions of human development do not pay enough attention to the dynamics and complexities of moral life in adulthood.

One thinker who has been sensitive to the ongoing and ever-changing dynamic of human growth through the adult years is Erik Erikson. Although he is usually identified with issues of adolescence and identity, his system as a whole has in fact emphasized the nature of human development throughout the adult years.[42] Moreover, Erikson has differentiated among different phases of adulthood, discussing the unique dimensions to and characteristics of early marriage, early parenting, middle parenting, late parenting, early grandparenting, late grandparenting, and old age. Although Erikson's system is seldom considered in the context of moral development or moral education, [43] his theory of human development is clearly linked with the moral life, and it points up some of the omissions of the existing work in this area.

The Problem of Measurement

Parents, educators, and public figures want to know whether moral education works — does it make a difference? We know that progress in education is very difficult to measure, but this does not relieve theorists in moral education of the responsibility to consider the results of the enterprise that they propose. With the exception of the Kohlberg school, contemporary moral education theory has neglected this area. Consequently, new approaches to moral education have generally been appraised by old (usually behavioral) standards and obviously therefore have been proved deficient. A product of a values-clarification classroom will not look more moral when tested on the number of good deeds performed, since that is not the goal of the values-clarification teacher. The situation is complicated by the fact that many of the new approaches to moral education are aimed at developing moral thinking or judgment, and these processes are difficult to measure. Thus, specific outcomes at any moment will only be temporary signposts, not conclusive statements about moral growth. In short, the theory of moral education must encompass conceptual clarity, practical directives, and evaluative procedures.

WHITHER MORAL EDUCATION?

This chapter has presented an overview of themes that have been emphasized and issues that have been neglected in the field of moral education in recent decades. What should be the emerging agenda for moral educational theory in the next quarter century? What are the issues that a budding Durkheim, Dewey, or Kohlberg should confront? What should moral education focus on in the coming years?

The first task of moral education in the next decades is to continue to ask the questions that have been asked in the past. The enterprise of moral education begins with the return to basic questions of morality: What is good? What is the role of reason in ethics? Who is the moral person? What is the relationship of community to the emergence of moral personality? How do reason, passion, and habit interact in the moral sphere? The discussion of these questions does not always result in definitive or convincing answers. The starting point of any good theory, however, is to raise anew old questions.

Still, it is not enough to ask and respond to philosophical questions; moral educational theory also depends on the contribution of the social sciences in the moral sphere. Empirical knowledge about many issues related to morality, education, and moral development is currently insufficient, and we need much work in these areas. Indeed, we do not always know what we do not know; and in some areas of moral education, we are like the young child who does not yet know what to ask.

The third body of questions critical to moral educational theory comes from the world of educational practice. Theorists in education must listen attentively to what teachers are saying, and they must take these teachers seriously. The questions of the teacher and the classroom are real, relevant, and reflective of deeper issues; but the academy tends to treat them as irrelevant, irreverent, and irritating. So we must keep in mind that the enterprise of moral education will advance very little unless the practitioner's questions are heard and answered. In the domain of moral education, practice is an indispensable partner and participant in the deliberative process.

This is a complicated agenda. It suggests, moreover, that moral education theory may have advanced to the point where it can no longer be defined by the disciplinary parameters of the past. Moral education may be ready to break out of established and well-defined constraints and to create new conceptual syntheses. The concern for moral education in future years will involve new integrations of philosophy, psychology, sociology, literature, art, cinema, and educational practice; it will also require new syntheses of academics and practitioners. Indeed, we may well find our new professors of moral education sitting in universities, local schools, recording studios, publishing firms, and laboratories. Hegemony over moral educational theory may no longer belong to the university in the traditional way.

Perhaps we will find a clue about the direction of moral education theory in the next decades by looking back to the innovative ideas of moral educational theorists of the past. What did a Durkheim, a Dewey, and a Kohlberg have in common? First, they all believed in education. They took it seriously, believing that it was worth studying, and they did not regard it as any less significant than philosophy, sociology, or psychology. Furthermore, they thought that the improvement of education was connected to the improvement of human society and the human condition. The new Durkheims, Deweys, and Kohlbergs must have the same kind of intellectual and personal commitment to education.

Second, they were thinkers of great expanse and broad scope. Dewey wrote in the areas of ethics, social philosophy, epistemology, aesthetics, social psychology, and education; he was also a social and educational activist. Kohlberg studied social psychology, taught the philosophy of moral development, conducted teachers' workshops, worked in prisons, and spent two days a week in difficult Bronx high schools for several years. Durkheim was a sociologist, philosopher, and professor of pedagogy. These innovators crossed many boundaries and wandered in many worlds in their attempt to understand morality and education. Their intellectual offspring will need the same — and even more — moral and educational wanderlust.

In the years to come, moral education theory will be framed by philosophy, informed by the social sciences, and tested in practice. But most of all, it will be fueled by the moral dilemmas and the moral prisons of the world. Some of these moral prisons periodically open, and a few of the morally oppressed are released. But until all the moral prisons of the world have been opened and all the beleaguered released, the task of moral education has only just begun.

NOTES

An early draft of this chapter was presented to a meeting of the Philosophy of Education Research Center at the Harvard University Graduate School of Education in March 1986, where I was a visiting fellow from 1985 to 1987. I am grateful to Israel Scheffler, Vernon Howard, and the late Lawrence Kohlberg for their helpful comments and warm hospitality.

1.   R. M. Hare, *The Language of Morals* (New York: Oxford University Press, 1964).

2.   Barry Chazan, *Contemporary Approaches to Moral Education* (New York: Teachers College Press, 1985), p. ix.

3.   See the following overviews and comparative analyses of some of the prominent schools: Chazan, *Contemporary Approaches to Moral Education*; Richard Hersh, John Miller, and Glen Fielding, *Models in Moral Education* (New York: Longman, 1980); Douglas Superka, Christine Ahrens, Judith Hedstrom, Luther J. Ford, and Patricia L. Johnson, *Values Education Sourcebook* (Boulder, CO: Social Science Education Consortium, 1976).

4.   I use the phrase "school of moral education" to refer to a comprehensive theory of morality and education that encompasses a theory of moral value, a theory

of moral justification, and a theory of education. There have been many proclamations about or programs of moral education in past decades; however, not every proclamation or program is a "school of moral education."

5. Chazan, *Contemporary Approaches to Moral Education*, ch. 6, "Against Moral Education," pp. 91–102; Paul Avrich, *The Modern School Movement: Anarchism and Education in the United States* (Princeton, NJ: Princeton University Press, 1980); Joel Spring, *A Primer of Libertarian Education* (Montreal: Black Rose Books, 1975).

6. Some of the relevant theories and projects not referred to here in great detail include the works of Martin Buber, Clive Beck, the British Schools Project, Erik Erikson, Carol Gilligan, and Nel Noddings.

7. John Wilson, Norman Williams, and Barry Sugarman, *Introduction to Moral Education* (Harmondsworth, England: Penguin, 1967), pp. 44–45.

8. Francisco Ferrer, *The Origins and Ideas of the Modern School* (New York: Arno Press, 1972); A. S. Neil, *The Problem Child* (New York: McBride, 1927); Lev Tolstoi, *Tolstoy on Education* (Chicago: University of Chicago Press, 1967).

9. John Dewey, *Theory of the Moral Life* (New York: Holt, Rinehart and Winston, 1960), p. 80.

10. Lawrence Kohlberg and Rochelle Mayer, "Development as the Aim of Education: The Dewey View," in *The Philosophy of Moral Development*, Lawrence Kohlberg, ed. (San Francisco: Harper & Row, 1981), p. 55.

11. Mary Warnock, *Ethics Since 1900* (London: Oxford University Press, 1960).

12. An interesting experiment in this direction was the Kentucky Movement, a program of moral education developed for the schools of Kentucky, that was aimed at teaching a set of virtues to children by using the total life of the school — the curriculum, sports, recreational activities, church attendance on Sundays, and the personal behavior of teachers. See William C. Bower, *Moral and Spiritual Values in Education* (Lexington: University of Kentucky Press, 1952).

13. Martin Buber, *Good and Evil: Two Interpretations* (New York: Scribner's, 1953), *Between Man and Man* (London: Kegan Paul, 1947), *Eclipse of God* (New York: Harper & Row, 1952); Maurice Friedman, *Martin Buber: The Life of Dialogue* (New York: Harper & Row, 1955), ch. 22, "Ethics," pp. 198–207.

14. Carol Gilligan, *In a Different Voice: Psychological Theory and Women's Development* (Cambridge: Harvard University Press, 1982).

15. Nel Noddings, *Caring: A Feminine Approach to Ethics and Moral Education* (Berkeley: University of California Press, 1984).

16. Martin Buber, "The Education of Character," in *Between Man and Man*; Gilligan, *In a Different Voice*; A. MacIntyre, *After Virtue* (Notre Dame: University of Notre Dame Press, 1981); Noddings, *Caring*.

17. Lawrence Kohlberg, "Educating for a Just Society: An Updated and Revised Statement," in *Moral Development, Moral Education, and Kohlberg*, Brenda Munsey, ed. (Birmingham, AL: Religious Education Press, 1980), p. 457; John Wilson, *Practical Methods of Moral Education* (London: Heinemann, 1972), p. 89.

18. Émile Durkheim, *Moral Education* (New York: Free Press, 1961), p. 59.

19. J. D. Salinger's Holden Caufield remains one of our best teachers about this subject. By now, Holden has spent many lifetimes pondering the disparity between what teachers, religionists, and parents say and what actually happens in city streets, bars, and school restrooms. See John D. Salinger, *The Catcher in the Rye* (Boston: Little, Brown, 1945).

20. John Dewey, *Moral Principles in Education* (Carbondale: Southern Illinois University Press, Arcturus Books, 1975).

24 / Chazan

21. Lawrence Kohlberg, "High School Democracy and Educating for a Just Society," in *Moral Education: A First Generation of Research*, R. Mosher, ed. (New York: Praeger, 1980).

22. Wilson, *Practical Methods of Moral Education*, p. 89.

23. Durkheim, *Moral Education*, p. 271.

24. John Wilson, *The Assessment of Morality* (Great Britain: Staples Printers, Ltd., 1973), pp. 38–39.

25. Durkheim, *Moral Education*, pp. 23–115.

26. John Dewey, "Theory of the Moral Life," in *Moral Principles in Education*, pp. 45–58.

27. Émile Durkheim, "The Role of the State in Education," in *Education and Society* (New York: Free Press, 1956), pp. 85–86; *The Evolution of Educational Thought* (London: Routledge and Kegan Paul, 1977), pp. 7–30.

28. For a catalogue of materials on moral education through the mid-1970s, see Superka et al., *Values Education Sourcebook*; see also Don Cochrane, ed., *Moral/Values Education in Canada: A Bibliography and Directory, 1970–1977* (Toronto: Ontario Institute for Studies in Education, 1978).

29. John Wilson, *Moral Education and the Curriculum* (London: Pergamon, 1969).

30. John Dewey, *The Child and the Curriculum: The School and Society* (Chicago: University of Chicago Press, Phoenix Books, 1963).

31. See R. Hersh, D. Paolitto, and J. Reimer, *Promoting Moral Growth* (New York: Longman, 1979), part 3.

32. Lawrence Kohlberg, "The Just Community Approach to Moral Education in Theory and Practice," in *Moral Education: Theory and Application*, Marvin Berkowitz and Fritz Oser, eds. (Hillsdale, NJ: Lawrence Erlbaum, 1985).

33. Ferrer, *The Origins and Ideas of the Modern School*.

34. Durkheim, *Moral Education*, pp. 228–35.

35. Samuel Bowles and Herbert Gintis, *Schooling in Capitalist America: Educational Reform and the Contradictions of Economic Life* (New York: Basic Books, 1976), chs. 1–7.

36. John Wilson, "Education and Indoctrination," in *Aims in Education*, T. H. B. Hollins, ed. (Manchester: Manchester University Press, 1969), pp. 24–46.

37. Carl Bereiter, *Must We Educate?* (Englewood Cliffs, NJ: Prentice-Hall, 1973), pp. 13–15.

38. I have reflected on this topic in "Holy Community and Values Education," in *Moral Development Foundations*, Don Joy, ed. (Nashville, TN: Abingdon Press, 1983), pp. 77–86.

39. Peter McPhail, *Great Britain Schools Council Moral Education Curriculum Project* (Harlow, Essex: Longman, 1978); Clive Beck, *The Moral Education Project* (Toronto: OISE, 1978); Clive Beck, Norma McCoy, and Jane Bradley, *Reflecting on Values: Learning Materials for Grades 1–6* (Toronto: OISE, 1978); Clive Beck, *Moral Education in the Schools: Some Practical Suggestions* (Toronto: OISE, 1971).

40. Durkheim, *Moral Education*, p. 271.

41. Mortimer J. Adler, *The Paideia Program: An Educational Syllabus* (New York: Macmillan, 1984).

42. Erik Erikson, *The Life Cycle Completed* (New York: Norton, 1982); Erik Erikson, Joan Erikson, and Helen Kivnick, *Vital Involvement in Old Age* (New York: Norton, 1986); Erik Erikson, *Adulthood* (New York: Norton, 1978).

43. Erikson wrote an essay that deals directly with education: "Psychoanalysis and the Future of Education," in *Erik Erikson: A Way of Looking at Things. Selected Papers from 1930 to 1980*, Stephen Schlein, ed. (New York: Norton, 1987).

2

Moral Character Education in the United States: Beyond Socialization versus Development

John Snarey and Thomas Pavkov

Moral character refers to those enduring aspects of personhood that are tied to an ethical normative orientation. Thomas Jefferson and other founders of the United States believed that schooling in a democracy should include moral character education — that is, it should aim to improve students' morality and minds so that they might become both "good and wise" (Lee 1961, pp. 95, 145, 163). The apparent evolution of students' moral character as seen by educators, however, has proceeded in ways that Jefferson never anticipated: "In the 1940s a survey listed the top seven discipline problems in public schools: talking, chewing gum, making noise, running in the halls, getting out of turn in line, wearing improper clothes, not putting paper in wastebaskets. A 1980s survey lists these top seven: drug abuse, alcohol abuse, pregnancy, suicide, rape, robbery, assault" (Will 1987, p. 64). When current educational policymakers in the United States consider how to stem the rising tide of these societal ills, moral character education consistently emerges as one of a number of policy options.

SHOULD PUBLIC SCHOOLS BE INVOLVED IN CHARACTER EDUCATION?

The primary questions that emerge from this ongoing discussion pertain to the role of the public schools in promoting moral character development. Should schools promote any form of morality? If this is a proper role for public education to play, how should it accomplish this educational task? Should the government mandate that a period of time each day be devoted to moral character education in the classroom? These questions loom ominously when one considers the diverse philosophical and pedagogical options being advocated and the potential ethical, political, and feasibility questions that these initiatives pose.

In a speech on moral character education, political scientist James Q. Wilson (1985a) stated, "We all value decency, but we find ourselves reluctant to use the word 'decency.' We all here condemn wrongful actions, but we are reluctant in public places to point to people and say 'that is wrong.' We value civility but think we can purchase it" (p. 4). Wilson's point illustrates what seems to be a pervading philosophy in our pluralistic society. We have been appropriately socialized to respect other people's values, but this leads to an inappropriate inhibition against evaluating the other's values, or standing up for our own values. A similar inhibition exists regarding governmental support of promoting moral character through the public schools. Concerns emerge at both ends of the political spectrum. Liberal critics warn of the dangers of legislating morality; they are fearful of the imposition of belief. Many conservatives are skeptical as well. Some religious fundamentalists, for instance, fear that moral character education in public schools will transmit to their children a valueless, liberal ideology (Baer 1982).

The reluctant voices are receding into the background, however, as a growing number of politicians and academics have expressed publicly their opinions on educational policy as a means for promoting moral character education (Beardsley 1980; Bennett 1980b, 1986a; Kohlberg 1981; Wynne 1986). The common point of their arguments is that public schools should and can act on behalf of the nation's citizens by aiming to promote the moral character of the citizenry. The general public, itself, has not been reluctant to call for greater attention to moral values in education. The annual Gallup Poll, over the last decade, has consistently indicated that an overwhelming majority of all major sectors of the population support teaching moral values and moral behavior in the public schools. When asked, for instance, Would you favor or oppose instruction in the schools that would deal with morals and moral behavior? 79 percent of all respondents and 84 percent of those with school-aged children favored moral character education (Gallup 1980).

Beyond arguments pro and con, we believe that morality is inevitably the business of education. Intentionally or unintentionally all educators are involved in moral character education. Some, like Martin Luther King, are intentional public educators for justice. As a Socratic moral educator of adults, King explicitly based his moral leadership upon the equality and universality of human rights. All teachers, however, live with the fact that moral character "comes with the territory" (Purple and Ryan 1976). If moral values are not rationally and explicitly objectified, they are still there as part of the hidden and unstudied moral curriculum (Jackson 1968). Given that value neutrality is a fallacy, public education does have a legitimate and inevitable role in fostering moral character. How to go about it, is more controversial, of course.

HOW DOES ONE PROMOTE MORAL CHARACTER?

A considerable amount of discussion on how moral character can be promoted has taken place over the last century. Building on this intellectual history, two approaches have moved to the forefront of the current debate: moral socialization and moral development. The differences between these two approaches underlie the current debate in educational and social policy circles. We will first discuss and then critique both approaches, concluding with educational policy recommendations.

The Socialization of Moral Aspirations

Do students aspire to be selfish or altruistic, reckless or disciplined? The central importance of this question seems self-evident from a moral socialization perspective, which emphasizes the social transmission of values. The focus is on a person's learning particular moral aspirations that serve as the value content of moral reasoning. The historical roots of moral socialization theory are found in Émile Durkheim's *Moral Education* ([1925] 1973). In this volume, Durkheim focused his attention on socialization: the process whereby a person learns what to think and feel and what one should do through instruction, explanation, role models, and group reinforcement. From a moral socialization perspective, education for moral character is primarily about social solidarity, group conformity, and mutual support. In Durkheim's words,

Far from there being some inexpressible kind of antagonism between [the individual and society], far from it being the case that the individual can identify himself with society only at the risk of renouncing his own nature either wholly or in part, the fact is that he is not truly himself, he does not fully realize his own nature, except on the condition that he is involved in society. . . . Man is the more vulnerable to self-destruction the more he is detached from any collectivity. (pp. 67–68)

The pleasure grows in proportion as we can say "we" with more assurance and conviction. The whole point [of moral education] is to give the child a taste for this pleasure and to instill in him the need for it. . . . [A] means that could awaken in the child the feeling of solidarity is the very discreet and deliberate use of collective punishments and rewards. . . . It is important that the group be conscious of its responsibility for the morality of its members. (p. 244)

In sum, Durkheim suggests that what is true of the larger society is equally applicable to the school classroom. Collective responsibility, applied with restraint and judgment, is central to promoting moral character in both settings.

A moral socialization approach in contemporary education generally assumes that students will learn prosocial moral aspirations if educators actively indoctrinate them regarding prosocial values and behavior. This process may be facilitated by two primary means. First, educators must teach by the example of their personal character and behavior. They should be open and assertive about their opinions about what is right and wrong and should enlist students in practicing prosocial conduct in and around the school. Second, prosocial moral character can be effectively socialized through exposure to literature that exhibits exemplary moral aspirations and behavior. This process is thought to be more effective if it is integrated into the entire education curriculum so children can be thoroughly inculcated with particular moral ideals and behavioral standards.

One vocal proponent of the socialization approach is William Bennett (1983). He claims that teachers should present traditional U.S. values — respect for adults, love of country, sacrifice, courage, honor, fidelity — with conviction, not with tentativeness; he claims that education needs to return to the "great texts, great minds, and great ideas" of the Western tradition (1985a, p. 15). He notes, for instance, that the study of the classics has been dropped in favor of catering to "contemporary fascinations" and suggests that a necessary component in promoting moral character is exposure to the humanities (1982):

Students who haven't been introduced to the magnificence of the Renaissance or the drama of the U.S. Constitutional Convention are invited to explore the legacy of the Sixties. Students who haven't studied Aristotle, Aquinas, or Kant are urged to examine ethical dilemmas on their own. We have arrived at this dismal state because we have yielded to the bullying of those fascinated with the merely contemporary. . . . Great works, important bodies of knowledge and powerful methods of inquiry constitute the core of the humanities and sustain the intellectual, moral and political traditions of our civilization. If we . . . permit the fragmentation of the humanities to continue, then we will jeopardize everything we are most about. (p. 10)

Edward Wynne (1986) also argues that a breakdown in society is occurring, in part because contemporary education has abandoned the great traditions, including the virtue-laden humanities. These writers contend that a return to the explicit indoctrination of students with traditional values and habits will achieve a return to the prosocial values of the Western tradition.

The Development of Moral Justifications

Do students justify the aspiration not to cheat on a test because they hold to principles of fairness or because they fear getting caught by an authority? The central importance of this question seems self-evident from a moral development perspective, which focuses on a student's actively constructing increasingly universalizable moral principles rather than on a teacher's actively indoctrinating conventional social norms. Moral character education, then, involves supporting students' development of autonomous inner standards of justice that overcome the dependence on external authorities. The historical roots of moral development theory are found in Jean Piaget's *The Moral Judgment of the Child* ([1932] 1965). Piaget emphasized moral judgment development — the process whereby a person constructs increasingly complex and universal reasons why one should or should not take a particular moral course of action. In Piaget's words,

The problem is to know what will best prepare the child for its future task of citizenship. Is it the habit of external discipline gained under the influence of unilateral respect and of adult constraint, or is it the habit of internal discipline, of mutual respect and of "self-government"? . . . For ourselves, we regard as of the utmost importance the experiments that have been made to introduce democratic methods into schools. We therefore do not at all agree with Durkheim in thinking that it is the master's business to impose or even to "reveal" rules to the child. (pp. 362–64)

How does classroom democracy replace the unilateral respect of authority by the mutual respect of autonomous wills?

With regard to [morality], cooperation is at first the source of criticism and individualism. For by comparing his own private motives with the rules adopted by each and sundry, the individual is led to judge objectively the acts and commands of other people, including adults. Whence the decline of unilateral respect and the primacy of personal judgment. But in consequence of this, cooperation suppresses . . . egocentrism

... and thus achieves an interiorization of rules. ... The adult must therefore be a collaborator and not a master, from this double point of view, moral and rational. (pp. 403–4)

Piaget argues that educators can promote the development of mature moral reasoning by talking with children as equal collaborators in the search for knowledge. Educators who speak with indoctrinative authority, however, will promote the consolidation of childish reasoning. Thus, it is not surprising that Piaget, writing less than seven years after the publication of Durkheim's book, considered the moral development approach to be at "the opposite pole from the Durkheimian pedagogy" ([1932] 1965, p. 362).

Building on the work of Piaget, current moral development theory postulates that moral reasoning about issues of justice proceeds through an invariant sequence of stages toward an increasingly adequate understanding of what is just or fair; education's aim is to provide the conditions that promote this natural development. The moral development approach has been the most fully elaborated by psychologist Lawrence Kohlberg. He postulates that, for the developmentalist,

The problem of offering a non-indoctrinative education which is based on ethical and epistemological principles is partially resolved by a conception that these principles represent developmentally advanced or mature stages of reasoning, judgment, and action. Because there are culturally universal stages or sequences of moral development, stimulation of the child's development to the next stage in a natural direction is equivalent to a long-range goal of teaching ethical principles. Because the development of these principles is natural they are not imposed on the child — he chooses them himself. (1981, pp. 75–76)

For Kohlberg, the problem of pedagogical indoctrination was further resolved by using democratic teaching methods:

A concern for the child's freedom from indoctrination is part of a concern for the child's freedom to make decisions and act meaningfully. Freedom, in this context, means democracy, i.e., power and participation in a social system which recognizes basic equal rights. It is impossible for teachers not to engage in value-judgments and decisions. A concern for the liberty of the child does not create a school in which the teacher is value-neutral and any pretense of it creates "the hidden curriculum." But it can create a school in which the teacher's value-judgments and decisions involve the student democratically. (1981, p. 76)

A developmental approach to moral education is based on knowledge of the order of moral development stages, and the implementation of democracy ensures that the means, as well as the aims, of education will be fair and just.

CRITICISMS AND CONTROVERSY: SOCIALIZATION VERSUS DEVELOPMENT

Critiques of Moral Socialization

Some Piagetians are tempted to conclude that a Durkheimian approach is only concerned with the welfare of mindless conformists. The primary developmental critique of moral socialization, however, has been based on a rejection of cultural absolutism (that is, ethics based on conformity to the requirements of society). Referring to moral socialization as a bag of virtues approach, Kohlberg (1981) explained the problem in the following way:

Although it may be true that the notion of teaching virtues, such as honesty or integrity, arouses little controversy, it is also true that a value consensus on the goodness of these virtues conceals a great deal of actual disagreement over their definitions. What is one person's "integrity" is another person's "stubbornness," what is one person's honesty in "expressing your true feelings" is another person's insensitivity to the feelings of others. (pp. 9–10)

Developmentalists suggest that moral socialization leaves the teacher with the philosophical illusion of teaching moral absolutes that, in the context of a pluralistic society, are often culture bound. Furthermore, a moral socialization approach does not provide the teacher with guidance in identifying other culturally nonrelative moral principles — values that are genuinely universalizable aims of education.

The pluralism of social norms also creates practical limitations for an indoctrinative pedagogy. Lacking truly universalizable ethical principles from which to evaluate competing claims, the proponents of indoctrination leave themselves vulnerable to the likes and dislikes of special interest groups. Pedagogically, who will judge the types of literature to be consumed by the students? How will individuals be judged as role models? For instance, "to identify morality with conformity is to be forced to take the position that a loyal Nazi was behaving morally" (Lickona 1976, p. 3). When the cultural relativity of many traditional norms is revealed, ethical relativity and ethical paralysis may result, instead of what is needed: a universalizable principle of justice that transcends cultural diversity.

Even if children are provided with moral role models and upright literature, developmentalists argue that it is illogical to assume that this alone will facilitate moral behavior. Beyond exemplary role models, moral behavior entails cognitive understanding and the exercise of free will. Even Durkheim was careful to indicate that "to teach morality is neither to preach nor to indoctrinate; it is to explain" ([1925] 1973), p. 120). The difference between persuasive explanation and oppressive indoctrination, the critics argue, sometimes seems to be lost on advocates of moral socialization.

A final major critique of the moral socialization approach is that its empirical support is quite limited. A long history of research has consistently demonstrated that simply being taught particular philosophical virtues — such as honesty, humility, and bravery — does not make students significantly more likely to act on those virtues; simply being exposed to a pedagogy of moral socialization — highly directive role models, upright literature, and courses in the humanities and social studies — does not significantly improve students' moral reasoning or behavior (Hartshorne and May 1928–30; Havighurst and Taba 1949; Milgrim 1974; Schlaefli, Rest, and Thoma 1985; Willging and Dunn 1982). What appear in the footnotes of articles by opponents of moral indoctrination are usually references to rhetorical arguments rather than empirical studies.

In defense of a socialization approach to moral character education, however, a few additional points can be made. First, the rejection of ethical relativism (that is, the supposed impossibility of universal ethical principles) is an important philosophical stand. Socialization-oriented educators accurately recognize that psychological theorizing about moral education cannot be value-neutral; all approaches to moral character education presuppose some standard of adequacy defining the direction of development. Not only can it not be any other way, it should not be any other way; when society cannot rest assured that some values are better than others, even civil disobedience becomes pointless.

Second, the claim that teachers should aim to help students become good, not just smart, is a courageous pedagogical call to moral literacy (Wynne 1986). As intellectuals from Ralph Waldo Emerson to Robert Coles have recognized, character is higher than, even if partly dependent upon, intellect (Coles 1986). Socialization advocates also make a significant point regarding the current inadequate educational focus on the humanities. They correctly claim that clarity can be brought to modern dilemmas when these are examined in light of past history. Studying the classics can also help students to anticipate forthcoming contemporary ethical dilemmas. Juxtaposing past and present ethical dilemmas further reminds us that many of the fundamental questions of the past and those of today remain essentially the same: "What is justice? What should be loved? What deserves to be defended? What is courage? What is noble? What is base?" (Bennett 1985a, p. 6). Ethical relativists who urge schools to avoid these questions and provide no direction toward better answers are in effect advocating an abandonment of moral responsibility.

Third, from an empirical perspective, it should be acknowledged that no program of evaluation research can ever prove the truth of a particular model of development or education; it can only provide support or fail to provide support. Short of proof, historical trend analyses do provide tentative societal-level support for a socialization perspective. The best historical research to date examining the role of moral character education in society has been completed by political scientist James Q. Wilson and psychologist Richard Herrnstein (1985). Citing trends perceived in crime statistics, they show a historic inverse relationship between individuals' criminal activities and society's moral character-building activities for young people: increased investment in moral character-building activities has coincided with lower crime rate during the last one hundred years. They point out that "in the mid-nineteenth century, childbearing advice emphasized the importance of inculcating moral and religious principles," and civic organizations directly promoted activities that encouraged virtuous behavior (p. 420). Wilson and Herrnstein contend that these activities had a positive effect in reducing crime in society. Demographer Peter Uhlenberg similarly notes increased levels of substance abuse, unintended pregnancies, and crime among adolescents, which he suggests can be understood as a function of declining levels of moral character (Uhlenberg and Eggebeen 1986).

Turning from societal-level research to studies of actual changes within particular individuals, it is also important to note that the failure of the latter to provide support for the effectiveness of a socialization approach may be caused by our asking the research questions too simply. For instance, although the positive effects of specific humanities classes alone upon moral reasoning are not evident empirically, perhaps humanities courses provide a necessary but insufficient condition for moral character development. From this perspective, in conjunction with other educational experiences, humanities courses would function as a catalyst in promoting moral maturity. Support for this interpretation can be found in the fact that the cumulative effect of formal education is strong; years in college, for instance, add significantly to the predictability of moral maturity in young adulthood (Rest and Thoma 1985).

Critiques of Moral Development

Some Durkheimians are tempted to conclude that developmentalists are only concerned with the welfare of powerless philosophers.

For instance, Paul Vitz's criticisms of U.S. education in general and of moral development education in particular also include a philosophical critique of liberalism (Vitz 1985). Socialization advocates, in general, have tended to assume that a developmental approach to moral education must be a purveyor of liberal ideology. This logical leap, of course, is the mirror image of a liberal logical assumption that moral socialization must inevitably be conservative, indoctrinative, dangerous, and inferior.

An educational methodology critique has also been raised. One common developmental approach to moral education uses classroom moral dilemma discussions as a means of promoting students' moral growth. Critics have characterized this method as dilemma mongering. Part of their rationale is as follows:

> In sum, students do not learn that there is an intimacy between moral reflections and their normally noncritical daily affairs. They do not learn that not all morally important matters are problems; they do not learn that reasonable people of good will have much in common and can disagree; and they do not learn that moral sophistication and the capacity to understand and discuss complex moral issues are not achieved instantly. (Bennett 1980a, p. 31)

Bennett, in particular, objects to the use of dilemmas because he believes that they are basically contemporary dilemmas, further reflecting the contemporary fascinations that he believes have blighted the humanities (1982).

Finally, critics indirectly attack the empirical support for the effectiveness of developmental interventions by arguing that, in fact, a moral development approach offers less than what it was intended to replace — indoctrination. Critics suggest, for instance, that it advances an approach that would force upon pupils an authority much more malevolent in its effects than any conventional form of authority. This malevolent authority, some fear, would emerge in the form of a tyrannical catering to minorities and special interest groups.

On behalf of a moral development approach to character education, a few replies can be offered. First, the philosophical labeling of modernist liberalism is a half-truth and, as such, is not accurate. For example, Kohlberg's discussion of the higher stages of moral reasoning is sometimes similar to a liberal moral or political view, such as his justification for opposing capital punishment (1981). Kohlberg has also stated, however, that "liberalism as an ideology which has dominated the West is in trouble and, to be viable, requires some reconstruction" (1984, p. 323). His modern conception of justice actually builds on a long philosophical tradition, ranging from the work of Socrates some 2,500 years ago, to Locke and Kant, and to his contemporary John Rawls (1971). This definition of justice is best described by the word *fairness*. Rawls's particular formalization of the justice principle ensures the equal consideration of the claims of each person affected by "choosing under a 'veil of ignorance' in which the chooser . . . must choose a principle or policy with which one could best live in any position" (Kohlberg 1984, p. 636). Most simply, justice is fairness. This moral principle represents a flexible guideline for identifying and balancing the perspectives of all persons involved. Neither socialization nor developmental advocates have a monopoly on the moral good. The adequacy of any approach to moral character education can be measured as a function of its ability to incorporate the principle of justice.

Second, the pedagogical critique of an overreliance on classroom discussions of hypothetical moral dilemmas is about ten years out of date. The first genuine venture in developmental moral education began with an experiment by Moshe Blatt (1969), who attempted to facilitate moral stage development among sixth-grade students through weekly classroom discussion of hypothetical moral dilemmas. Blatt found that over one-third of the students in the experimental group advanced in their stage of moral development during the year, whereas few of the students in the control group exhibited any stage change. Subsequently, developmentally oriented educators implemented this methodology through dilemma discussions that were integrated into the curriculum of classes on the humanities (for example, literature) and social studies (for example, history). These programs produced statistically significant gains in moral maturity, but their pedagogical significance was generally modest in that students' gains were typically small (Blatt and Kohlberg 1975). Such findings led developmentalists to broaden their view of a moral education pedagogy. As Kohlberg recalls:

> Continuing work in the schools led me to a view . . . that moral education must deal directly with action and not just with reasoning, with "real-life" situations and not just with hypothetical ones. . . . It led me to the formulation of a participatory democracy or "just community" as the context for moral discussion and moral education. Our theory of moral education then, is changing and . . . developing through an interchange between psychological theorists and practitioners. (1983, p. xiii)

The broadening of their educational pedagogy led developmentalists to establish classroom and school governance through direct participatory democracy in a number of settings (for reviews, see Berkowitz and Oser 1985; Power 1981; Reimer, Paolitto, and Hersh

1983). The teacher's role in these schools is not as a facilitator but as an advocate, and this advocacy must operate within the constraints of students' democratic participation. Through these methods, students and teachers ideally share the responsibility for decisions regarding issues of fairness. In sum, the current developmental approach to moral character education involves two elements: integrating the discussion of hypothetical and historical moral dilemmas into the classroom curriculum and instituting developmentally appropriate democratic school governance programs that allow students to participate directly in the decision-making process.

Socialization advocates' empirical critique (for example, Vitz 1985) of a developmental approach to moral education is also quite dated. In the early years, much of the research done in this field was rather sloppy, and it quite appropriately came under heavy criticism. During the last decade, however, hundreds of reliable empirical studies have been conducted, and, most recently, several systematic evaluative reviews of Kohlbergian research have been published. These reviews have drawn the following conclusions:

Developmentally, moral stage change among individuals is invariant, in sequence, and proceeds one stage at a time (for reviews, see Colby et al. 1983; Snarey 1985; Walker 1982).

Cross-culturally, the first four stages are found in virtually all cultural groups, and the highest measured level (stage 5, principled reasoning) is found in all complex cultural groups (that is, societies with elaborate systems of education), such as India, Japan, and Taiwan (for reviews, see Snarey 1985; Edwards 1986). This is not to deny, of course, that there may be genuine ethical principles held in other cultures in addition to those currently documented.

Despite the controversy regarding possible gender differences in moral judgment (see Gilligan 1982; Lyons 1983), the current empirical evidence indicates that there are no significant differences between males and females in moral development when measured by the current standardized scoring systems (for reviews, see Walker 1984; Thoma 1986). This is not to deny, of course, that there is more to moral development than justice reasoning.

Moral behavior and moral reasoning are positively and significantly associated. In both laboratory and real-life settings, moral reasoning has been demonstrated to be a significant predictor of moral action, including honesty, altruistic behavior, resistance to temptation, and nondelinquency. For instance, persons at higher moral stages are significantly more likely to give assistance to a stranger who needs medical attention (McNamee 1978; for reviews, see Blasi 1980; Kohlberg and Candee 1984). Pedagogically, the dilemma discussion approach has been shown to produce modest but definite educational effects upon moral development, while all other types of intervention programs produce smaller effects, and individual academic courses in the humanities and the social sciences produce no measurable effects. In addition, more substantial effects upon moral judgment development, including lower levels of school theft and drug abuse, have been produced by educational programs using a just-community approach to school governance. (For reviews, see Berkowitz and Oser 1985; Reimer, Paolitto, and Hersh 1983; Schlaefli, Rest, and Thoma 1985.)

Many important research questions, of course, remain to be addressed. In sum, the empirical support for a developmental approach to moral character education is substantial but not exhaustive.

CONCLUSIONS

U.S. education during the 1960s and 1970s embraced value neutrality and attempted to dissociate itself from moral character education (Ryan 1986). During the 1980s, "the most important change in how one defines the public interest," observes James Q. Wilson (1985b), "has been a deepening concern for the development of character in the citizenry" (p. 3), especially through public education. Socialization advocates tend to attribute this renewed interest to a need to address the rising crime rates and declining adherence to traditional norms. Developmental advocates tend to attribute it to a rediscovery of the principles underlying the Declaration of Independence and the Constitution. We believe that both are correct; both the ethical bill we continue to pay for our Irangates and each generation's rediscovery of the Bill of Rights are involved. Beyond this, we believe that a movement toward consensus is not only possible but crucial for the success of moral character education. In outlining what we see as a growing consensus, we will focus on the common philosophical and pedagogical ground between socialization and developmental approaches to moral character education, using Bennett and Kohlberg as exemplars of their respective approaches.

Toward Consensus

U.S. philosopher and educator John Dewey (1911, 1916) viewed the endpoint of development as the building of a free and powerful moral character. As Bennett and other socialization advocates have noted, "John Dewey's forceful and highly influential writings concerning the interdependence of democracy, education, and moral character, are a modern reformulation of the old belief that 'virtue' can and should be taught in the schools" (Bennett and Delattre 1979, p. 81). Similarly, developmentalists have commended Dewey's perspective on the aim of education as centered on moral development and on the concordance of moral action with moral judgment (for example, Kohlberg and Mayer 1972). From a philosophical perspective, furthermore, both socialization and developmental advocates join Kant in rejecting ethical relativism. For instance, both Kohlberg and Bennett have critiqued Sidney Simon's (1971) pedagogical approach — values clarification — as regrettably based on ethical relativity. Both camps suggest that relativistic pedagogues leave the teacher without any guidance in transmitting values and communicate the logical implication that values cannot be taught in the classroom (Bennett and Delattre 1978; Kohlberg and Mayer 1972). It appears that both approaches share a commitment to promoting moral growth as an aim of education. Their philosophical differences involve different emphases on ethical principles and traditional values.

In this regard, it is important to note that a Durkheimian approach need not be based upon an indoctrinative pedagogy. Bennett, for instance, rejects this approach: "It is important that students learn more principles and rules, but at the same time, it is essential that they discover the good or right reasons for holding to any such principles and rules" (Bennett and DeLattre 1979, p. 8). "I am not talking about browbeating students into accepting [a] point of view. That is simply indoctrination, which we all deplore. I am talking about intellectual honesty and ethical candor" (Bennett 1985b, p. 5). The concern that students discover better reasons for holding particular values points to a common ground with a developmental perspective, insofar as moral education facilitates students' ability to engage in a rational construction and assessment of moral values and to achieve a consistency of reasoning and action (compare Boyd 1986). For instance, Bennett's discussion of the study of history on the elementary school level acknowledges that "we must recognize that children need to develop certain cognitive skills before they can handle abstract . . . concepts" (1986b, p. 128). The perspective is also reflected in socialization advocates' discussions of the state of humanities courses at colleges and universities; they have stressed that students should read original texts, not just secondary sources, and should be expected to reflect on them, discuss them, and write about them in order to discover the power of ideas. They obviously have more in mind than a passive learner. In sum, both approaches acknowledge that moral character education must be sensitive to the student's present level of development.

A socialization educator's emphasis on including particular Western values in education is also consistent with a developmentalist's perspective to the extent that both view these values as the concrete expression of more abstract universal ethical principles that underlie "our own and other civilizations" (Bennett 1985a, p. 6). For instance, Bennett's view of the U.S. Constitution as a core statement of these universalizable Western values is consistent with Kohlberg's view that the U.S. Constitution is a stage 5 or morally principled document (Bennett 1980b; Kohlberg 1984). In short, both claim that the Constitution contains universal moral values, and both support a philosophy of education that claims that these values should be taught in the public schools.

From a pedagogical perspective, both socialization- and developmental-oriented educators view the formation of moral character as relevant to the total curriculum and view the group as a means of promoting moral character development. A concrete example of this area of agreement can be found when we compare Kohlberg and Bennett. Kohlberg's reluctance to isolate moral education as a separate component of the curriculum and his call for democratic discussion and decision making in schools are not dissimilar to Bennett's claim that "moral education properly belongs in every part of the programs and curriculum of the school; matters of moral import should be discussed when they arise, as they inevitably will, as real issues" (Bennett and DeLattre 1979, p. 6).

Differences in philosophy revolve around different conceptions of the educator's role and authority in the group. In this regard, it is crucial to note that the conclusions Kohlberg reached during the last decade of his life were very Durkheimian. In one of the first public statements of his revised perspective, he said:

It [a developmental model] is not a sufficient guide to the moral educator, who deals with concrete morality in a school world in which value content as well as structure, behavior as well as reasoning, must be dealt with. In this context, an educator must be a socializer, teaching value content and behavior, not merely a Socratic or Rogerian process-facilitator of development. In becoming a socializer and advocate, the teacher moves into "indoctrination," a step that I originally believed to be invalid. . . . I no longer hold these negative views of indoctrinative moral education, and I now believe that the concepts of guiding moral education must be partly "indoctrinative." This is true, by necessity, in a world in which children engage in stealing, cheating, and aggression and in a context wherein one cannot wait until children reach the fifth stage to deal directly with moral behavior. . . . I now believe that moral education can be in the form of advocacy or "indoctrination" without violating the child's rights *if* there is an explicit recognition of shared rights of teachers and students and as long as teacher advocacy is democratic, or subject to the constraints of recognizing student participation in the rule-making and value-upholding process. (1978, pp. 14–15)

Moral education, according to the revised Kohlberg, involves both the socialization of moral aspirations and developmental promotion of moral justifications (compare Kohlberg 1978, 1985). In Kohlberg's words we hear a stress on behavior as well as on reasoning, on educators serving as Durkheimian socializers as well as acting as Piagetian developmental facilitators. Kohlberg's stress on the learner as a member of a democracy can also be heard in the words of Bennett: "The most important teaching of morality is done by living example. Students learn about how to treat others through the ways in which they themselves are treated" (Bennett and Delattre 1979, p. 6). It follows that, if we want to prepare students to function as mature adult members of a democratic society, then the educational means of achieving this aim must also be democratic. The style in which democratic methods are implemented must also vary according to the students' age and developmental readiness.

There is clearly a growing interaction between developmental and socialization approaches — between learning about the depths of human depravity and about the heights of human ideals, between concern with school morality and school solidarity, between responsibilities and rights, between society and the individual. Developmentalists have acknowledged that students must first learn to obey society's rules before they can reasonably understand when it is ethically required not to be obedient; socializationists have acknowledged that there are better and worse reasons for students to follow the rules. Both agree that, even though normative values should generally be upheld for the good of society, there are times when disobedience to authority is ethically required. In sum, we find that developmental versus socialization approaches represent distinct but paradoxically complementary emphases rather than unbridgeable dichotomies (compare Gibbs and Schnell 1985). Educational policy and practice must encompass both developmental and socialization perspectives as interdependent approaches to a common aim; neither approach can carry the full weight of moral character education.

Toward Policy Recommendations

Educational policy must do two things. First, it must renew the public schools' mandate to help students rediscover the universal principles underlying the United States' core documents: the Declaration of Independence, the Federalist Papers, the Constitution, and the Bill of Rights. Second, it must renew the public schools' mandate to help each generation of students experience these universal principles through democratic decision making regarding issues of fairness; schools can play an important role in renewing our commitment to participatory democracy as a central cultural value. Practically speaking, this means that students must be socialized to understand the values embodied in the U.S. Constitution and the Bill of Rights through formal instruction, and students must develop their ability to be democratic through a system of classroom and school governance based on direct participatory democracy. The Constitution and Bill of Rights articulate moral principles that subsume even interpersonal qualities such as fairness, honesty, and charity.

How might schools embody a concern for the establishment of curricula that promote a growing understanding of the principles upon which the U.S. government is founded? Most simply, the content of current social studies and humanities curricula should focus on the U.S Constitution (for example, the Bill of Rights as an outline of natural rights prior to law and society) and upon actual ethical dilemmas encountered during the course of the nation's history (for instance, President Truman's decision to use the atomic bomb in World War II, or constitutional-era farmers' decision to count slaves as three-fifths of a person). A keystone of this curriculum is that students be introduced to the emotionally compelling history behind the U.S. Constitutional Convention. Ladenburg (1977), for instance, has developed a curriculum unit that helps students to understand the excitement and importance of the writing of the U.S. Constitution by having students study and assume the roles of the nation's founders. "The exercise of writing a constitution is really an experience in arriving at a social contract," he states. "By playing the roles assigned to them in the convention, students . . . partake in their nation's political-historical culture [and] they gain the ability to see the situation from another point of view which is an essential factor in [achieving] . . . a responsible adult perspective" (pp. 193–94). Such an approach recognizes the U.S. Constitution as a core, classic document that is able to provide unity and continuity to the mission of public education in the United States (Fowler 1984). Such approaches also illustrate that the discussion of moral questions must be integrated into the context of the historical data and the school's curriculum. Constitution-based education will promote students' ability to understand both their responsibilities and their rights in their constitutional democracy and to develop a loyalty to the democratic process. As Kohlberg has also argued, in agreement with political figures from Jefferson to Bennett, "a central purpose of public education is the development of an active and enlightened citizenry, that is, a citizenry that has an understanding of the principles of justice which are the presupposition of our constitutional democracy" (1978, p. 13).

How might a school embody a concern for the establishment of democracy and promote the re-creation of the principles of the Constitution in everyday life? Most simply, a school should practice governance by developmentally appropriate, direct participatory democracy and should encourage a sense of community conscious-ness and group responsibility among its members. Such a curriculum would focus on the ethical relations among students and between students and staff (Giroux and McLaren 1986). Every school day, at every grade level, ethical decisions are confronted: being responsible with homework assignments, not cheating on a test, confronting a fellow student who is cheating, responding to acts of violence, and obeying a teacher's request. All of these situations provide the content — the practical concerns and daily dilemmas — for group discussion and decision making, for teachers to explain their opinions on ethical issues, and for all to experience being democratic.

The keystone of such a just-community school would be a weekly community meeting — a gathering of students and staff to decide upon classroom or school rules, policies, and practices that deal with issues of fairness. These meetings can be organized on the classroom level for all grades, with regular schoolwide meetings also held at the higher grade levels. Even young children can be exposed to "some limited choices and 'votes' within the classroom" (Shaheen 1986). The general aim would be to help students achieve a sense of community solidarity and, within this context, to arrive democratically at fair decisions, to implement these decisions through action, and, as necessary, to change their decisions democratically (Jennings and Kohlberg 1983; Reimer, Paolitto, and Hersh 1983, pp. 236–61; Snarey 1987). The particular aims include the formation of the following characteristics:

1. Concern for people, or respect for persons as such. The person of good will is committed to just treatment of all and not to special consideration in his own case.
2. The capacity to take the place and point of view of another person as though it were one's own. This amounts to the moral imagination required to understand the views, beliefs, and feelings of others, and the diligence to think about personal conduct and treatment of others as they would be likely to perceive it.
3. Respect for the relevant factual information (evidence) which must be considered in moral deliberation and

judgment, and for the kinds of reasons that merit attention in moral life.

4. Finally, the presence of aspirations that reach beyond considerations of what is [minimally] universally obligatory under a given set of circumstances. The goal here is to achieve a conception of what is worthy of oneself, in light of one's worthy commitments and interests (Bennett and DeLattre 1979, p. 6).

Just-community schools provide an avenue for teachers and administrators to embody these ideals in their treatment of students and each other. It is not our aim to prescribe a detailed moral character pedagogy but rather to indicate that such a pedagogy is needed and possible. The differences between socialization and developmental approaches to moral character education are reconcilable. The movement that both socialization- and developmental-oriented educators have shown toward more balanced positions may also represent movement toward the achievement of the educational aim of socializing our students to aspire with Dr. Martin Luther King (1963) that one day our children "will not be judged by the color of their skin, but by the content of their character" (p. 42). And, furthermore, the movement may develop in our students the ability to justify with Dr. King that we hold these aspirations because of the principle that all persons have the same human rights and should be treated with dignity, as free and equal autonomous persons. It is now time for socialization and developmental educators to work together.

REFERENCES

Baer, R. A. (1982). Parents, schools and values clarification. *Wall Street Journal,* April 12, p. 22.

Beardsley, E. (1980). Moral development as an objective of government. In *Moral Development and Politics,* edited by R. Wilson and G. Schochet, pp. 41–54. New York: Praeger.

Bennett, W. J. (1980a). The teacher, the curriculum, and values education development. *New Directions for Higher Education* 31 (3): 27–34.

___. (1980b). What value is values education? *American Educator* 4 (3): 31–32.

___. (1982). The shattered humanities. *Wall Street Journal,* December 31, p. 10.

___. (1983). A question of values. *National Review,* September 30, pp. 1209–10.

___. (1985a). To reclaim a legacy. *American Education* 21 (1): 4–15.

___. (1985b). Education and character: Educators in America. *Current* 275 (September): 3–7.

___. (1986a). The condition of American higher education. Address given at the 350th anniversary convocation, September, Harvard University, Cambridge, Mass.

___. (1986b). First lessons. *Phi Delta Kappan* 68 (2): 125–29.

Bennett, W. J., and E. J. DeLattre. (1978). Moral education in the schools. *The Public Interest* 50 (Winter): 81–98.

———. (1979). A moral education: Some thoughts on how best to achieve it. *American Educator* 3 (4): 6–9.

Berkowitz, M., and F. Oser, eds. (1985). *Moral education: Theory and application*. Hillsdale, N.J.: Lawrence Erlbaum.

Blasi, A. (1980). Bridging moral cognition and moral action: A critical review of the literature. *Psychological Bulletin* 88: 1–45.

Blatt, M. (1969). Studies on the effects of classroom discussion upon children's moral development. Ph.D. diss., University of Chicago.

Blatt, M., and L. Kohlberg. (1975). Effects of classroom discussion on children's level of moral judgment. *Journal of Moral Education* 4 (2): 129–61.

Boyd, D. (1986). Beyond Bennett. Paper presented at the annual conference of the American Educational Research Association, April, San Francisco.

Colby, A., L. Kohlberg, J. Gibbs, and M. Lieberman. (1983). A longitudinal study of moral judgment. *Monographs of the Society for Research in Child Development* 48 (1–2): 1–124.

Coles, R. (1986). Beyond the IQ: Education and human development. Symposium paper presented at Harvard University, September, Cambridge, Mass.

Dewey, J. (1911). *Moral principles in education*. Boston: Houghton Mifflin.

———. (1916). *Democracy and education*. New York: Free Press. Reprinted 1966.

Durkheim, É. (1925). *Moral education: A study in the theory and application of the sociology of education*. New York: Free Press. Reprinted 1973.

Edwards, C. (1986). Cross-cultural research on Kohlberg's stages: The basis for consensus. In *Lawrence Kohlberg: Consensus and controversy*, edited by S. Modgil and C. Modgil, pp. 419–30. Philadelphia: Falmer Press.

Fowler, J. (1984). Pluralism, particularity, and paideia. *Journal of Law and Religion* 2: 263–307.

Gallup, G. (1980). *The Gallup poll: Public opinion 1980* (12th annual). Wilmington, Del.: Scholarly Resources.

Gibbs, J., and S. Schnell. (1985). Moral development "versus" socialization: A critique. *American Psychologist* 40 (10): 1071–80.

Gilligan, C. (1982). *In a different voice: Psychological theory and women's development*. Cambridge, Mass.: Harvard University Press.

Giroux, H., and P. McLaren. (1986). Teacher education and the politics of engagement: The case for democratic schooling. *Harvard Educational Review* 56 (3): 213–38.

Hartshorne, H., and M. A. May. (1928–30). *Studies in the nature of character*. 3 vols. New York: Macmillan.

Havighurst, R. J., and H. Taba. (1949.) *Adolescent character and personality*. New York: Wiley.

Jackson, P. (1968). *Life in the classroom*. New York: Holt, Rinehart and Winston.

Jennings, W., and L. Kohlberg. (1983). Effects of a just community program on the moral development of youthful offenders. *Journal of Moral Education* 12 (1): 33–50.

King, M. L. (1963). I have a dream. Speech delivered at the Lincoln Memorial, August 28, Washington, D.C.

Kohlberg, L. (1978). Moral education reappraised. *The Humanist* 38 (November–December): 13–15.

———. (1981). *Essays on moral development*. Vol. I, *The philosophy of moral development*. San Francisco: Harper and Row.

———. (1983). Foreword. In *Promoting moral growth*, edited by J. Reimer, D. Paolitto, and R. Hersh, pp. ix–xviii. New York: Longman.

____. (1984). *Essays on moral development*. Vol. II, *The psychology of moral development*. San Francisco: Harper and Row.

____. (1985). High school democracy and educating for a just community. In *Moral education: A first generation of research and development*, edited by R. Mosher, pp. 20–57. New York: Praeger.

Kohlberg, L., and D. Candee. (1984). The relationship of moral judgment to moral action. In *Morality, moral behavior, and moral development*, edited by W. Kurtines and J. Gewirtz, pp. 52–73. New York: Wiley-Interscience.

Kohlberg, L., and R. Mayer. (1972). Development as the aim of education. *Harvard Educational Review* 42 (4): 449–96.

Ladenburg, T. (1977). Cognitive development and moral reasoning in the teaching of history. *History Teacher*, March, pp. 184–98.

Lee, G., ed. (1961). *Crusade against ignorance: Papers of Thomas Jefferson on education*. New York: Columbia Teachers College Press.

Lickona, T., ed. (1976). *Moral development and behavior*. New York: Holt, Rinehart and Winston.

Lyons, N. (1983). Two perspectives on self, relationships, and morality. *Harvard Educational Review* 53: 125–45.

McNamee, S. (1978). Moral behavior, moral development and motivation. *Journal of Moral Education* 7: 27–31.

Milgrim, S. (1974). *Obedience to authority*. New York: Harper & Row.

Piaget, J. (1932). *The moral judgment of the child*. New York: Free Press. Reprinted 1965.

Power, C. (1981). Moral education through the development of the moral atmosphere of the school. *Journal of Educational Thought* 15 (1): 4–19.

Purple, D., and K. Ryan, eds. (1976). *Moral education: It comes with the territory*. Berkeley, Calif.: McCutchan.

Rawls, J. (1971). *A theory of justice*. Cambridge, Mass.: Harvard University Press.

Reimer, J., D. Paolitto, and R. Hersh. (1983). *Promoting moral growth: From Piaget to Kohlberg*. New York: Longman.

Rest, J., and S. Thoma. (1985). Relation of moral judgment to formal education. *Developmental Psychology* 21 (4): 709–14.

Ryan, K. (1986). The new moral education. *Phi Delta Kappan*, November, pp. 228–33.

Schlaefli, A., J. Rest, and S. Thoma. (1985). Does moral education improve moral judgment? A meta-analysis of intervention studies using the defining issues test. *Review of Educational Research* 55 (3): 319–52.

Shaheen, J. (1986). Steppingstones toward citizenship: Little children speak up for fairness. *Moral Education Forum* 11 (2): 1–16.

Simon, S. (1971). Value clarification versus indoctrination. *Social Education* 3 (December): 902–5, 915.

Snarey, J. (1985). Cross-cultural universality of social-moral development: A critical review of Kohlbergian research. *Psychological Bulletin* 97 (2): 202–32.

____. (1987). Promoting moral maturity among adolescents: An ethnographic study. *Comparative Education Review* 3 (2): 241–59.

Thoma, S. (1986). Estimating gender differences in the comprehension and preference of moral issues. *Developmental Review* 6: 165–80.

Uhlenberg, P., and D. Eggebeen. (1986). The declining well-being of American adolescents. *The Public Interest* 82 (Winter): 25–38.

Vitz, P. (1985). Ideological biases in today's theories of moral education. In *Whose values? The battle for morality in pluralistic America*, edited by C. Horn, pp. 113–38. Ann Arbor, Mich.: Servant.

Walker, L. (1982). The sequentiality of Kohlberg's stages of moral development. *Child Development* 53: 1330–36.

_____. (1984). Sex differences in the development of moral reasoning: A critical review. *Child Development* 55: 677–91.

Will, G. (1987). Three balls, two strikes. *Newsweek*, January 5, p. 64.

Willging, T., and T. Dunn. (1982). The moral development of law students. *Legal Education* 31: 306–58.

Wilson, J. Q. (1985a). Why we should teach character. *Thomas Jefferson Research Center Newsletter* 216 (March-April): 1–4.

_____. (1985b). The rediscovery of character: Private virtue and public policy. *The Public Interest* 81 (Fall): 3–16.

Wilson, J. Q., and R. Herrnstein. (1985). *Crime and human nature*. New York: Simon and Schuster.

Wynne, E. (1986). The great tradition in education: Transmitting moral values. *Educational Leadership*, January, pp. 4–9.

3

Shaping an Acceptable Child

Nel Noddings

Feminists have begun the important process of examining intellectual life — both its processes and concepts — from the standpoint of women. As we look at a particular theory, situation, or problem, Gerda Lerner advises us to ask, "If women were central to this argument, how would it be defined?"[1] Women do not, however, have to be the objects of argument. Rather, the idea is for the investigator to take up the standpoint of women and see what the world looks like from this perspective.[2] But one cannot speak only as a woman, for whatever else one is also may color the argument, and a danger arises that the world of epistemological subjects will be broken down into many radical subjectivities.[3] There is, however, protection against this fragmentation. Writing as a woman, one can be careful to choose experiences that cut broadly across the lives of most women; note situations, opinions, or problems that are affected by membership in other groups; and couch one's conclusions in language that is moderate and makes claim only to a contribution toward a cumulative universality — not to universality itself.[4]

In an article entitled "Maternal Thinking," Sara Ruddick gives us a way to start thinking about moral education from the standpoint of women.[5] She identifies three interests that guide maternal practice: preserving the child's life, fostering the individual growth of the child, and shaping an acceptable child. "The interest in preservation, growth, and the acceptability of the child," Ruddick warns, "are frequently and unavoidably in conflict."[6] This conflict gives rise to analysis and reflective thought. In this chapter, I want to see what can be learned by approaching moral education with these interests in mind. What conflicts arise? What intellectual advantages are gained? What tasks are posed? How should acceptability be defined?

TRADITIONAL THINKING: THE
INDIVIDUAL VERSUS SOCIETY

"Each of us is in a pitched battle with the rest of mankind," says Frazier, the protagonist of B. F. Skinner's *Walden Two*.[7] Not only must we compete for the necessities of physical life, but our faulty educational methods encourage us to compete — do literal battle — for every sort of good. The everybody else with whom we struggle is called society, says Frazier, and the dogged fight of the individual for a taste of freedom is doomed. Because the individual is inevitably a product of the environment, the solution must be to plan the society so that individuals with acceptable characteristics will be produced, and acceptability must be judged by a person's effects on others and their needs and desires.

In most political and educational philosophies, we find a sharp dichotomy between the interests of the individual and those of the society. The problem is defined, explored, and resolved in a variety of ways. Skinner lays down as a postulate the idea that man is not free, and he traces all human behavior to the conditioning of the environment. If happiness for individuals is agreed upon as an appropriate goal, then the society must be arranged in such a way that it will induce only those behaviors compatible with the happiness of all involved. No soul building in Skinner's utopia!

In direct contrast, the great idealist philosopher, Hegel, held that only the mind is real. Hegel envisioned the mind as a collective rationality, a highly conscious, concerted effort to coalesce toward the infinite. From this perspective, a powerful, well-ruled state is both an end to be pursued by thoughtful citizens and a sign of progress toward Absolute Mind.[8] Inevitably, in such a state, those less gifted intellectually will be somewhat baffled by their condition and must be directed by those intelligent and courageous enough to take risks. Society (defined as the state) is supreme here not because it shapes and conditions, but because it is the highest expression of mind. Allegiance is owed to it, and progress comes out of the battle engaged to construct it.

Rousseau also explored the conflict between the individual and society, but instead of casting the state as a representative of Absolute Mind, he castigated existing governments for their propensity to crush individual freedom and induce inequalities. Again, we have a sharp dichotomy between individual and society. Indeed, Rousseau believed that interdependence itself generates slavery and misery.[9] His educational philosophy is, as a result, deeply pessimistic, for the education of a free individual can never be entirely compatible with that of a citizen.

In contrast to the long-standing supposition that conflict is inherent in the relation between individuals and society, John

Dewey's philosophy locates individuality itself in the life of the community, thus obliterating the traditional dichotomy. It is not that Dewey denies the existence of conflicts among actual individuals or between particular individuals and their governments, but he denies that there is an inherent conflict between the individual and society.[10] Using the powerful concepts of interaction and transaction, Dewey describes the relation between individual and society as one of mutual construction. The ideal society treasures its individuals (including dissidents) because they raise issues and provide opportunities that lead to inquiry and, thus, to deeper knowledge and progress.

Dewey's attempt to break down the old dichotomy was only partly successful. His claim that the conflict is not inherent opens the door to a new exploration of social policy and to a whole new way of looking at education. But although Dewey asserts that the enlightened society treasures its dissidents (which implies that a society striving toward enlightenment *should* treasure its dissidents), he does not tell us convincingly *why* persons in power should give way to plans that might reduce or constrain their power. Presumably persons in power would behave this way out of commitment either to inquiry itself or to the common good. But the idea of commitment to the common good, coupled with a firm belief in progress, has a familiar Hegelian ring to it. We are led to believe that all conflict can be resolved and used to move us collectively forward. We are not encouraged to examine the varieties and passions of the actual conflicts, nor the possibility that some conflicts must simply be lived and others resolved in a way that may be satisfactory for some individuals yet highly problematic for the contemporary society or vice versa. What is missing in Dewey's framework is a compelling interest that can unify thought and focus attention on nonviolent resolution or acceptance of conflicts.

The feminist view that I will advocate also denies the dichotomy between individual and society, but it does so by starting with a basic relation — one between mother and child — that compels a natural interest. It recognizes the conflicts that arise as one considers how best to raise a child in his or her particular society, but it also suggests a transformation of society for the sake of its children. The perspective here is that of the mother — one who has never been seen as representative of either state or individual; the starting point is the child.

THE MATERNAL PERSPECTIVE AND ITS CONFLICTS

The maternal perspective is constrained by three great interests: preserving the life of the child, fostering its growth, and shaping an acceptable child. Because mothers are concerned first with preserving the lives of their children, they must think relationally.

Clearly, the safety and well-being of our own children depends in large part on the decency and generosity of those around us. We have a significant stake in keeping other people reasonably comfortable and content. Conflicts arise, of course, but they are not initially conflicts between individuals or between the individual and society. The conflicts that do arise are of two sorts: clashes among maternal interests (for example, between preservation and acceptability) and clashes between motherhood and personhood. Both must be examined carefully, but let's start with the latter.

Today's women, both mothers and nonmothers, are often put off by a concentration on maternal thinking, because motherhood has long been associated with stereotypes of femininity and with powerlessness.[11] Further, nonmothers are likely to feel that claims about maternal thinking exclude them from a pseudoelite set of thinkers. This, of course, is not what Ruddick intends. She writes:

> In articulating and respecting the maternal, I do not underwrite the still current, false, and pernicious identification of womanhood with biological or adoptive mothering of particular children in families. For me, "maternal" is a social category: Although maternal thinking arises out of actual child-caring practices, biological parenting is neither necessary nor sufficient. Many women and some men express maternal thinking in various kinds of working and caring with others.[12]

The view that Ruddick expresses has its roots in what has been called social feminism[13] or maternal feminism.[14] It was a popular position among early feminists. Jane Addams, for example, held such a view. Because her mother died when Addams was very young, Addams was far more directly influenced by her father than by her mother. But she knew that her mother had been eulogized as a person who would be "missed everywhere, at home, in society, in church, in all places *where good is to be done and suffering relieved.*"[15] Although she herself never became a mother, Addams explicitly accepted the "old ideal of womanhood." In Addams, we find a line of thought compatible with maternal thinking: an insistence on "independent thought and action" directed toward the welfare and growth of others toward "good works and honest toil."[16] Thus nonmothers are not and historically have not been excluded from either an ideal of womanhood or from maternal thinking.

The problem for modern women is aggravated by talk of an ideal of womanhood. Such an ideal can too easily be used to enforce a pernicious stereotype of woman. It has been used as a nucleus — admirable in itself — around which all sorts of less admirable attributes have been clustered. Thus the ideal woman becomes a soft, kind, beautiful, silent, obedient, and often vacuous creature. Further, any woman who fails to measure up on whichever attributes are currently most admired somehow fails at womanhood itself. The language is clearly dangerous. The ideal detached from "womanhood," however, should be acceptable. It should be admirable for anyone to be guided by an ideal of good works and honest toil directed by independent thought and action. It should also be acceptable for a woman or a man to be guided by some other defensible ideal or by a combination of ideals used as regulatory mechanisms.

Because women have been relatively powerless in male-defined and dominated societies and because this powerlessness has been associated with motherhood and the ideal of womanhood, there is a strong temptation to reject any line of thought that seems to extol the traditional condition of women. Articulating the logic of female work and caring is, however, not the same as advocating or extolling the traditional condition. Ruddick comments on the mistake:

In their fight to preserve their nonmaternal aspirations and projects, mothers may belittle the importance of maternal experience in their lives. Or out of fear of their own anger at a limiting social identity as well as out of legitimate fury at the devaluation of mothers and motherliness, they may over-identify with the maternal identification foisted upon them, letting their nonmaternal working and loving selves die. Whichever we mothers do, and frequently we do both, the cost to our maternal and nonmaternal works and loves is enormous.[17]

Anyone who wants to use maternal thinking as a foundation for social, political, or ethical argument must face the substantial fears just discussed. For men attracted to this line of thinking, a comparable problem arises. Because maternal thinking is associated through use of the word *maternal* with women, it is automatically relegated to inferior status. To be accused of thinking or being like a woman is a fearful insult to a male's manhood. Thus we find ourselves in the odd predicament where neither men nor women in contemporary society are eager to be judged as maternal thinkers. We seem to have two choices (if we do not accept the traditional dichotomy): abandon such talk entirely, or undertake the monumental task of making maternal thinking respectable for both men and women, for persons. Ruddick has courageously chosen the latter, and I join her enthusiastically in this.

One might reasonably ask, however, why the dichotomy should be rejected in just this way. Why, that is, should both women and men adopt maternal thinking? Why not advocate parental thinking? Ruddick has been sharply criticized by J. C. Walker and M. A. O'Loughlin, among others, for equating parental thought with maternal thought.[18] Their objection is that her view denigrates the role of fathers. But Ruddick is actually quite clear on this. She wants both fathers and mothers to share equally and actively in the daily care and psychological parenting of children. When that day comes, Ruddick says, "there will be no more 'Fathers,' no more people of either sex who have power over their children's lives and moral authority in their children's world, *though they do not do the work of attentive love*" (emphasis added).[19] Her capitalization of *Fathers* is meant to signify what she rejects — the traditional patriarchal pattern of fathering.

There is no doubt that such a pattern has existed, and indeed, it has long been construed as natural. It is rooted in two important beliefs: first, that men have a natural superiority to women (one enhanced by Eve's role in the Fall)[20] and, therefore, should have authority over both women and children; and, second, that women are more deeply attached to their children than are men. The first belief seldom appears explicitly in contemporary writing; I will, therefore, set it aside. The second, however, often appears. In his essay on fatherhood, Gabriel Marcel, for example, expresses this belief:

> But what we can perhaps be right in saying is that in general there is a network of much closer connections and much more delicate innervation in the woman than in the man between the strictly sexual modes of experience and the special aspects of emotional activity opened up by the existence of the child. In this respect we should be tempted to say that the man is perhaps more naturally detached than the woman; or, more exactly, detachment which generally is of a morbid character in the woman, is on the contrary almost normal in the man, for in him it comes down to the originally distinct existence of modes of experience which can, and . . . should harmonize without encroaching on each other.[21]

Marcel locates the strength to father — to accept responsibility for offspring — in a creative vow to God. In contrast, most women find the strength to mother directly in the child. This is, in part at least, a physiological response. Nowhere in Marcel's lovely essay, however, do we read anything about the child or about passionate attachment. Marcel considers the possibility of feeling tenderness and compassion in the presence of this new being but says this is likely as not to give way to "a growing irritation in the presence of a mewling, unclean creature who demands ceaseless attention and exercises a veritable tyranny over its relations."[22] He describes fatherhood as a test to be passed,[23] as a "more or less hazardous conquest . . . full of ambushes,"[24] and finally as "a self-spending which can be compared to a gift."[25] "This pure act [of fatherhood] is inconceivable," he says, "without what I propose to call the *vœu créateur*."[26] Marcel presents a picture of the hero-father, one who recognizes his duty and vows to God that he will do it. There is no sign that he expects to gain strength, love, and lasting delight from his interaction with the child. The child and his own fatherhood are for him symbols of "quivering anticipation of a plenitude"[27]; he is first connected to God and through God to the child — a symbol of God's power. Indeed, Marcel sees power and its just use as the central problem of fatherhood.

Do all these considerations enable us to get a glimpse of how to set about solving the ethico-religious problem which here towers above all others: the problem of knowing to what extent the father can and should regard himself as invested by God himself with the authority which he is bound to exercise over his own children? It seems as though the *vœu créateur* can help us to avoid the excesses of a fatherhood oriented in a theocratic direction.[28]

The creative vow helps a man to avoid these excesses by reminding him continually that his own power derives from God and that, since God's power is tempered by mercy and justice, so should his own be so tempered. The authority itself is unquestioned, and the obligation of fathers is construed mainly as a just exercise of authority. The child is a symbol of eternity and as such, proof of both God's creativity and his delegation of proper authority.

I have spent considerable space on Marcel's essay because I believe it raises a possible problem for Ruddick's program. On the one hand, it underscores the point she has made so well — that Fathers are first and foremost inclined toward holding power and authority over their children. On the other hand, it may be that a different form of "attentive love" can be exercised by fathers. Perhaps physiological differences are greater than most feminists want to believe. It seems prudent to remain agnostic on this for the present and invite further analysis on both maternal and paternal thinking. If Fathers must go (and I agree with Ruddick on this), there may still be a form of thinking that is parental and yet not maternal; Fathers may have something distinctive to contribute. I would welcome the participation of men in the analysis of attentive love. It remains clearly reasonable in the meantime to develop a conception of maternal thinking and its influence on moral education. One ought not to assume, however, that maternal thinking is the only form of thinking that leads to a better, more moral conception of human interaction. As a defensible view of paternal thinking is developed, women may be attracted to it since we now hope men will be attracted to maternal thinking.

Let us consider next the conflicts that arise within maternal thinking. One can think of all sorts of examples of conflict between maternal interests in preservation and growth. It is quite natural to worry whether a child is ready for certain forms of experience that signify both possible danger and possible growth. Conscientious mothers inform themselves about developmental needs and readiness, and although we cannot banish every trace of fear when our children take their first plane trip alone or ride their first ocean wave on a surfboard, we seek a way to encourage independence with just the right note of caution. This is difficult, sensitive work in which mothers must avoid both carelessness and overprotection. The latter is a temptation not only because mothers are charged with the protection of their children but also because mothering represents an enormous opportunity for the exercise of power, and women have traditionally occupied few other areas of power.[29] Women who give way to the temptation to exercise unnecessary power over their offspring fall into pathologies of mothering.

The conflicts I am most interested in for present purposes are those between preservation and acceptability and between growth and acceptability. We are frankly concerned with the moral development of our children. Are there situations or occasions in which good people should put their own lives at risk? If so, should we prepare our children to be willing to do so? How? Can personal growth sometimes be a sign of selfishness, or is this way of putting things a contradiction in terms? Finally, if we agree that the acceptability of our children is an important maternal interest, to whom should children be acceptable? To what sort of persons and groups should our children be acceptable?

CALLING TRADITIONS INTO QUESTION

When we consider the conflict between preservation and acceptability, we must question traditions that define honor or acceptability so as to put the lives of our children at risk. In particular, the warrior model must be challenged. Ruddick has suggested that maternal thinking is in logical opposition to militarism.[30] Interpreting Ruddick, Grimshaw says "that the *task* of mothering is necessarily in contradiction to that of waging war; the objectives of each are in conflict with each other."[31] It seems right, for reasons that will become clear shortly, to concentrate on the logic of maternal thinking — including both the tasks to which it is applied and the interests that guide it — but the challenge to militarism cannot be a simple rejection of war as a solution to international quarrels. It must, rather, be cast as a thorough examination of the moral codes by which and to which we shape acceptable children.

Women, like men, can be fierce in defense of their young. Total pacifism is not congruent with what remains of our maternal instincts. If it appears that violence is the only means of protecting hearth and home, most of us — women and men — would use it. It will not do to argue that women are peace-loving and men warlike, although there is considerable evidence that women in general are more likely to oppose war and violence than men in general.[32] The point is not to paint one sex virtuous and the other villainous but to show how maternal thinking is logically incompatible with the traditional warrior code.

Maternal thinking and warrior thinking have at least one aim in common: preservation of those persons and ways of life held dear. The image of the warrior, however, has been developed in isolation from the instinct to preserve; it has escaped the purpose it once shared or might have shared with maternal thinking. For centuries, the warrior model has comprised a set of aggressive virtues and competitive skills defining manhood. To be acceptable in societies that adopt this model, a young man must be prepared to be a warrior, and a young woman must be prepared to support and to sacrifice her men in war. Even now, the model and the code are invoked officially as a call to honor — in the service of preservation — but their manifestations are destructive. One is hard put to argue that Rambo and Dirty Harry (or, in an earlier time, Odysseus and Achilles) act in the service of preservation.

War and warriors have long been glorified. Seth Schein remarks, "The earliest poetry extant in several major Indo-European language families — poetry which presumably reflects earlier, originally moral traditions — includes stories of the exploits of warrior-heroes who fight both for the benefit of their people and for their own glory."[33]

Possibly no one has written more eloquently on the virtues of the warrior and the horrors of war than William James. In both *The Varieties of Religious Experience* and "The Moral Equivalent of War," James extols the virtues and energy that accompany a just war but deplores its destruction and horror. Recognizing the great attractions of war and the romantic role it plays in our national histories and literature, James advises us to find "the moral equivalent of war: something heroic that will speak to men as universally as war does, and yet will be as compatible with their spiritual selves as war has proved itself incompatible."[34]

James had an opportunity here to explore the common interests of just warriors and mothers. He might have launched a careful analysis of virtues exercised by each in the interest of preserving the lives of sons and daughters. Surely courage, hardiness, and the willingness to take risks — all virtues praised by James — take on new coloration when examined from these two very different perspectives. James, however, does not undertake this sort of analysis. Even though he clearly saw the dreadful nature of war itself, he does not seem to have seen the connection between war and the model of manliness that supports and encourages it. He writes:

> History is a bath of blood. The *Iliad* is one long recital of how Diomedes and Ajax, Sarpedon and Hector *killed*. No detail of the wounds they made is spared us, and the Greek mind fed upon the story. Greek history is a panorama of jingoism and imperialism — war for war's sake, all the citizens being warriors. It is horrible reading, because of the irrationality of it all — save for the purpose of making "history" — and the history is that of the utter ruin of a civilization in intellectual respects perhaps the highest the earth has ever seen.[35]

James, like so many other writers, does not consider the challenge that Greek behavior directs to Greek intellect. How can a civilization so highly rated in intellectual respects be also governed by irrationality? In his admiration for the achievements of art and abstract thought, James overlooks the possibility that a way of life guided by the *Agon* was in part responsible for both the achievements and the irrationality. Maternal thinking was despised (denied altogether might be more accurate), and paternal thinking concentrated on the production of sons who would emulate and eventually surpass — even physically overcome — their fathers. Schein comments:

> *Aristeia* is a word used in later Greek for "excellence" or "prowess," including, in particular, the excellence or prowess of a Homeric warrior when he is on a victorious rampage, irresistibly sweeping all before him, killing whomever of the enemy he can catch or whoever stands against him. . . . [*Aristeuo*] is used by Glaukos when he tells Diomedes (6.207-9; cf. 11.783) that his father sent him to Troy and told him "always to be best and bravest and to surpass all others, / and not to disgrace the line of my fathers, who were / much the best."[36]

The words *good, excellent,* and *best* thus have a long association with striving in the sense of struggling with a contender for victory or supremacy. This sense of striving is still pervasive in contemporary U.S. culture and is widely perceived as virtuous. Everywhere we hear the importance of being number one. If this attitude, this worship of striving, gives rise to hate and fear in other people, we might do well to reexamine striving and related terms. In what sense are striving, hardihood, and risk taking virtuous? The answer for James had to be inextricably bound up with the idea of manliness. James shared the widespread fear of being like a woman, which he reveals in his discussions of both war and poverty. Recommending voluntary poverty as a virtuous and arduous way of life, he asks, "Does not the worship of material luxury and wealth, which constitute so large a portion of the 'spirit' of our age, make somewhat for effeminacy and unmanliness?"[37] Voluntary poverty — asceticism — is considered by James to be a challenge worthy of manliness. It requires fortitude. But he then notes that asceticism is not congruent with human nature, whereas war and fighting are so congruent. "But," he continues, "when we ask ourselves whether this wholesale organization of irrationality and crime [war] be our only bulwark against effeminacy, we stand aghast at the thought and think more kindly of ascetic religion."[38]

The fear of being like a woman has prevented a careful reevaluation of virtues associated with hardihood and has trapped wise, compassionate men like James in a dilemma that simultaneously deplores war and extols many of the behaviors that induce it. Maternal thinking, in contrast, begins by asking: Will this mode of behavior preserve the lives of my children? Will it foster their growth? Will it make them acceptable? To *whom* do I want them to be acceptable? Here questions begin to arise about the nature of our communities, but they are driven by interest in our children, not by devotion to some abstract conception of the state.

Male children are directly and obviously influenced by traditional conceptions of manliness and its associated virtues, but girls are also affected, if somewhat indirectly. Women have been asked to support the warrior model and to help their men meet the painful obligations of manhood. Indeed, failure to provide this support for a way of life defined in deliberate opposition to their own has been considered a moral failure on the part of women. M. Esther Harding writes, "The typical story is that he must join his regiment. When he goes to say goodbye to her she coaxes him to remain or is so alluring that he forgets his obligation, and the army entrains without him."[39]

Such incidents are not analyzed as possibly rational moves to deter men from violence (and, indeed they are not usually initiated in a fashion that would induce such analysis) but, rather, as a failure to complement the male sense of honor by admiring and supporting it. Harding makes this clear when she says, "All true women blame the woman who acts this way, rather than the man. They know that such an action takes unfair advantage of the man's vulnerability."[40] Thus, on the one hand, to be a man requires assiduous avoidance of any traits that resemble those of women, and, on the other hand, to be a woman requires a worshipful commitment to complementing men in their quest for manhood. As many feminists have pointed out, this requirement pushes women to uphold a model of manhood that holds them in contempt.

Because we want to preserve the lives of our children and foster their growth, we must ask fundamental questions about the group to whom they will be acceptable. If we do not assume a position of advocacy for an existing state and if we refuse to be seduced by philosophical and ideological abstractions of political life, we see that the group must, logically, be one that values preservation and growth. This gives us something to work toward in the larger social world — what Ruddick calls a transformed maternal thought — that will "make the preservation and growth of *all* children a work of public conscience and legislation."[41] Further, recognizing that it is the desire of all maternal thinkers to promote the preservation and growth of their children, we are led to seek cooperative and considerate international relations. It would be of little use to teach our children to eschew the warrior model if it were to be thrust on them as a logical outcome of hostile relations on the larger scene. Our children have to be acceptable in some sense not only as individuals but also as members of the social, political, religious, and ethnic groups to which they belong.

The problem of resolving conflicts between the first two maternal interests and acceptability becomes one of defining and describing kinds and levels of acceptability. One kind of acceptability that we seek is vital for intimate love; we want our children to be acceptable to a loving inner circle. We also want them to be acceptable in a less intimate way to a wide circle of colleagues, friends, and acquaintances; this kind of acceptability requires a description of the groups to which the children will be acceptable. Finally, we want our children to be at least minimally acceptable to all other well-intentioned people; that is, we would like to educate them for nonhostile relations in the world. To educate for these kinds of reflectively and interactively defined acceptabilities requires a careful study of relations and relational virtues. I will, therefore, turn to that discussion after examining the problem of acceptability.

ACCEPTABILITY

In challenging traditions from the perspective of maternal thinking, we question the ways in which people have allocated their energy and devotion. Because warrior thinking threatens the lives of our children, we would like to transform it — to refocus it on preservation and growth. With James we want to abolish war, but we do not start by seeking its moral equivalent, for it is not immediately clear what this could mean. James sought morally admirable activities that would require manliness, hardihood, a sense of adventure, and a willingness to take risks. It may be, however, that whatever activities call forth these qualities also induce war, and so we need to ask what it is men really want when they extol the virtues of manliness and hardihood. Then perhaps we can tease apart the traditional virtues and see which parts remain virtuous.

It is often said that men go to war out of devotion to God and country; they fight to end war because they love peace; they fight to make the world safe for democracy; and they fight to overcome evil. But perhaps the deepest reason for an individual man to join a fighting force and display his prowess is to achieve or to maintain acceptability. It is usually called something more glorious, of course — duty or honor. But the main motivation seems to be acceptability in the eyes of one's peers and elders. One may be terribly afraid to die or to kill but even more afraid to let down one's outfit, to be disgraced, and thus to lose something more precious than life. I do not intend to argue that this is the only motive that places or keeps a man on the battlefield; clearly there are others — some admirable, some not. But surely one powerful motive is to forge relations, to remain or to become part of a circle of acceptability.

The problem is that the group and its assigned tasks define acceptability. In war, behavior that was once completely unacceptable becomes acceptable, even admirable. Often all that remains of acceptability is the fact of it. So long as people are acceptable to each other, many can hide from themselves the true nature of what they are doing. H. D. Duncan remarks, "[A]s we wound and kill our enemy in the field and slaughter his women and children in their homes, our love for each other deepens. We become comrades in arms, our hatred of each other is being purged in the sufferings of our enemy."[42]

Young men, raised to try themselves against an abstract model in daily contest with each other, nevertheless long for acceptability. Raised to scorn and even despise those who must try to please all the people they encounter, males have to earn the respect of their comrades in order to have the positive relations with others that females achieve in their own direct efforts to please. At the bottom, paradoxically, there is still the desire to please someone — other males, superiors, God — and thus be acceptable.

Sometimes the desire to be acceptable leads individuals to give over whatever autonomy of conscience they might have possessed. Such people make conscious decisions to pledge their devotion to organizations or other persons who will decide for them what is good and right or bad and evil. Terrible acts performed out of duty or obedience are categorized by Barry Clarke as heteronomous evil and by S. I. Benn as heteronomous wickedness.[43] Adolf Eichmann has become the paradigm case of heteronomous wickedness. His conscious choice to join the Nazi party and to seek acceptability from an organization that overtly embraced evil ends committed him to deeds that he did not himself believe in (or so he said). The judgment of the world (for the most part) has been that Eichmann was nevertheless responsible for his evil acts because he knowingly chose an evil group as his domain of acceptability.

Benn differentiates between heteronomous wickedness, in which the evil-doer may insist that he or she would not have chosen to do evil if not so ordered, and conscientious wickedness. In the latter, evil-doers commit evil deeds because they believe in the ends sought or, even, in the means chosen. Some Nazis, for example, believed that the expulsion or extermination of Jews was good for Germany. Some of these conscientious evil-doers were even disgusted or appalled by the means chosen and recommended more merciful ways of killing or alternatives to killing. In contrast, prosecutors of witches in the sixteenth and seventeenth centuries often deliberately inflicted the most painful of tortures because they believed, first, that God would protect the innocent from pain and second, that pain in the guilty might induce confession and thus save the soul.[44] The deeds of both Nazis and witch prosecutors are examples of conscientious wickedness.

Categorizing wickedness as Benn does is enormously interesting and useful for philosophical discussion. Benn lays out for us a full array of wickedness: selfish, conscientious, heteronomous, and malign. He also provides a discussion of moral luck which suggests rather convincingly that many people are saved from wickedness by chance, as it were: the nasty situations that make some people conscientiously or heteronomously wicked just never arise in their lives. This raises the interesting question of whether we can do something to enhance moral luck — whether in fact we should look more kindly at Skinner's recommendations to transform the social world so that it will be easier for people to live peaceably together.

Thomas F. Green has recently made an argument that is compatible with a recommendation to enhance moral luck.[45] Arguing that prudence is "prior to morality in the order of learning," he suggests that the cost of behaving virtuously should be small and the benefits of doing evil slight.[46] This sort of social scheme would make virtue accessible to many and reduce the need for moral heroics.

Recognizing that we all live at least partly heteronomous lives — we all belong to groups that prescribe our behavior — underscores the wisdom of Green's remarks. Organized groups and institutions, especially schools, should pay careful attention to their effects on the moral behavior of their members and should invite continual scrutiny of their ideals and practices. It is self-defeating for a society or institution to make virtue a matter of heroism. Rather, it should be a requirement for basic acceptability.

Discussion of moral luck and prudence also raises a question about the experience of maternal thinkers — women in particular. Perhaps women have been less violent and more concerned about the welfare of others because their situations have protected them from events that lead men to fight and compete. This sort of explanation was used in Victorian times to continue the isolation and dependence of women.[47] It was women's moral luck — with a good deal of coercive effort from men — to live in situations that brought out the beautiful, the tender, and the compassionate. Further, as we have already seen, the nurturing qualities thus induced were supposed to be and usually were passive and nonjudgmental with respect to men's moral lives. The morality of women left the immorality of men firmly in place.

Moral luck of the Victorian sort cannot, however, explain the relatively nonviolent and altruistic lives of working-class women and women of color. Maternal thinking transcends class and race, although, of course, maternal style may not. Elements of moral luck remain: women have not been trained as warriors; they have been expected to care for children, and most have themselves expected to do so; they have been largely responsible for the physical care of the elderly and incapacitated. Women's situations and the tasks in which they have been immersed do suggest a sort of moral luck, but, more importantly, these activities give rise to maternal thinking. If maternal thinking is ethically valuable and if its growth has been in part a product of moral luck — a result of the situations its users have been immersed in — then perhaps we should consider providing all people with the life experience that induces such thinking. Thinking maternally need not continue to be a matter of moral luck. It might be conscientiously cultivated.

So far in this section, I have discussed the apparently innate longing for acceptability that is susceptible to the constant defining and shaping forces of socialization. Human beings need to belong and to be acceptable in the eyes of some norm groups. Society and its subgroups decide on the criteria of acceptability. If one has the moral luck to be born female, one is less likely to encounter situations that require a violent response in order to maintain one's acceptability. This is not to say, of course, that women do not experience situations in which violence is inflicted on them and might be used by them for protection. Women have been subject to such violence for millennia, but it has only recently become acceptable for women to fight back. In the past, women were expected to struggle against or resist rape, for example, but the real heroine was one who died resisting, not one who physically overcame her attacker. The acceptability of men has been bounded by expectations for the use of active and righteous physical force; the acceptability of women has been constrained by expectations of passivity, gentleness, and complementarity. This last, of course, requires women to support in others what they must reject in themselves.

The education of both women and men has been guided by faulty standards of acceptability. We must now seek new models, new standards. Neither traditional man nor traditional woman will do. Ruddick would like all human beings to be capable of maternal thinking, and as we have seen, her conception of such thinking goes well beyond the stereotypical sentiments of tradition-bound mothers — it is not exclusionary with respect to gender or actual motherhood. Such a recommendation raises questions about the experience that induces maternal thinking, about how this thinking may be cultivated, and about the groups for whom our children should be made acceptable. How do we educate for forms of acceptability not yet firmly established?

EDUCATING FOR ACCEPTABILITY

Human beings are not totally at the mercy of moral luck or of any form of conditioning. They resist, adapt, and transform; they place themselves in new situations. Maternal thinking suggests working from the beloved child outward. At least in theorizing, we can put aside the criteria of acceptability established by various groups. We can ask what criteria should guide our judgments of acceptability. Logically, the groups to which our children must be acceptable should be committed to preserving life and fostering individual growth. Starting here, we might engage in the fascinating project of constructing a social utopia based on maternal thinking.[48]

It is also possible to apply maternal thinking to the world as it is and to suggest both concrete improvements in current patterns of socialization and criteria of acceptability that provide our children with some measure of protection from hostility. The attributes we decide to cultivate in our children should contribute to positive relations, and these may be discussed in the three large categories mentioned earlier.

First, our children should be acceptable in an inner circle of intimate love. This means that boys as well as girls should be prepared to do the work of attentive love. Allowing for the possibility explored earlier that paternal attentive love may differ in some respects from maternal, the shaping of an acceptable child must be guided by this goal. Children must learn not only the attitudes and behaviors that will enable them to do the work of attentive love, but they must also learn to assess this capacity in others. Maternal thinking always looks outward from the child. Young women should be prepared to do this work, but they must also be competent to select mates who are similarly prepared.

The psychic agonies of women who take total responsibility for the condition of their relationships have been well documented by Carol Gilligan and several others.[49] One might argue that this phenomenon points to a weakness in women and that girls should, therefore, be socialized more in the pattern of males: to be assertive, independent, and less concerned with the welfare of others and the strength of relations. The argument of maternal thinking runs somewhat differently. Girls and boys should be raised to believe that the work of attentive love is a human obligation and that the capacity for such work should be a primary criterion in the selection of a mate or partner. As parents teach their children to do the work of attentive love, they shape them for acceptability in an intimate circle that shares commitment to this work. Hence children are not socialized to an ideal that may set them up for abuse and exploitation.

Parents have long put emphasis on teaching their children to be polite and to consider the desires and feelings of those around them, but at a certain age boys have been allowed to separate themselves from tasks associated with the direct care of human beings and the maintenance of positive relations. Pleasing others is displaced as a moral aim by the development of rational problem solving.[50] Virtues become more firmly attached to the individual and less naturally associated with relations. Even the custom of allowing males to retire after dinner to the smoking room, ballfield, or back porch while females clean up contributes to the odd notion that men's work is defined by locating and solving sequential problems or earning money and not in the mere doing of repetitive, unpaid tasks. If, however, maternal thinking arises out of experience with such tasks — pleasing others by maintaining a clean and comfortable environment, preparing appetizing meals, taking tender care of the ill and infirm — then we cannot expect it to develop in people deprived of opportunities to do such work.

This is part of what Jane Roland Martin is addressing when she claims that the standard forms of liberal education ignore the reproductive functions of society — those functions associated with bearing and rearing children, maintaining a home, teaching the ordinary tasks of life, and caring for the ill, poor, and aged. Her assessment is that liberal education provides

No place . . . for education of the body, and since most action involves bodily movement, this means there is little room in it for education of action. Nor is there room for education of other-regarding feelings and emotions. The liberally educated man or woman will be provided with knowledge about others but will not be taught to care about their welfare or to act kindly toward them.[51]

Martin is not claiming that all liberally educated people lack qualities of human warmth and kindness. She is, rather, pointing to the fact that these qualities are neither the primary aim nor the logical outcome of such an education. Education for public life, for citizenship, has concentrated on the development of intellectual achievement and individual virtue. One may indeed learn to treat others justly (and this is no small achievement), but one does not necessarily learn to evaluate the impact of justice on human relations. To treat others with justice measured by abstract criteria may invite hatred and deep enmity from those who define justice differently or invoke a different perspective on the events to be judged. To turn an old expression around, we might say that kindness should be tempered with justice. This means that the well-being and feelings of the other are steadily regarded as we try to work out just arrangements and persuade each other of their justness.

Working out what is just in a particular situation implies attention to building and maintaining relations of trust. The reason that we can often dispense with justice in our private lives is that we love and trust each other. As relations become less personal, love becomes at best an abstraction, but trust need not disappear. Indeed a relation of trust seems to be a precondition for any exercise of justice that is recognized by all participants as justice. If this is so, then moral education must involve not only the training of reason in principles of justice but also — and perhaps more importantly — the development of interpersonal reason. This form of reasoning is best learned, as Norma Haan has said, "within the context of moral dialogue between agents who strive to achieve balanced agreement, based on compromise they reach or on their joint discovery of interests they hold in common."[52] This is, in short, the kind of reasoning that develops in situations where people care as much about pleasing others as they do about pleasing themselves.

Besides preparing children to be acceptable in an inner circle where they will do the work of attentive love, we must also prepare them for acceptability in a circle of friends, coworkers, and neighbors. Schools have traditionally put great emphasis on educating for productive work and good citizenship, but little attention has been given to the social interactions that might increase both productivity and job satisfaction, nor to the forms of citizenship that matter to all of us in our daily lives. At some level it matters, of course, whether our neighbors are equipped to vote intelligently and whether they understand and support our system of government. But to most of us it is even more important that our neighbors be considerate people: kind to children and animals, reasonably quiet, reasonably clean, nonviolent in their interaction with us, and respectful of our property. Yet, although we attempt to enforce rules that support these qualities in our schools, we make no attempt to study seriously the situations and patterns involved in coming to cherish these values and in committing ourselves to live by them. They often seem to be patterns of behavior insisted upon by mothers and teachers but not by the people who have real power in the world and do exciting things.

Even in areas where a form of moral education is taken seriously — in, for example, drug education — emphasis is usually on the responsibility of the individual moral agent and, sometimes, on his or her self-esteem. The slogan Just say No is an example of our concentration on the individual and on his or her power to say no to drugs. Overlooked in this well-intentioned campaign is the fact that people say yes or no to other people, not to the materials they ingest. An effective form of education has to include a careful study of relations and the effects that accompany them. Human beings have always sought ways to enhance mental acuity, induce spiritual experience, heighten sexual pleasure, restore youth, and extend life. Further, we have always been influenced by each other and especially by those who seem to share our experience. To be capable of saying no to drugs, young people must be able to explain their views to others; interpersonal reasoning is required. It helps to know that we all share substantial parts of the human condition, and if adults are to be effective in persuading young people toward healthy and moral ways of living, they must demonstrate in their interactions that they care enough to share their experience and to listen to what others are going through.

Commenting on the great human need for this sort of listening, Ruddick draws on Simone Weil:

In the first legend of the Grail, it is said that the Grail . . . belongs to the first comer who asks the guardian of the vessel, a king three-quarters paralyzed by the most painful wound, "What are you going through?"

The love of our neighbor in all its fullness simply means being able to say to him: "What are you going through?" . . . Only he who is capable of attention can do this.[53]

Again we see that the problem of acceptability has two faces. It is part of our parental and pedagogical task to shape acceptable children, but it is also our task to teach them how to evaluate the groups from whom they will seek acceptance. To be a good friend or cherished colleague, one must be capable of attention; to be capable of attention, one must have experienced it from others, and it must be expected in return. This implies practice in both speaking and listening — elements of interpersonal reason.

Experience shapes mind. It is common to speak of the military mind, business thinking, or police mentality. When such expressions are used, it is recognized that not only do aptitudes and attitudes suggest lines of work but lines of work also shape attitudes. There is, of course, a good bit of stereotypical thinking that accompanies such attributions, but insofar as these expressions capture something real, their existence raises another caution for those shaping children. The sort of single-mindedness represented by these labels is dangerous. Those who are accurately so judged are highly acceptable within narrowly defined domains and are often feared or mocked outside of them. As shapers of children, we want it to be possible for a child to become a business professional or a police person without exhibiting business thinking or a police mentality in every sphere of life or with narrow exclusivity even within the professional domain.

Maternal thinking may be an effective antidote to single-mindedness. Extended to all our encounters, it becomes caring in its most sensitive form.[54] It too is shaped by experience, and once acquired, it in turn shapes all subsequent experience. Thus it seems reasonable to suggest that all children be enlisted early in the work of attentive love and caring, and perhaps the easiest way to do this is to involve them in what has been called for centuries women's work: child tending, cooking, cleaning, and attending. In each of these tasks, however, children should be encouraged to develop autonomy and creativity. They should be apprentices in caring, not mere servants. This means that they must be encouraged to think about the people for whom they are doing this work: those who enjoy certain items of food, whose comfort and efficiency are enhanced by tidiness, whose daily pleasure is at least in part contingent upon their attentiveness. Contributing to household work is not merely a matter of earning one's keep; more importantly, it is a way of learning to live considerately and creatively with each other. It is a way of developing maternal thinking and the capacity to sustain caring relations.

As we consider educating our children away from single-mindedness, we can expand our thinking into the larger domains of national and international life. Before doing so, however, the possibility that maternal thinking can itself become single-minded should be discussed. An objection might be raised that maternal thinking logically belongs to the same odd family as the military mind and police mentality. Ruddick herself has ably discussed this possibility, and it is clear that she is not recommending maternal thinking in a narrow, particularistic sense. She urges, rather, the extension of maternal thinking into the world of public affairs. Here it retains its interest in preservation, growth, and acceptability, but it also embraces all whom it encounters and guides policy at the level where direct encounter is impossible or unlikely. Because it is directed at children — first at one's own, then at all children

— it provides the compelling interest needed to reshape the public world.

In national and international life, acceptability often depends as much or more on the groups with which we are identified as it does on ourselves individually. U.S. citizens are sometimes seen as rich and friendly customers (tourists), but we are also seen as citizens of a dangerous nation. The United States often behaves like a swaggering braggart on the international scene. Any individual who constantly trumpeted his desire to be number one in everything and put all his energy into accomplishing this would be feared, disliked, and found excruciatingly boring. Yet this is the way the United States behaves on the international scene. U.S. citizens have not given a great deal of thought to making the United States acceptable. Power and money have been our badges of respectability. But nations, like individuals, should create domains of acceptability that value the preservation of life and the fostering of individual growth.

It is not possible to explore here the enormous topic just introduced. New conflicts arise immediately. Many political thinkers and ordinary people would respond to these comments by insisting that the United States does, in fact, stand for the preservation of life and the fostering of growth. Growth, indeed, is our national byword! But now we must ask what is meant by growth, what criteria can be used to assess it, and how its demands might conflict with those of preservation and acceptability.

Growth that depends on the creation of enemies is anathema to maternal thinking. It risks the lives of our children. Maternal thinkers want their grown children to be at least minimally acceptable in most circles, including those circles that are themselves barely acceptable. Their children should be able to differ and argue their cases persuasively with persons of vastly different beliefs and attitudes without creating enemies or depending on the continuance of enmity for their own growth. This is a way of life that has not been well taught by either traditional religion or public education. In both, personal virtue, sacrifice of self and others, and heroism in great causes have far outweighed the kind of relational virtues valued by maternal thinkers — those that might enable all of us to walk safely, speak gently, and live sensitively in shared domains of existence.

SUMMARY

Interest in preserving the lives of our children and fostering their individual growth provides a compelling interest in moral life and moral education. We want to shape acceptable children so that they can give and receive love, live full professional and civic lives, and move about sensitively and safely in the world. Concern for our own children is extended through empathy with other maternal thinkers to concern for all children; but even if it were not, we would be constrained to behave ethically in order to make the world safe for our children. This concern leads us to describe and identify domains of acceptability and to teach our children to consider carefully the groups from which they will seek acceptance.

Maternal thinking is accessible to all mature human beings, but it grows most obviously out of the direct care-taking activities that have in the past been called woman's work. I have left open the possibility that the attentive love of fathers may be qualitatively different from that of mothers. If that possibility is real, we may anticipate a form of paternal thinking that rejects traditional patriarchal modes of control. In any case, care-taking activities properly designed to encourage autonomy and empathy in caring should be required of all children. Both girls and boys should develop the capacity to do the work of attentive love.

Finally, maternal thinking at its best is not single-minded. It does not create separations; it is not exclusive.[55] It accompanies other modes of thinking as a safeguard against single-mindedness. As we work to achieve something in the world, we are keenly aware of the effects other people have on us. The better they are, the better we can be. Therefore, as we try to shape acceptable children, we try simultaneously to shape acceptable environments and to teach our children how to maintain them.

NOTES

I would like to thank Pam Tyson and Sarah Erickson for valuable suggestions on the first draft.

1. Gerda Lerner, *The Creation of Patriarchy* (New York: Oxford University Press, 1986), p. 228.
2. See Sandra Harding, "Why Has the Sex-Gender System Become Visible Only Now?" in *Discovering Reality: Feminist Perspectives on Epistemology, Metaphysics, Methodology, and Philosophy of Science*, ed. Sandra Harding and Merrill Hintikka (Dordrecht: Reidel, 1983). See also Dorothy Smith, "Women's Perspective as a Radical Critique of Sociology," *Sociological Inquiry* 44 (1974): 7–13.
3. See Sandra Harding, *The Science Question in Feminism* (Ithaca: Cornell University Press, 1986).
4. See Nel Noddings, "Ethics from the Standpoint of Women," in *Theoretical Perspectives on Sexual Difference*, ed. Deborah Rhode (New Haven: Yale University Press, 1990).
5. Sara Ruddick, "Maternal Thinking," *Feminist Studies* 2 (1980): 342–67.
6. Ruddick, "Maternal Thinking," p. 349.
7. B. F. Skinner, *Walden Two* (Toronto: Macmillan, 1962), p. 104.
8. For an introduction to Hegel's ideas, see H. B. Acton, "Hegel," in *The Encyclopedia of Philosophy*, vol. 3, ed. Paul Edwards (New York: Macmillan 1967), pp. 435–51.

9. Jean-Jacques Rousseau, *Discourse on Inequality*, trans. Maurice Cranston (Harmondsworth, Middlesex, England: Penguin, 1984).

10. John Dewey, *Democracy and Education* (New York: Macmillan, 1916).

11. See the discussion in Jean Grimshaw, *Philosophy and Feminist Thinking* (Minneapolis: University of Minnesota Press, 1986).

12. Ruddick, "Maternal Thinking," p. 346.

13. See Naomi Black, "Virginia Woolf: The Life of Natural Happiness," in *Feminist Theorists*, ed. Dale Spender (New York: Pantheon, 1983), pp. 296–313.

14. See the historical account in Jessie Bernard, *The Future of Motherhood* (New York: Penguin, 1975).

15. *Jane Addams on Education*, ed. Ellen Condliffe Lagemann (New York: Teachers College Press, 1985), p. 7. Lagemann cites James Weber Linn, *Jane Addams: A Biography* (New York: Appleton, 1935), pp. 22–23.

16. Addams spoke of this allegiance to the traditional ideal in her address to the class of 1881 at the Junior Exhibition, Rockford Seminary. See *Jane Addams on Education*, p. 13.

17. Ruddick, "Maternal Thinking," p. 363, n. 11.

18. J. C. Walker and M. A. O'Loughlin, "The Ideal of the Educated Person: Jane Roland Martin on Education and Gender," *Educational Theory* 4 (1984): 327–40.

19. Ruddick, "Maternal Thinking," p. 362.

20. For a description of patriarchal thinking on the subject of man's superiority to woman and its possible circularity, see Rosemary Radford Ruether, "Misogynism and Virginal Feminism in the Fathers of the Church," in *Religion and Sexism*, ed. Rosemary Radford Ruether (New York: Simon, 1974), pp. 150–83.

21. Gabriel Marcel, "The Creative Vow as Essence of Fatherhood," in *Homo Viator*, trans. Emma Craufurd (New York: Harper Torchbooks, 1962), pp. 103–4.

22. Marcel, "The Creative Vow," p. 108.

23. Ibid., p. 107.

24. Ibid., p. 110.

25. Ibid., pp. 116–17.

26. Ibid., p. 117.

27. Ibid., p. 124.

28. Ibid., p. 122.

29. See Dorothy Dinnerstein, *The Mermaid and the Minotaur: Sexual Arrangements and Human Malaise* (New York: Harper, 1976).

30. Sara Ruddick, "Preservative Love and Military Destruction: Some Reflections on Mothering and Peace," in *Mothering: Essays in Feminist Theory*, ed. J. Trebilcot (Totowa, NJ: Rowman and Allanheld, 1984), pp. 231–62.

31. Grimshaw, *Philosophy and Feminist Thinking*, p. 241.

32. For a discussion of both women's opposition and their occasional enthusiastic endorsement of war, see Jean Bethke Elshtain, *Women and War* (New York: Basic, 1987).

33. Seth Schein, *The Mortal Hero* (Berkeley: University of California Press, 1984), p. 16.

34. William James, *The Varieties of Religious Experience* (New York: Mentor Books, 1958), p. 284.

35. William James, "The Moral Equivalent of War," in *War and Morality*, ed. Richard A. Wasserstrom (Belmont, CA: Wadsworth, 1970), p. 5.

36. Schein, *The Mortal Hero*, p. 80.

37. James, *Varieties of Religious Experience*, p. 282.

38. Ibid., p. 284.

39. M. Esther Harding, *Woman's Mysteries* (New York: Harper, 1971), p. 81.

40. Ibid.

41. Ruddick, "Maternal Thinking," p. 361.
42. Hugh Dalziel Duncan, *Communication and Social Order* (New York: Bedminster, 1962), p. 132.
43. See Barry Clarke, "Beyond 'The Banality of Evil,'" *British Journal of Political Science* 10 (1980): 417–39; S. I. Benn, "Wickedness," *Ethics* 95 (1985): 795–810.
44. See Joseph Klaits, *Servants of Satan* (Bloomington: Indiana University Press, 1985).
45. Thomas F. Green, "The Economy of Virtue," *American Journal of Education* 96 (1988): 127–42.
46. Ibid., p. 127.
47. See Jessie Bernard, *The Future of Motherhood* (New York: Penguin, 1975); also Berthold Brecht, *The Mother* (New York: Grove, 1965).
48. Charlotte Perkins Gilman made such an attempt in *Herland*, 1915 (New York: Pantheon, 1979), but her thinking was heavily influenced by Marxism.
49. Carol Gilligan, *In a Different Voice* (Cambridge, MA.: Harvard University Press, 1982); see also, for example, Larry Blum, Marcia Homiak, Judy Housman, and Naomi Scheman, "Altruism and Women's Oppression," *Philosophical Forum* 5 (1975: 222–47); and Phyllis Chesler, *Women and Madness* (New York: Avon, 1971).
50. Kohlberg's stages of moral development are, of course, illustrative of this tendency.
51. Jane Roland Martin, *Reclaiming Conversation* (New Haven: Yale University Press, 1985), p. 190.
52. Norma Haan, "Two Moralities in Action Contexts: Relationship to Thought, Ego Regulation, and Development," *Journal of Personality and Social Psychology* 36 (1978): 303.
53. Quoted in Ruddick, "Maternal Thinking," p. 359. From Simone Weil, "Reflections of the Right Use of School Studies with a View to the Love of God," in *Waiting for God* (New York: Putnam's, 1951), p. 115.
54. See the analysis in Nel Noddings, *Caring: A Feminine Approach to Ethics and Moral Education* (Berkeley: University of California Press, 1984).
55. Feminists are paying increasing attention to the evils of separation. See, for example, Catherine Keller, *From a Broken Web* (Boston: Beacon, 1986) and Nel Noddings, *Women and Evil* (Berkeley: University of California Press, 1989).

4

Two Moral Orientations: How Teachers Think and Act in the Classroom

Kay Johnston

In some of my earlier work, I have explored the relationship between moral orientation and methods of problem solving (Johnston 1988). Working with preservice teachers has enriched my understanding of this relationship and led me to the topic to be examined here: there seem to be two distinct moral orientations, and the way in which they are understood influences how teachers think about teaching and how they behave in the classroom. This connection works through classroom interaction, through diversity in the classroom, and through the content actually taught. The context of interactions in the classroom are discussed in this chapter.

TWO MORAL ORIENTATIONS IN DEFINITIONS

The field of moral development was first defined by Lawrence Kohlberg, whose work grew from the cognitive developmental tradition of Piaget and who equated moral development with the development of the idea of justice (Kohlberg 1976). Kohlberg describes moral development as a series of stages, with each stage leading to a more comprehensive understanding of the moral ideal of justice. This is one moral orientation.

Gilligan's ground-breaking work, which focused on women describing moral problems, identified a second moral orientation (Gilligan 1977, 1982). Later work by Gilligan and her colleagues explored how people use the two orientations in thinking about real-life moral conflicts (Gilligan and Attanucci 1988; Lyons 1982, 1983) and in solving hypothetical dilemmas (Langdale 1983). This work offers a theory about the morality of care — the second moral orientation.

Lyons (1983) devised a coding method to identify these two orientations in discussions of real-life moral conflict, defining the difference between justice- and care-based moral considerations, which she calls the moral orientations of rights and response. She defines the morality of rights as construing moral problems involving "issues/decisions of conflicting claims between self and others (including society). These issues are resolved by invoking impartial rules, principles, or standards which consider one's obligations, duty, or commitment or standards, rules, or principles for self, others, and society." In contrast, the morality of care and response construes problems as issues of how to respond to others in situations of conflict. In responding, one must consider how to "maintain relationships" or to "promote the welfare of others or prevent them from harm or relieve their burdens, hurt, or suffering, physical or psychological" (p. 134). (See Brown et al. 1987 for a complete reading guide on this subject.)

REAL-LIFE MORAL DILEMMAS: ONE TYPE OF STUDY

The discovery and exploration of moral orientation has largely been confined to studies in which subjects are interviewed and asked to discuss their real-life moral conflicts. The questions about moral conflicts and their elaboration generate data called real-life moral dilemmas. Although both justice and care orientations appear in descriptions of moral conflict, people typically focus on one or the other. Furthermore, in descriptions of real-life moral conflict, care-focus dilemmas are more likely to be presented by females and justice-focus dilemmas by males (Gilligan and Attanucci 1988; Lyons 1983). These studies showed that an individual who focused on one orientation might spontaneously use the other in his or her description of a moral conflict, but no attempt was made to explore systematically the moral orientation that the subject did not focus on or use spontaneously.

THE FABLE STUDY

My own fable study (1985) was predicated on the notion that a person's spontaneous use of one orientation does not preclude use of the other orientation if prompted. The study considered how males and females could use both moral orientations to reason through the same dilemma. The question was addressed by following a standard method (Johnston 1983) to investigate the ability to use both orientations in solving moral dilemmas, which were embedded in fables.

The study varied age and gender to test the premise that 11- and 15-year-old boys and girls could use both the justice and care orientations. Subjects who were asked the same questions could solve the problem in different ways, and each participant was asked to evaluate the different ways of solving the problem. Based on previous work (Gilligan 1982; Lyons 1983; Johnston 1983), it was predicted that gender differences would occur spontaneously and would be found in the best solutions to the problems. It was also predicted that most subjects would be able to use both moral orientations. (See Johnston in Gilligan, Ward, & Taylor 1988 for a complete description of this study.)

The results of the original study (Johnston 1985) demonstrate that, by at least age 11, both males and females know and can use both moral orientations. The results also showed a consistent gender difference in the preferred voice — that is, in the orientation the subject chose as best for solving the moral dilemmas in fables. This work explicitly connects these moral orientations to systems of problem solving. The justice orientation is associated with a hierarchical or linear method of problem solving in which priorities are ordered and variables are excluded until only the most important one remains. The care orientation, however, is associated with a method of problem solving that has been described metaphorically as a web (Gilligan 1982, p. 88). Such a system includes many variables and integrates them into a solution (Johnston 1983, p. 88).

The results of this study contribute to the discussion of gender and moral orientation in moral psychology, but they also suggest a way to think about education: since moral orientations seem clearly related to methods of problem solving, they have applications in the classroom.

TEACHING AS A MORAL ACTIVITY

Using the two moral orientations as tools to help teachers in classroom problem solving requires two linked assumptions: first, that there is a moral dimension in teaching, and second, that the classroom contains many different relationships. Alan Tom addresses the moral dimension of teaching by suggesting that a teacher is a moral craftsperson. He argues that the metaphor of craft is fitting for teachers since craft learning involves a skill but also "entails the mastery of analytic knowledge and ability to apply this knowledge to specific situations" (1984, p. 144). Because a teacher must not only learn skills but also go beyond to a level of thinking and reflection on the application of these skills, he sees the craftsperson as a fitting analogy. Tom adds a moral dimension to his metaphor because it "encourages us to favor a reflective, diligent, and skillful approach toward the pursuit of desirable ends" (p. 144). Thus the term *craftsperson* makes clear that a teacher perfects and improves his or her teaching abilities. The teacher not only thinks about and changes lessons that don't work well but also reflects on and tries to change interactions that do not go well. Teaching is not defined as a technique or a skill to be learned and filed for later use. The logic of the moral orientations can help perfect a teacher's craft of problem solving.

Zeichner and Liston (1987) stress the idea of teaching as a moral activity, and they refer to Tom's central moral questions, "which are mediated by concerns for justice, equity, and concrete fulfillment, and [the question of] whether current arrangements serve important human needs and satisfy important human purposes" (p. 25). They see these concerns as one of the levels of reflective teaching that students are encouraged to use. They agree with Tom — as do I — that teaching has a moral dimension, and they use Tom's definition of moral, "a concern for the rightness of conduct and a broader concern for what is deemed important or valuable, provided that these valuational situations clearly entail desirable ends" (1984, p. 79).

However, in both these cases, morality is defined in terms of rights — that is, as concern for issues of fairness and equality. This definition of morality is certainly important, and anyone who has been in a classroom is certainly impressed by the number of times students use the word *fair* to describe classroom interaction, but this definition is not complete. I would add that an understanding of the teacher as a moral craftsperson should also include the dimension of morality described by the orientation of care. In this view, the teacher is concerned not only with the moral imperative of justice, which is to treat everyone equally and fairly, but also with the moral imperative of care which is not to abandon relationships. Such an orientation might change the way the teacher reflects on and deals with the relationships in the class because it redefines morality. When the definition of morality is expanded in this way, the two moral orientations can offer problem-solving alternatives for teachers who reflect on classroom interactions.

RELATIONSHIPS WITHIN A CLASSROOM

If we take seriously the idea that the classroom contains both a teacher-student relationship and the connection of a teacher with an entire class, the teacher must be seen as a moral craftsperson. Thinking of these connections in a classroom provides another perspective on classroom interaction: what can be constructed as a problem of fairness can also be thought of as a problem in relationships. Noddings (1984) supports this view when she describes the teacher as the one caring; Belenky et al. (1986) discuss similar ideas. Clearly the teacher and the student are in a relationship. It may not be a long-term relationship, but it is characterized by the interaction in a particular classroom. And while interactions differ for each teacher and class, a relationship does emerge. To take seriously Piaget's contention that there can be no moral necessity without relationship ([1932] 1965, p. 196) is to acknowledge the moral nature of the classroom.

This is not to say that relationship is ignored in talking about teaching. Quite frequently relationship is seen as important, especially in the early grades. The primary-grade teacher is generally acknowledged as the nice person while the secondary-grade teacher is expected to be serious, knowledgeable, and concerned about content. Hence the break between primary and secondary education has been seen as moving away from relationship toward preparation for the future. (See Simmons 1987 for an interesting discussion of how the structure of schools supports this idea.)

Teachers also develop important relationships with individual students. Often these individual relationships enable the students to function in the classroom. All teachers, of course, have good relationships with many students, but they see them as individual relationships — teachers do not characterize themselves as "in relationship" with their classes. Yet if teachers are moral craftspeople, then all classrooms are characterized by teachers being in relationship with their classes. The question thus becomes, In what moral terms do we construct the relationship? It is often a distant and respectful one because the logic of the justice orientation usually characterizes the relationship in a classroom of many students. Fair treatment is important in the student's school career and is judged by the teacher's objectivity in dealing with each member of the class. May Sarton has written that one maintains this objectivity by keeping the subject between the students and the teacher (1976). This distancing is a major consideration in how teachers have been taught to think about their students: if a teacher does not get too close to any one of her students, if she does not have a pet, then she will treat each student fairly.

Although this approach is useful for some classes, there are other ways to characterize the teacher-students relationship — by using both moral orientations, for example. The relationship can be perceived as one in which people strive to treat each other fairly and equally or as a context for learning to respond to each other as individuals with different needs. The question to be asked in the first construction is how to be fair; the question for the second is how to integrate individual needs without slighting anyone. Both moral orientations must be used to solve problems that come up in that relationship, and it is in solving these problems that reflective thinking is used in a classroom. This should be discussed in teacher-training classes to emphasize that there is more than one way to construct the relationship and to encourage other perspectives.

REFLECTIVE THINKING AND MORAL ORIENTATION

In recent years, the literature on teacher training has shown a trend toward teaching teachers to be reflective (for example, Schon 1983; Cruickshank 1987) through the process of deliberation. Recall the discussion about the metaphor of craft. In one of the most provocative works in this area, Zeichner and Liston (1987) describe the training program at Wisconsin, which teaches student teachers to reflect. This work and Tom's (1984) offer useful models for teaching reflection, but neither model addresses both moral orientations. Their narrow focus limits the moral domain and the alternative for problem solving. So, while we can use the terms and ideas, we need to broaden the definition of morality.

Zeichner and Liston begin by outlining the goals of the Wisconsin teacher-training program and note specifically that "reflective teaching is the central goal of the curriculum." They use Dewey's distinction between routine and reflective action:

> *Reflective action* entails the active, persistent, and careful consideration of any belief or supposed form of knowledge in light of the grounds that support it and the consequences to which it leads.
> *Routine action* is guided primarily by tradition, external authority, and circumstances. (p. 24)

Routine action also consists of habits of behavior, which teachers fall back on when the classroom presents a difficult problem. Since they are under constant pressure, there is a strong temptation to respond to problems with routine action. If a classroom teacher has been trained to reflect, however, then more thoughtful solutions to the problem may be reached. Of course, some problems do not allow time for reflection. If a child is in danger, one acts immediately, but there is time to reflect on a way to solve the problem when the situation is again under control. It is at this point that a teacher can use both moral orientations in reflecting and can attend to concerns of both justice and care. Thus the development of reflective thinking is critical for preservice teachers.

THE IMPORTANCE OF SCAFFOLDING

In the earlier discussion defining two moral orientations, I emphasized two things. The first is that this work is in the cognitive-developmental tradition and these orientations guide individuals' thinking about morality. The second is that people know and use both orientations. Thus the orientations are logics that all people can use in moral problem solving. One task of the teacher-educator is to break the limiting routine of thinking about classroom interaction using only the logic of the justice orientation. It is important to distinguish between routine that is a prescribed course of action and useful and one that is mechanistic. To do this, I use *limiting routine*. It may be counterintuitive, but teachers can learn to routinely ask themselves questions that can lead to reflective thinking. The reflective thinking will not be routine; it will be serious thought and contemplation, but the questions that promote this thinking can be learned as a way to promote reflective thinking. We can learn to break the limiting routine of "justice only" thinking. Of course, if "care only" thinking were routine, this limiting routine could also be broken. How? One way would be to teach the logics of the two moral orientations and the questions that arise from the recognition of both logics. This teaching might be done by providing what Bruner calls scaffolding, by which he means that the person teaching must ask questions that help the learner reach a new place in his or her thinking.

HOW SCAFFOLDING WORKS: TWO EXAMPLES

The questions arising from the logics of the two moral orientations provide a kind of scaffolding to help problem solving in classroom interaction. For example, if a child is hitting another child, the teacher first stops the hitting and then reflects on resolving the issue of why a child sees hitting as an appropriate way to solve a problem. The teacher could reflect on the problem as a matter of unfairness and ask the child, "Would you want someone to hit you?" Or the teacher could construct the problem in the care orientation by asking the child, "Do you want to remain friends with the child you hit?" Then the teacher could ask if hitting seems to be a way to maintain friendships and could begin to help the child construct alternative ways to solve this problem in relationships. This approach offers an explicit way for the teacher to talk about how to maintain friendships and take care of others in the context of the classroom.

In this example, the two moral orientations scaffold the teacher's reflection on the problem. They provide the questions that may help the teacher reach a new place in her thinking. Before the teacher asks the child about the problem, she must think through ways to help the child see this as behavior that does not attend to or maintain relationships, as well as not being fair to another child. Such reflective thinking about relationships in the classroom may not provide separate solutions to the moral dilemma — both moral orientations would say not to hit in the situation described — but in other instances, the two orientations might provide different ways of seeing the problem, and these alternative visions might lead to different solutions.

In a study on adolescence,* a seventh-grade girl was asked to discuss a classroom problem using both moral voices. In the discussion of the problem, she reached a solution that had previously escaped her. In this project, the moral voice of justice was pursued by asking each student, "Have you ever been in a situation where something happened to you or someone else that was unfair?" The question prompted the following exchange:

> *Student*: Unfair? Well, sometimes just in school, it can be . . . just the teachers sometimes. If the teacher doesn't have a good side of you, that is kind of unfair.
> *Interviewer*: What do you mean by not having a good side of you?
> *Student*: Well, if they don't explain things to you and you don't understand, and it doesn't seem like they want you in class.

The interviewer continued by asking whether the teacher is unfair to the whole class or to just one person. The student responded that the teacher was unfair to one person and then revealed that the anonymous person was she, the student herself. She "maybe" doesn't understand something about the lesson, and the teacher does not take the time to explain it to her:

> *Student*: It throws that person off when she doesn't understand.
> *Interviewer*: What is unfair about that?
> *Student*: I don't know if this is good, but the teacher is at school to teach the students and she's getting paid to teach the students, and so if a student doesn't understand, it should be — it's only fair for them to explain it so she [the "she" the student describes is herself] does understand, but then she's going to go out of class and she's not going to understand it, and she's going to get so mad at the teacher that she's not going to want to come in for extra help and then she's going to blow her test, and so it leads up.
> *Interviewer*: What would be the fair thing to do?
> *Student*: Well, she could start the class on something. . . . Well, not really. She could say to the student that she could come in for extra help. She could . . . right after class she will explain it to them, or she could have someone, another student, explain it to her quietly, and that helps.

The student's anger at the teacher kept her from seeking extra help. She went on to explain that she didn't say anything to the

*My thanks to Lyn Brown, who is directing this project, for the use of these data.

teacher because she was afraid the teacher did not like her. This student saw the relationship as vital to her understanding of the material, but she did not take the relationship with the teacher seriously enough to say anything to her. She constructed the problem in the fairness mode and accused the teacher of unfairness, but she failed to see her own obligation in the relationship. She was rendered silent (Gilligan 1986) by looking at the problem in one way and deciding that the teacher should be fair. The student finished this part of the interview by saying,

> *Student*: I still keep quiet because I still know that she would not stop for me, and it still feels that way.

The same problem was later reconstructed in the same interview through a question designed to elicit a care orientation.

> *Interviewer*: Have you ever been in a situation where you or someone else was not being listened to?
> *Student*: Well, kind of the [subject is deleted]. Just when I ask her what I still don't understand, it seems like she rushed the class or is rushing, so she's not taking it slowly.

As the interview progressed, the student was asked,

> *Interviewer*: Do you know why you weren't being listened to?
> *Student*: I think it's because everyone else understands. . . . I think she gets aggravated that she has to stop for one person, one or two people.
> *Interviewer*: What do you think should happen?
> *Student*: Between us?
> *Interviewer*: Yeah, in that situation where she is not listening to you.
> *Student*: I think we should talk about it.

The student had been asked to use both moral orientations to discuss the problem. In the process of answering the questions, she came to the conclusion that she should talk to her advisor and that they would then talk with the teacher. In this conversation, which constructs the problem using each moral orientation, the student discovered that the teacher is not solely responsible when a student has a problem. She realizes that she is part of the student-teacher relationship and has a responsibility for finding a voice in the relationship. She must tell the teacher that she does not understand.

In this example, the student saw the problem in the teacher-student relationship from both the justice and the care orientations. From a perspective of justice, she saw a problem of unfairness and chose the solution of anger and silence. In contrast, the perspective of care focused on a problem of relationship. It implied a speaker and a listener because the question asked if there had ever been a time when she or someone else was not listened to. The student then saw that the problem could not be judged solely as one of the distant other, the teacher. When thinking about the problem from the care orientation, she acknowledged her role in the problem and in the relationship, a responsibility that is not always acknowledged if the relationship is negotiated only through the impartial standards of the justice orientation. Reflecting on the problem from both moral orientations gave the student alternative ways to see the problem, and the alternatives provided a solution.

This example of reflection shows the student's perspective, but it also demonstrates how questions derived from the logic of the two orientations provide scaffolding for thinking through a moral problem from more than one perspective. Seeing the problem in a different way allowed this student to get beyond her initial angry response and find a solution. Clearly the logics of the two orientations provide a kind of scaffolding as a strategy for moral problem solving. In this case, it was provided by the interviewer, who asked questions that did not allow the thinker to settle on one answer. Indeed, this conversation could serve as a model for an internal dialogue to promote the reflective moral thinking that teachers might do.

Teachers can also learn to routinely ask questions about a classroom dilemma to provide a scaffolding for the kind of reflective thinking that is necessary in a classroom. There are three types of questions that are derived from the logics of the two moral orientations and that may help teachers break a routine of thinking in only one moral orientation.

The first type asks, How can I construct this problem from a justice orientation? How can I solve this problem? and Is there another way to think about this problem in terms of fairness and equality? The second type asks, How can I construct this problem from a care orientation? How can I solve this problem? and Is there another way to think about this problem in terms of maintaining this relationship?

Finally, the third type of question asks, Of all these constructions and solutions, which provides the best solution?

MORAL ORIENTATION AS
PROBLEM-SOLVING STRATEGY

Why should the two moral orientations be taken seriously as problem-solving strategies by teachers? Teachers are asked to attend to many issues in today's classroom. They are held accountable for students' mastery of basic skills; they are asked to teach critical thinking; and they are required to deal with issues that affect both the personal and academic lives of their students. The classroom is a place where children and adolescents learn academic lessons and a place where they learn about being in relationships with other people, some very different from themselves. The relationships contained in the classroom are important, as is the teacher's role as a model in forming, negotiating, and maintaining those relationships. The teacher is thus a moral craftsperson, for whom the two moral orientations offer alternatives for thinking about these relationships.

PROBLEM SOLVING AND THE JUSTICE ORIENTATION

Tom suggests that "the 'moral basis' of the student-teacher relationship is grounded in the inherent inequality of this relationship" (1984, p. 80). This view of teaching is at the core of liberatory education. Viewing the teacher as powerful and the student as needing to be freed from that power calls for the moral craftsperson to solve problems by using the moral orientation of justice. Ideally, the rules are democratically derived and apply equally to everyone in the classroom. In fact, as has been previously discussed, the justice orientation seems to be the most common way of solving problems in a classroom. Hendrickson (1987) investigated teachers' use of both moral orientations in a study modeled on the fable study. She asked teachers to solve both hypothetical and real teaching dilemmas and found that both male and female teachers spontaneously solved most problems using the justice mode.

The teachers in Hendrickson's study may have used the prevailing justice orientation for routine classroom problem solving, or they may have preferred this orientation for problem solving after considering both in a reflective way. The teachers simply may not have talked about care alternatives for classroom problem solving that they, in fact, used or considered. But it is equally possible that these teachers may have been guided by traditional methods of classroom problem solving and thus were unaccustomed to examining the assumptions underlying the justice orientation. Although the justice mode may be adequate for solving many classroom problems, it is not the only way for a teacher to construct the teacher-student relationship.

PROBLEM SOLVING AND THE CARE ORIENTATION

To ignore the power dimension of the teacher-student relationship would be naïve. To ignore the satisfactory results a teacher achieves by routinely applying fair rules to classroom situations would be to fail to understand useful and appropriate classroom dynamics. But suppose this relationship is examined in another way. We may think about it from the perspective of the care orientation, which holds as its central moral imperative the importance of not abandoning relationships. What does this mean in the context of the relationships in a classroom?

When the seventh-grade girl quoted earlier was asked about her relationship with her teacher, she said it should be close, and she defined close in this context not only as "when a teacher tries to draw you out in class" but also as "feeling close is feeling close all the time, and not just in that class, [but] when you walk down the hall, you know you can stop right there and they'll talk to you." Defining close in these terms acknowledges self and other in the relationship, not in teacher-student roles but as two people who can meet in the hall and talk. Of course the definition has its problems — the teacher has too many students to be close to all of them, and the care orientation may not work as a way to think through the problem of maintaining individual relationships with 25 students.

Even so, we should not conclude that the solution is to think about the teacher-student relationship only in terms of being fair to these numerous students. That is not what this girl is saying; she is simply asking to be acknowledged as a person. She is not saying that the teacher must be the best friend of every student in the class but that her relationship with the teacher should allow her to think that she can approach the teacher to talk about things, even in the hall.

In the context of this interview, as the student discussed what she meant by the teacher's being close to her, she began to see her own responsibility in the problem; she had to acknowledge her obligation in the relationship with the teacher. She had to see the teacher as a person who could not read her mind but must be told that she is having trouble.

USING BOTH ORIENTATIONS IN THE CLASSROOM

Just as perceiving the problem through one orientation was limiting for the student in this discussion, it may also be limiting for the problem solving that teachers do. Kagan suggests that we tutor our students to "search for and use appropriate rules and strategies, to reflect on alternative solutions, and to know why the solution chosen was best" (1984, pp. 239–40). If alternatives are required in problem solving, then teachers need them too. Although the logic of the moral orientation of justice seems to provide the base most frequently used in thinking about the moral dimension of teaching, the logic of the orientation of care provides a needed alternative. It liberates students as well as teachers. This means, according to Noddings, that "what I must do is to be totally and nonselectively present to the student — to each student — as he addresses me. The time interval may be brief, but the encounter is total" (1984, p. 180).

Our seventh-grade problem solver is asking for this kind of encounter when she wants to feel all right talking to the teacher in the hall.

We can assume that teachers, like the 11- and 15-year-olds in the fable study, know and use both orientations in their relationships outside of school, but can we bring the moral orientation of care into their thinking about in-school relationships? Can we use the moral orientation of care as a base for reflective thinking? This would result in the reflective action that Zeichner and Liston describe as "the active, persistent and careful consideration of any belief or supposed form of knowledge" (1987, p. 24). Using the logics of both moral orientations could provide a scaffolding for reflective thinking that would offer a way for the teacher to reflect on solutions to problems. This in turn could help the teacher avoid routine action, "action [which] is guided primarily by tradition, external authority, and circumstance" (p. 24).

Consider this *New York Times* headline: "Rochester Asks Teachers for 'Extra Mile'" (February 18, 1988). The story reported that one element of this "extra mile" was that "every teacher and administrator in a school [would] take personal responsibility for a group of 20 or so students for several years," the idea being that adding this element of personal responsibility might help "end the failure of the schools to educate poor inner-city children." In the context of our discussion of the two moral orientations, this program of establishing long-term relationships among students, teachers, and administrators clearly seems to align with the care orientation. This relationship is not about treating everyone equally or about empowering students; it is about establishing and maintaining a relationship with students.

The connection of actual educational practice and moral theory is enlightening. Although the newspaper story describes this program as one in which teachers accept increased accountability and responsibility, the program can also be seen as bringing relationships to the foreground of educational discourse. In this setting, there is not only a power dimension in the teacher-student relationship but also a relational dimension. Both are necessary.

The moral orientations of justice and care are crucial elements in mature moral thinking. The teacher must be thought of as a moral craftsperson, and that moral craftsperson must be a mature moral thinker. To solve problems in the classroom, teachers must have alternative strategies in their repertoire. The logics of the two moral orientations provide these alternative strategies.

REFERENCES

Belenky, M. F., B. M. Clinchy, N. R. Goldberger, and J. M. Tarule. (1986). *Women's ways of knowing*. New York: Basic Books.

84 / Johnston

Brown, L., D. Argyris, J. Attanucci, C. Gilligan, D. K. Johnston, B. Miller, R. Osborne, J. Ward, G. Wiggins, and D. Wilcox. (1987). *A guide to reading narratives of moral conflict and choice for self and moral orientation*. Unpublished manuscript. Harvard Graduate School of Education.

Bruner, J. (1973). *Beyond the information given*. New York: Norton.

Cruickshank, D. R. (1987). *Reflective teaching: The preparation of students of teaching*. Reston, Va.: Association of Teacher Educators.

Gilligan, C. (1977). In a different voice: Women's conception of the self and of morality. *Harvard Educational Review* 47: 481–517.

_____. (1982). *In a different voice: Psychological theory and women's development*. Cambridge, Mass.: Harvard University Press.

_____. (1986). Exit-voice dilemmas in adolescent development. In *Development, democracy, and the art of trespassing: Essays in honor of Albert O. Hirschman*, edited by A. Foxley, M. McPherson, and G. O'Donnell, pp. 283–300. South Bend, Ind.: University of Notre Dame Press.

Gilligan, C., and J. Attanucci. (1988). Two moral orientations: Gender differences and similarities. *Merrill Palmer Quarterly* 34 (3): 223–37.

Gilligan, C., J. V. Ward, and J. Taylor, eds. (1988). *Re-mapping the moral domain: A contribution of women's thinking to psychological theory and education*. Cambridge, Mass.: Harvard University Press.

Hendrickson, L. (1987). Teachers' uses of moral orientation: Kids in the classroom. Unpublished manuscript, Colgate University.

Irwin, C. E., Jr., ed. (1987). *Adolescent social behavior and health: New directions for child development*. San Francisco: Jossey-Bass.

Johnston, D. K. (1983). Moral problem-solving: A pilot study of adolescents' ability to use both moral orientations. Unpublished manuscript, Harvard Graduate School of Education.

_____. (1985). Two moral orientations — two problem-solving strategies: Adolescents' solutions to dilemmas in fables. Ed.D. diss., Harvard University.

_____. (1988). Adolescents' solutions to dilemmas in fables: Two moral orientations — two problem solving strategies. In *Mapping the moral domain*, edited by C. Gilligan, J. V. Ward, and J. M. Taylor with B. Bardige. Cambridge, Mass.: Harvard University Press.

Kagan, J. (1984). *The nature of the child*. New York: Basic Books.

Kohlberg, L. (1976). Moral stages and moralization: The cognitive-developmental approach. In *Moral development and behavior: Theory research and social issues*, edited by T. Lickona. New York: Holt, Rinehart, and Winston.

Langdale, S. (1983). Moral orientations and moral development: The analysis of care and justice reasoning across different dilemmas in females and males from childhood through adulthood. Ed.D. diss., Harvard University.

Lickona, T., ed. (1976). *Moral development and behavior*. New York: Holt, Rinehart, and Winston.

Lyons, N. (1982). Conceptions of self and morality and modes of moral choice: Identifying justice and care in judgments of actual moral dilemmas. Ed.D. diss., Harvard University.

_____. (1983). Two perspectives: On self, relationships, and morality. *Harvard Educational Review* 53: 125–45.

Noddings, N. (1984). *Caring*. Berkeley: University of California Press.

Piaget, J. (1932). *The moral judgment of the child*. New York: Free Press. Reprinted 1965.

Rochester Asks Teachers to go Extra Mile. *New York Times*, February 1988, p. 112.

Sarton, M. (1976). *The small room*. New York: Norton.

Schon, D. A. (1983). *The reflective practitioner*. New York: Basic Books.

Simmons, R. J. (1987). Social transition and adolescent development. In *Adolescent social behavior and health*, edited by Charles E. Irwin, Jr. San Francisco: Jossey-Bass.

Tom, A. (1984). *Teaching as a moral craft*. New York: Longman.

Zeichner, K. M., and D. P. Liston. (1987). Teaching student teachers to reflect. *Harvard Educational Review* 57: 23–48.

II

MORAL EDUCATION
IN PRACTICE

5

Schools and Families: Partners or Adversaries in Moral Education?

Thomas Lickona

Renewed interest in moral education has turned a spotlight on the role of the family in the child's moral growth and on the relationship between families and schools. In a pluralistic society, are families and schools natural allies or adversaries in moral education?

This chapter will attempt to show that they can be either or both. To sort out the conditions affecting the relationship, I will examine four areas: parallel forms of moral education that can be carried out in both home and school; distinctive, complementary contributions that the school and family each make to the child's moral growth; tensions and conflicts between home and school around issues of moral education; and instances where schools and families have deliberately and successfully collaborated as partners in moral education.

There are several compelling reasons why moral educators should be concerned about the relations between schools and families. To teach moral values, schools need not only community permission but also families' active support of those values and standards. James Coleman (1985), a University of Chicago sociologist who has long studied public and private schools, believes that the primary cause of the downtrend in youth character — a downtrend evidenced, for example, by an increase in destructive behavior toward oneself and others — lies outside the school in changes that have taken place in the family. Schools can no longer assume that a strong, cohesive family supports and teaches the school's value norms such as honesty, hard work, delay of gratification, respect for property, and respect for legitimate authority. Nor can schools assume cohesive communities; parents today often do not know their neighbors or the parents of their children's friends. Isolated from each other, many parents have a hard time knowing what limits are appropriate for their children at particular ages and consequently are insecure about setting rules and expectations.

Faced with this situation, Coleman says, schools have a formidable new task: they must try to create a moral community surrounding the school by bringing parents together in ways that allow parents to discover shared values. In this way, schools can help to bring into being the norm-generating structures — the external support systems — that they used to take for granted. Such support structures are vital, Coleman argues, for holding in place the character development that the school is trying to bring about.

Finally, just as schools need families, families more than ever need schools. In growing numbers of families, the whole job of parenting falls on one parent's shoulders. In increasing numbers of two-parent families, both parents work outside the home and must struggle to protect time for family life and guiding children. In view of these trends, it is not surprising that public opinion polls in both Canada and the United States show that 80 percent of parents want the schools to teach morality to their children.

PARALLEL FORMS OF MORAL EDUCATION IN THE SCHOOL AND HOME

One powerful form of home-school cooperation is an invisible partnership. This happens when families and schools spontaneously do parallel things that foster moral growth.

Self-esteem is a case in point. The Ontario Ministry's guide to values education, *Personal and Societal Values* (1983), lists developing the student's self-esteem as the first of 12 school objectives. Good teachers do that in a variety of ways: by treating children with respect, listening to them, giving them individual attention, helping them feel valued as members of the class, and helping them succeed at the work of the school. Good parents foster children's sense of worth in similar ways: spending the kind of time that makes a child feel valued and important, helping children develop talents and skills that are a source of self-esteem, and pointing out good qualities and strengths children might not be able to see in themselves.

Conscientious parents also try to set an example for their children — to practice what they preach as much as humanly possible — and they want teachers to do the same. Besides modeling, wise parents and teachers do a lot of direct moral teaching. Both teachers and parents can teach children that it is wrong to call people names because names hurt; the hurt is invisible, but it is real. It is wrong to lie because lying undermines trust, and trust is needed to enable people to believe each other. It is wrong to cheat because cheating is a lie — it deceives another person and it is unfair to all the people who are not cheating. It is wrong to steal because there is a person behind the property, and stealing violates the rights of that person.

Conflicts go with the territory of both home and school. Tempers flare between two third graders because one cut ahead of the other in line. At home, a brother and sister get into an argument over what TV show to watch. In all such disputes, there are opportunities to learn to take another's perspective — how does the other person see it? And there are opportunities for developing moral reasoning — what is a fair way to solve the problem, one that takes account of both points of view? In both families and classrooms, conflict is part of the moral curriculum.

Discipline is another parallel process. Diana Baumrind's studies (1975; see also Maccoby 1980), among others, have helped to establish that parents who rear self-confident, prosocial children are authoritative disciplinarians. They listen to their child's feelings and encourage give-and-take, but they also make high maturity demands and set and enforce clear rules. Discipline is an essential part of moral education in the school as well. Durkheim (1925) reminds us that the function of school discipline is to create the morality of the classroom, not simply to maintain order for learning. Hence the moral meaning of rules — their function in governing the collective life — must be made clear to children both in school and in the family.

Open discussion of moral issues, in the classroom or around the family dinner table (Lickona 1985), is still another parallel process. What should you do if you see somebody cheating? If someone asks to copy your homework? If you are with kids who start teasing a retarded boy? If a friend is pregnant but afraid to tell her parents?

Both home and school can foster the development of responsibility. Whiting and Whiting's cross-cultural research (1975) found that U.S. families typically assigned children much less responsibility for contributing to the life of the family than is the case in other countries. Wise parents, however, take pains to give children other-oriented responsibilities such as supervising, playing with, or reading to a younger sibling, or helping with work in the house or yard. Similarly, elementary schools can give youngsters opportunities to carry out classroom responsibilities or to tutor a younger child, and secondary schools can provide opportunities for service to the school or community. Such reponsibilities help children learn to care by giving care, teach them to value others, and deepen their sense of membership in the human community.

These examples make it clear that moral education is not restricted to classrooms. Rather, it is a process that goes on wherever adults — parents or teachers — are trying to teach children what it means to be human.

DISTINCTIVE CONTRIBUTIONS OF
FAMILIES AND SCHOOLS

It would be a mistake to think that parents and teachers make identical contributions to a child's moral growth. The contributions of school and family are also distinctive.

Schools, for example, focus on learning. Although learning certainly takes place in the home, the school assigns the child a structured role in a social system whose chief business is learning. Children carry out that role well or poorly. Do they listen to directions? Do they apply themselves to the task at hand? Do they get their work in on time? Do they try to learn from the teacher's criticisms and corrections? Do they follow the rules of classroom conduct that facilitate their learning and the learning of others? In short, do they do their best?

It is significant that virtually all the recent national critiques of U.S. schools call for developing students' orderly conduct, self-discipline, sense of purpose, and capacity for hard work — all of which can be seen as qualities of character underlying a responsible commitment to make the most of one's education. From this perspective, learning itself is a kind of moral activity — the application of the will toward a good end — and all schooling is a form of moral education. This view breaks down the distinction between cognitive and moral education; if you create schools where students mobilize their energies for the task of learning, you have accomplished a moral aim.

Thomas Green, professor of cultural foundations of education at Syracuse University, extends this line of thinking. Green writes that there are four "voices of conscience," one of which is the "conscience of craft." To have a conscience of craft, he says, is to have acquired the capacity for satisfaction for a job well done and for shame at slovenly work. A sense of craft underlies our concern with excellence, which is what the Greeks meant by virtue. It is conscience of craft that motivates a mechanic to repair a car not only to the owner's satisfaction but also to his own. Green even suggests that it may be in the acquisition of a sense of craft that the formation of conscience takes place most clearly: "If we cannot teach children that it matters whether they craft a good sentence, then why should we be surprised when they do not craft a good life?" (Green 1984, p. 5). Developing a conscience of craft, he concludes, is a major part of what we should routinely think of as moral education.

Whether or not they call it moral education, effective schools foster conscience of craft and thereby make a distinctive contribution to children's moral growth. What else do schools do that is distinctive? They make the child a citizen of a small society, the classroom, which is bigger and more complex than the family. The rules needed to govern the shared life of the classroom are typically more numerous and salient than the rules of the ordinary family. Classroom rules are also based on a more impersonal kind of authority — fair is fair, the same goes for all — and that kind of impersonal social structure demands a new level of social accommodation from children.

Classroom authority, in the hands of a skilled and confident teacher, can be shared with students, who act as cocreators of their moral community. That is harder to do in a family, where shared decision making can occur to some degree but where a child is born into an already existing group and parents exercise, of necessity, a lot of unilateral control during the child's early years. The classroom also typically provides a richer mix and a greater range of values and viewpoints than those available to children within their own families. In the hands of a sensitive teacher, the pluralism of the classroom can be a helpful preparation for the pluralism of society at large.

The most distinctive contribution of the family to the moral growth of the child is love. Urie Bronfenbrenner (1976) says that two things are necessary for the optimal development of a child: a social environment that draws the child into roles of increasing variety, complexity, and responsibility; and somebody who is crazy about the kid. A parent is crazy about a kid in a way that nobody else is. That kind of irrational love not only nourishes a child's self-esteem but also creates a deep bond between parent and child. That bond, as Selma Fraiberg points out in *The Magic Years* (1959), makes a child responsive to a parent's approval and disapproval — a responsiveness that is crucial for the child's socialization and development of self-control. When parents are not making this contribution at home, teachers often see the negative effects in the classroom. A kindergarten teacher, for example, tells of a little boy, a child from a very affluent family, who repeatedly stole things in the classroom. An inquiry into his home situation revealed that his father was usually on the road, his mother was preoccupied with her own problems, and the boy hungered for attention and love. Research (for example, Staub 1978, 1979) finds that lack of parental love is a salient feature in the background of delinquents, while the presence of love is prominent in the constellation of factors that appear to bring children to moral maturity.

A second distinctive contribution of the family is to offer a child a spiritual heritage, a coherent vision of life that speaks to life's ultimate meaning. Often that vision is religious. Here, for example, is a Catholic mother, responding to the question, What values or heritage do you hope to pass on to your children that you don't expect them to get from public school?

She said, "Faith in God. The value of an interior life. Prayer. A religious view of the universe."

When I asked her, "How does your faith in God translate into what you teach your children about morality?" she answered,

If you see God as the center of the universe, it affects everything. It affects *why* you behave in certain ways and not others. There is a standard of behavior. It comes partly from people who have tried to discern the mind of God over the ages. We also have our own hearts to listen to. There is someone who has created us to behave in a certain way — so much so that if we don't behave in that way, we are unhappy, we create problems for ourselves. We are called to goodness, to live our lives according to a very high standard.

Clearly, the distinctive contributions of school and family are not conflicting but are complementary. Families can be grateful to schools for their distinctive contributions to the child's moral development, and schools can be grateful to families for theirs.

TENSIONS AND CONFLICTS BETWEEN SCHOOLS AND FAMILIES

When parents protest moral values education in the schools, they are usually objecting to one or more of the following:

Exercises they regard as emotionally distressing and potentially destructive to children — An example is the infamous "life raft," in which children are asked to pretend they are in an overcrowded boat. Each must make a case for why he or she should stay in the boat, and then there is a vote on which child should be thrown overboard.

Exercises that confuse children — One father reported that a moral dilemma discussion confused his elementary school-age son about the rightness or wrongness of stealing from a store.

Exercises that invade the child's or family's privacy — Examples of this type of exercise are children being asked questions like these: Do you love your parents? or Is there something you did once that you are ashamed of? (questions recommended in the values clarification activity, "Public Interview," Simon, Hower, and Kirschenbaum 1972).

Exercises that undermine respect for parents — These ask questions such as What disturbs you most about your parents? or employ exercises that encourage students to question their parents' values. One workshop allegedly began by telling students, "Your parents' values are different from yours. They grew up at a different time and have a different field of experience" (Schlafly 1984, p. 50).

Activities that teach students decision-making skills without teaching substantive moral values to guide decision making

Activities or materials that directly or indirectly promote a moral standard that may be contrary to values taught at home — One tenth-grade health textbook, for example, states that "there are two qualifications for joining in any kind of sexual activity — that an individual feels it is right for him or her at the particular time with the particular person, and that he or she is fully able to handle the sex, the love, and the consequences" (Schlafly 1984, p. 160). A mother objected to this text on the grounds that it taught situational ethics without mentioning chastity or marriage as values that would be relevant for some people in deciding issues of sexual behavior.

Approaches that promote moral relativism — These include open-ended moral discussions that begin with the teacher telling the students, "There are no right or wrong answers."

Approaches that parents believe undercut family influence by promoting children's autonomy — These questions include telling children to "make your own decisions" about moral questions.

Approaches that, in the view of some parents, are based on a philosophy of secular humanism — This approach holds that there is no God and that human beings are the sole source and judge of morality.

Values education activities that are presented to children without the prior knowledge and consent of their parents.

One mother gives voice to the feelings of parents upset about these issues: "We do not send our children to school to have their morals, values, ethics, beliefs, thoughts, and feelings questioned, scrutinized, prioritized, and rearranged by the group. We do not abdicate our right to raise our children according to our own moral, cultural, and ethical beliefs when we send them off to school every day" (Schlafly 1984, p. 58).

Many of these parental objections may no longer be live issues in Canada. It has been several years since the publication of *Yes, Virginia, There is Right and Wrong* (1980), in which Kathleen Gow charged that some Canadian values educators were promoting moral relativism in the schools. In 1981, the Ontario Ministry of Education issued a directive stating that life raft and bomb shelter dilemmas condoned moral relativism, upset students, invaded their privacy, and were to be avoided. In the Canadian systems I have been able to learn about, school boards have taken pains to build community support, to base programs on consensual values, and to affirm the home as the primary moral educator of the child.

In the United States, most parents continue to tell the Gallup Poll that schools should teach morals to their children. But with regard to values education, there is still controversy, which is fueled by the Hatch Amendment. Passed in 1978, this amendment says two things: that parents have the right to inspect all instructional materials used in federally funded school programs designed to develop "unproven teaching methods"; and that parents' prior written consent is required for students to participate in any program or testing whose primary purpose is to reveal information about such things as psychological problems potentially embarrassing to the student or his family, sexual behavior and attitudes, self-incriminating behavior, and critical appraisals of persons with whom students have close family relations (Lewis 1985). In March 1984, hundreds of parents attended federal hearings in seven cities to testify that regulations were needed to enforce the Hatch Amendment because, in the experience of these parents, schools were continuing to violate the amendment, often flagrantly. Transcripts of the hearings were published in a book edited by Phyllis Schlafly, *Child Abuse in the Classroom* (1984). As a result of the hearings, the Hatch Amendment now has teeth: schools stand to lose federal funds for programs judged to be in violation.

Many dismiss Schlafly's arguments because they disagree with her politics or with her sweeping attacks on values clarification, mastery learning, moral reasoning, critical thinking, sex education, death education, drug education, family life courses, character education, global education, and programs for the gifted and talented all as forms of educational therapy (Schlafly 1984, p. 14). And the transcripts of the Hatch hearings are sometimes hard to evaluate because they do not include a school's defense. However, if the parents' accounts are accurate, real problems do exist that responsible schools should correct. Even without the requirement of law, schools should, ethically, inform parents about values education programs being used. They should seek parents' consent for their children's participation in programs where the issues treated are controversial and where some parents would be likely to object. Schools should put a stop to exercises that embarrass students, invade their privacy, suggest that their parents' values are obsolete, promote values that are not universal, teach decision making devoid of moral content, or foster the view that morality is just a matter of personal opinion. Teachers should not introduce moral discussions by saying, There is no right or wrong answer, when in fact they mean, There is no *single* right answer or There may be several answers, some of which are better than others.

Other issues that concern parents are more complex, at least at first glance. Autonomy is one. Autonomy is typically defined as "independence, freedom, or self-government." Many parents don't think their children are ready to be independent or self-governing when it comes to morality. They don't want schools giving their children open-ended moral dilemmas and telling them to make up their own minds about whether Heinz should steal the drug.

It is true that autonomy is a goal of moral education. William Frankena, in his classic book *Ethics* (1963), points out that morality has a social and an individual side. Morality is social in that it exists before the individual and is meant to serve the social good. But it is also individual in that it promotes rational self-guidance or self-determination. Philosophers since Socrates have stressed that morality "calls for the use of reason and a *kind of autonomy* on the part of the individual. It asks him, when *mature* and normal, to make his own decisions," but to do so in a way that respects the rights of others (Frankena 1963, p. 26; emphasis added). With maturity, the rule of reason replaces the rule of authority. Internal control, or what Frankena calls "rational self-guidance," replaces external control. Most parents would agree that the replacement is a good thing; they wouldn't want a 21-year-old child who still needed parents to tell him or her not to cheat, vandalize, or steal from a neighbor.

However, parents might reply, Frankena says people should make their own decisions when they are mature. My 8-year-old is not mature enough to decide his own values about cheating or stealing. Until he is mature enough to make his own decisions, I want him to follow the values we're teaching at home.

Schools in turn might respond, We agree you have a right to teach your child the values you believe in, such as honesty. We are trying to teach the same value by helping children learn to reason about why honesty is a good thing. For example, we might give fourth graders a moral dilemma about a girl named Marie, who sees a soccer ball under a bush and is tempted to take it home. To get students thinking, the teacher doesn't tell them what Marie should do but asks them, What should Marie do? Then the teacher follows up with questions such as, If others found your soccer ball, what would you like them to do? What would happen if all the boys and girls did what you suggest Marie should do? Would school be a better place or a worse place? These questions help children think that they wouldn't want someone to steal *their* belongings and how the school would not be a very nice place if everybody took whatever they pleased. So, although the discussion begins by asking students what they think, it guides them, through reasoning, to the values of honesty and respect for others. In this way, it makes them more autonomous, in that their conscience is based on good reasons not to steal and not just on an adult's forbidding it. (For the full dilemma and discussion questions, see *Personal and Societal Values* 1983.) In short, schools and families can find common ground regarding moral autonomy if the discussion of this term moves from the abstract to the concrete.

In the case of secular humanism, an issue that has sometimes bitterly divided families and schools, conciliation is possible if both sides are committed to reason and fairness. About ten years ago, the Catholic Bishops of Pennsylvania offered a helpful distinction among three kinds of values: religious values, which are rooted in a belief in God and a religious view of life and human destiny; authentic secular values such as democracy, equality, and social justice, which concern the temporal life and are fully compatible with religious values; and secularistic values, which either exclude any reference to religion or explicitly reject a religious worldview (*Public Education and Student Conscience: A Dilemma for Concerned Citizens* 1976).

Do secularistic values prevail in U.S. public schools, as the bishops suggested? Not perhaps in the sense of explicitly rejecting religious values. The U.S. Supreme Court in *Abington* v. *Schempp* said that the state could not establish a religion of secularism by showing hostility to religion. But schools and textbook publishers, at least in the United States, often ignore religion altogether. One U.S. history text, for example, in describing life in colonial New England, omits all reference to Sunday activities (Davis 1984). So parents concerned about secularistic values — in the sense of excluding all teaching about religion — have a point. Public schools, for their part, could teach religious traditions as an important part of the culture and national history, as many Canadian schools do. Religious parents, for their part, should recognize that the schools have a right and a duty to teach authentic secular values — liberty, equality, democracy, and justice — that can be taught without appeal to religious belief. Even in this difficult area, then, it may be possible to make peace between dissident parents and the public schools.

CASE STUDIES OF COLLABORATIONS
BETWEEN FAMILIES AND SCHOOLS

Let me turn now to cases where schools and families have deliberately collaborated as partners in moral education.

Many schools and parents are concerned about the growing impact of television as a moral educator. For example, at an inner city parochial school on the south side of Chicago, the principal surveyed K–8 students to determine their viewing habits. The average fifth grader, she found, watched seven hours of television a day, and children at other grade levels watched nearly as much. Most students said they had television sets in their bedrooms and could watch any program they pleased. This fall, with the support of the parent Advisory Board, the principal is asking every parent to sign a contract limiting his or her child's TV viewing to two hours a day and specifying those programs that a child may watch.

In Washington, D.C., an independent K–12 school has formed parent peer groups that meet twice a year, sometimes at school and sometimes in a parent's home. A teacher or a principal participates in each group. The format is informal: each meeting begins with parents introducing themselves, giving their children's names, and suggesting one or two topics they would like to address. In the lower school (K–4), the group discusses such questions as How do you get your kids to help around the house? or What TV programs are right for young children? Middle school parents ask questions like What would you do if you sent your sixth grader to a birthday party where the entertainment was a R-rated movie your family had already decided not to see? High school parents ask each other, What do you do when your child goes to an open party but doesn't know whether any parents will be chaperoning or whether liquor is going to be served? What rules do you have about using the car? (Harter and Lodish 1985).

After attending parent peer groups for four years, parents are better acquainted and more often work together to plan events in the school and community. Parents feel helped by being able to communicate their values and standards to each other, and many have found support for their stance on a given issue. One thinks of Coleman's exhortation to bring parents together so they can discover and affirm shared norms that in turn will support the school. Here is a school that is doing just that.

An urban elementary school in Ontario was concerned about the school atmosphere and the vandalism rate, one of the worst in the city. As a first step, the Parent-Teacher Council organized a series of neighborhood meetings, one for every neighborhood served by the school. Each meeting was hosted by a school parent, who invited everyone on the block — not just school parents but other members of the community as well. The principal, vice principal, and a teacher attended each gathering. They presented clear, specific objectives for improving student behavior and values and asked for comments and suggestions. They also asked, What would you like the school to start doing? Stop doing? Continue doing? How can we work together? What can parents do at home to reinforce the school's effort to foster students' self-esteem and good citizenship?

Suggestions were taken back to the whole school staff and implemented as much as possible. Students were asked to "join 'The Force' for positive values in our school" (*Star Wars* was big at the time). School goals included helping students develop responsibility for their actions, social skills, a greater sense of belonging in the school, and school pride. Each goal was treated as a special theme during its own five-week period, with assemblies and schoolwide projects developed to illustrate them. An awards program recognized good citizenship. Clear rules were established for classroom cleanup at day's end. Parents and students worked together to design and raise money for an adventure playground. Parents tried out some of the activities suggested by the school — for example, a family home evening once a week when all family members stayed home for talk, games, and other shared activity.

What were the results of all this effort? Teacher morale went up. Parent volunteers in the school increased. Discipline problems in the school and on the playground decreased. Parents said they saw changes in the children's neighborhood behavior; children got into fewer fights as they played ball hockey in the streets and showed better ways of solving conflicts that did arise. Pride in the school soared; both students and community members reported any acts of vandalism they saw being committed by an outsider. Vandalism declined drastically; during the last half of the program's third year, there was not a single broken window. This school had created a cohesive moral community within and around the school, and the results were evident everywhere (for further details, see *Personal and Societal Values* 1983).

In an elementary school in Scarborough, Ontario, parents and teachers planned an in-service day on values education. Together they chose the topic — self-esteem — and selected speakers. At the conference, attended by both parents and teachers, they discussed the implications of the talks for classroom and family. The opportunity for this kind of common experience and thoughtful communication was viewed as highly valuable by all participants.

San Ramon, California, is the site of the child development project, the most comprehensive, well-researched character development program in the United States. The project seeks to enhance prosocial motives and behavior in children through five components promoted in both the school and the home: cooperative activities, helping roles, setting positive examples and reducing children's exposure to negative examples, developing social understanding, and developmental discipline aimed at using adult authority in ways that foster children's self-control.

Parents are involved in a variety of ways. At each of the three program schools (all elementary), parents share the leadership for planning how the school will implement project goals during the year. Families turn out in large numbers for school events like family fun festivals and family film nights; at the latter, parents and children see a movie with a prosocial theme and talk about it together afterward.

I had a chance to visit this project recently and interview parents about their involvement in and perceptions of the program. One mother told of a workshop on helping in the home that she and her sixth-grade daughter attended; following the workshop, they were able to work together on a strategy that got the daughter to keep her room picked up. Another mother told of how her family — with children aged four, five, and nine — had lapsed into a pattern of screaming their wants at each other. She and her husband went to a school workshop on family meetings, came home, and held a successful meeting on "how we can all make this a happier family." Another mother said simply that she had more empathy in her dealings with her children after attending classes on parenting.

A project evaluation finds that nearly half of all families in the three schools say they have made changes in family life as a result of their involvement with project activities. The project's research design does not separate home effects and classroom effects, but early assessment of overall program effects is encouraging. Children in program schools are more considerate, show higher levels of interstudent cooperation, and show more complex reasoning in solving social problems than do children in the project's comparison schools (*Child Development Project Progress Report* 1985).

My next example of collaboration between schools and families regarding moral education comes from a rural community in northern Ontario. It was shared with me by a principal who left his school for two years to head a systemwide effort in values education. He said teachers and administrators knew they had to do something in the area of values. Society was changing, families were breaking down, elementary school children were coming to school with hardcore pornography, and students at all levels seemed to have little self-esteem. "We started," the principal said, "with the faith that ordinary people can come up with answers. We firmly believed that human beings could reach common consent through discussion."

They began by building consensus among the school board trustees. Then they created a subcommittee of trustees to take the leadership. This group went to the high schools and met with senior students. "What was good about your elementary schools?" they asked. "What would make them better?" They used a circle format to conduct these meetings so as to facilitate democratic participation.

"Next," the principal said, "we met with the clergy, and I'll tell you, that was a sweaty one. We have every shade of religion here from fundamentalist to liberal, and they locked horns right away. But they saw the dilemma — the schools had to do something with values, and we didn't have the luxury of sitting on our differences. We asked the clergy, 'What are the common elements in our traditions? If our goal is to foster students' understanding of moral responsibility, what are appropriate topics for classroom discussion? What are *not* appropriate topics?' Trust and consensus came slowly, but it came."

The trustees met with parents, using the same process. Before inviting discussion, they presented sample goals and sample lessons showing different approaches to moral values education. They asked parents, "Do you see a need for the school board to develop programs in this area? Would you prefer religious education classes a couple of times a week, or values integrated into academic subjects, or nothing at all? If clergy are to be involved, what role should they play?" Parents were asked to respond to these questions in writing, and responses were collected.

Finally, the trustees met with teachers in schools throughout the system. After all this, the principal, who was the lead consultant to the board, sorted and sifted all the responses from students, clergy, parents, and teachers, searching for common themes. Once he identified common values, he presented them to a newly formed committee of six parents, six clergy, and six high school students. Another committee of teachers was formed to develop curricular materials based on the values approved by the larger steering committee. They identified 100 such values that now form the basis for education exercises used to open the school day in all the schools. Sometimes these exercises use scripture, but always text that bears on shared values, such as the parable of the Good Samaritan. Controversial issues are deferred to the high school level, where a debate format is used to give equal time to both sides.

When asked how the values program affected students, the principal responded, "We probably won't know that for twenty years. But we had to make the effort, and I believe the process itself was of great value. We showed we could use reason to reach agreement about basic values and how to teach them in our schools. And that process has affected how we handle discipline in our schools. Many teachers now use the circle meeting in their classrooms, allowing students to help with forming rules and solving problems. It gives them a voice. We think if this process was valuable for us as adults, it will be valuable for students too. . . . And if it's working, I think it's because people feel ownership; they have been consulted."

This system's experience is helpful, I think, not only because it exemplifies a process of consultation but also because it reminds us that the community is more than just parents. Involving other groups as well — for example, clergy, teachers, and students — broadens the base of community support for a values program and maximizes its chance for long-term success. The dialogue that takes place as community groups try to define their values enables them to discover an important truth: that even in a changing and pluralistic world, there are moral norms on which we can agree and on which we can build our schools, our communities, and our society.

My last example of a partnership between families and schools comes from Scotia-Glenville, a small working-class community in upstate New York. This school district calls its program "An Integrated Approach to Responsible Behavior" and gives credit for help with its design to Herman Williams of Union College's Character Research Project. The program has two main goals: to educate students to be the kind of people anybody would like as neighbors, and to develop students' ability and willingness to be participating citizens in a democracy. Implementation of the program involves the following steps:

> The school district states clearly that its role is to support the family, which is viewed as the child's primary moral teacher.
>
> The character development curriculum is home grown. It has been either adapted by teachers, as in the case of the primary materials, or developed from scratch, as in the case of materials for grades four through six. This practice stems from the district's belief that indigenous materials have the best chance of long-term success.
>
> The curriculum is written by a team of parents, teachers, and administrators.
>
> The district has moved slowly, implementing the first-grade curriculum in 1981–82 and adding one grade level each year.
>
> At each grade level, parents receive a family guide, which contains all the classroom lessons for their child's grade level. For every classroom lesson there is a suggestion on how to follow through on the lesson in the home.

For every grade level there are 12 curriculum units, each one week long. The units begin in late October and run through mid-April. Each unit features daily lessons that take 15 or 20 minutes of instructional time. During the rest of the day, teachers refer to the lesson as they teach other subjects or deal with classroom situations that arise.

The first-grade curriculum focuses on membership in groups — being a family member, a peer group member, or a member of the classroom and school — and the responsibilities that go with being a member of these groups. The very first lesson in first grade deals with family responsibilities. The teachers asks, "What responsibility can you take that will help your family?" and the children respond with their ideas. Then the teacher gives each child a personal learning activity (PLA) worksheet, which is part of every lesson and which the child takes home at the end of the day. The PLA for this first-grade lesson is entitled "I Belong." The teacher says, "At the top of your worksheet, draw a picture of something you can do to help your family. The picture you draw can remind you of your responsibility." Beneath the picture are the days of the week and spaces that children can check off to show that they fulfilled the responsibility for a given day.

At the end of the classroom lesson, the teacher reads the family note that is printed at the bottom of the child's PLA. For this lesson, the note reads, "Please help your child to remember this responsibility. The same responsibility, or a new one, may be chosen each day" (*Family Guide for First-Grade Students* 1981). Other family notes that go home with first graders on their PLAs are:

> We are all teased sometimes. Record two incidents when your child was teased. Ask your child to tell you how he or she felt at the time. Talk about the four positive responses to teasing.
> Role-play a teasing situation with your child.
> Talk about how another child would feel if your child teased him.

The grade-two curriculum centers on good work habits. Grade three stresses self-confidence, empathy, and good sportsmanship. Grade four teaches how to make good decisions. Grade five tries to help students develop the courage and skills to carry out their convictions while respecting the dignity of others and their right to be different. The grade-six curriculum being implemented this year will try to help students develop the imagination needed to find ways they can contribute to their communities and to humanity. The curriculum steadily builds toward the ideal of active, democratic citizenship and global awareness.

Ruth Kellog, assistant superintendent for instruction, explained how the schools get parents to use these materials: "At our back to school night in September, each teacher gives the family guide to parents and explains the purposes of that year's curriculum. About 90 percent of the parents turn out for that. In November, in parent-teacher conferences, teachers talk individually with parents about the program and the family's role. And about 90 percent of the parents come out for a conference."

It is harder to tell how many parents do the family guide activities with their children because the schools have been sensitive to family privacy. Kellog says, "We've been very careful not to embarrass children whose parents may not be using the at-home materials. Therefore a teacher will never ask, 'How many did the family activity last night?'" The district gets a rough measure of parent participation from a questionnaire sent to all parents at the end of each year's program. It asks them to evaluate the program and indicate how often they used the home materials. Between 50 and 55 percent of the parents return the questionnaire; of those who do, most say they use the at-home materials on a regular basis.

The survey also asks parents to evaluate the character development curriculum for that year. Questions are tied to the objectives that were pursued at the child's grade level. For example, parents of first-grade children are asked to agree or disagree, on a five-point scale, with statements such as My child has learned to handle teasing in a constructive way. Parent responses typically indicate that they see progress. In response to open-ended questions, parents often write, for example, that their first grader is less likely to get angry over teasing from siblings or peers. Sometimes parents write that they haven't seen a lot of behavior change, but that their child is more aware of what is appropriate. Often parents also report closer family ties, even though only one child may have been directly involved in the family guide activities.

Finally, the evaluation asks parents, What did your child like best in this year's program? What things did your child like least? What suggestions do you have for improving the program? (parent suggestions are, in fact, used), and Should the program be extended through grade twelve? (every year, virtually 100 percent of the parents have said yes).

CONCLUSION

I have tried to show that parents and schools are often partners in moral education in parallel, unplanned ways. They also each make distinctive, complementary contributions to a child's moral education, and there is a whole range of ways, big and small, in which they can deliberately collaborate to teach children positive moral values. Where there are conflicts, reasonable and honorable people can take steps to solve them; the common ground is broad and firm.

Moral education in these times is too big a job for schools or families to tackle alone. Working together, they have the best possible chance of helping children become moral people and of creating a good and just society for us all.

REFERENCES

Baumrind, D. (1975). Early socialization and adolescent competence. In *Adolescence in the life cycle*, edited by S. E. Dragastin and C. H. Edler (pp. 117–43). New York: Wiley.
Bronfenbrenner, U. (1976). *The ecology of human development*. Cambridge, MA: Harvard University Press.
Coleman, J. (1985). Reflections on developing character. Paper presented to the Symposium on Developing Character, Annual Conference of the American Educational Research Association, April, Chicago.

Davis, E. D. (1984). Should the public school teach values? *Phi Delta Kappan* (January): 358–60.

Durkheim, É. (1925). *Moral education.* New York: Free Press. Reprinted 1961.

Family guide for first-grade students. (1981). Union College Character Research Project, 266 State Street, Schenectady, NY 12305.

Fraiberg, S. (1959). *The magic years.* New York: Scribner's.

Frankena, W. (1963). *Ethics.* Englewood Cliffs, NJ: Prentice-Hall.

Gow, K. (1980). *Yes, Virginia, there is right and wrong.* Toronto: Wiley.

Green, T. (1984). The formation of conscience in an age of technology. *American Journal of Education* (November 1985): 1–38. John Dewey Society Lecture. Available from the School of Education, 263 Huntington Hall, Syracuse University, Syracuse, NY 13210.

Harter, N., and R. Lodish. (1985). Parent peer groups at Sidwell Friends. *Independent School* (May): 21–22.

Lewis, A. C. (1985). Washington report. *Phi Delta Kappan* (June): 667–68.

Lickona, T. (1985). *Raising good children.* New York: Bantam Books.

Maccoby, E. (1980). *Social development: Psychological growth and the parent-child relationship.* New York: Harcourt Brace Jovanovich.

Personal and societal values: A resource guide for the primary and junior divisions. (1983). Toronto: Ministry of Education.

Public education and student conscience: A dilemma for concerned citizens. (1976). Harrisburg, PA: Pennsylvania Catholic Conference.

Schlafly, P., ed. (1984). *Child abuse in the classroom.* Alton, IL: Père Marquette Press.

Simon, S., L. W. Hower, and H. Kirschenbaum. (1972). *Values clarification.* New York: Hart.

Staub, E. (1978, 1979). *Positive social behavior and morality.* Vols. 1, 2. New York: Academic Press.

Watson, Marilyn, et al. (1984). Child development project progress report. In *Moral development and character education,* edited by L. Nucci. Berkeley: McCutchan Publishing Corp. Available from Developmental Studies Center, 111 Deerwood Place, Suite 165, San Ramon, CA 94583.

Whiting, B., and J. Whiting. (1975). *Children of six cultures.* Cambridge, MA: Harvard University Press.

6

Teaching Moral Reasoning in the Standard Curriculum

Robert Swartz

In Howard Fast's novel *The Hessian*, Hans Pohl, a Hessian drummer boy, is placed on trial for murder. He was attached to a troop of Hessians brought by Britain to help quell the rebellion in the American colonies, and his troop has now dispersed. It is near the end of the Revolutionary War, and Hans's trial, conducted in a revolutionary court by local military officers, takes place in Ridgeway, Connecticut. Hans, sick and wounded, has been sheltered by a schoolteacher and nursed back to health. Now even the schoolteacher and the doctor who treated him are accused of treachery.

Hans speaks some English but has trouble understanding complex uses of the language. Nevertheless, he understands that he is on trial for the murder of Saul Clamberham, a member of the Ridgeway community executed as a spy by the Hessians, who were working their way through Ridgeway when they found Saul following them and making strange marks on a slate. He was summarily hung. Any semblance of a trial would have been futile at any rate, since none of the soldiers understood English and they could hardly, in the interests of justice, linger deep in colonial territory when the tide of battle had shifted against them. Saul, in fact, had the mental age of a small child and lacked the ability to conduct even the crudest of reconnaissance missions. Hans now stands accused, even though he was a noncombatant member of the troop. Hans, of course, is luckier than Saul. He can try to defend himself, using the little English that he knows, and there are a number of people at the trial who value justice more than revenge.

For Michelle Commeyras, this fictional situation presents a challenge. She wants to help her seventh-grade students develop critical and creative thinking skills, and this means helping them develop two things: a broad range of skills and attitudes derived from the profile of a good thinker and the ability to use these skills in their lives. The skills fall into three basic categories: skills for generating ideas, clarifying ideas, and assessing their reasonableness. These core skills of creative and critical thinking are motivated by attitudes of openness to new ideas, by sensitivity to the need for having good reasons, and by willingness to change one's mind in light of new considerations. They blend together and have application in contexts calling for thoughtful problem solving and decision making. Practiced well, such thinking can counter the tendency in our culture to make routine and hasty judgments founded on little evidence, to succumb to bias and stereotyping, and to accept uncritically almost anything voiced by people in positions of authority.

The educational technique that Michelle employs again and again in her classroom is the infusion of critical and creative thinking into standard subject area instruction by restructuring the material she normally teaches (Swartz 1987a). This involves embedding instruction in critical thinking skills in broad problem and decision contexts that already exist in the standard curriculum. Michelle believes that the curriculum already contains sufficient opportunity to practice good thinking and that it is unnecessary to use or create a separate program or course on critical thinking. In fact, the natural place for teaching good thinking in school is in the material to which students are exposed every day. Teaching good thinking through a separate course or program gives students a message that it is not important enough to apply to the standard information taught in regular classrooms.

What is especially challenging about the story of Hans Pohl is that it provides an opportunity to engage students in careful, reflective thought about a host of choices involving morality and responsibility — and there is no substitute for good thinking about such choices, for otherwise we would be easily swayed by bias, closed-mindedness, and uncritically accepted values.

Michelle's strategies derive from well-supported approaches to teaching critical thinking. She guides her students through the story of Hans Pohl and helps them apply organized and appropriate forms of thought to the questions that arise. The critical thinking skills that her students learn in this process involve the reflective application of critical standards in making a careful and well-founded decision about what Hans should do. She tries to fix these forms of thought by helping her students engage in metacognitive reflection on how such skills are exercised and applied to analogous examples, thereby encouraging them to transfer these forms of thought to issues that arise in their own lives.

One important characteristic of teaching critical thinking in this way is that one of Michelle's primary goals is instruction in specific, relevant, critical thinking skills. This goal can be contrasted with situations where teachers encourage students to think about issues that arise in standard curriculum materials but do not focus on helping students to develop the specific habits of organized thought that is so important in using good thinking. In some high school social studies programs, students are challenged to think about genocide through the study of the Holocaust in World War II; in other classrooms, students consider less cosmic issues — how they feel about the antics of Tom Sawyer's friends, for example. There is no doubt that students in these classrooms engage in thinking that involves more than the simple recall of facts, but there is a real question about whether enough is done to encourage students to assimilate good thinking strategies and skills into their lives for use outside classroom context.

Some of the specific thinking skills that Michelle emphasizes include distinguishing reliable from unreliable sources of information, using causal explanation, making well-founded predictions, uncovering assumptions, and applying inferential skills related to valuing. She is concerned about helping her students to use these skills in activities like decision making. Embedding their instruction in rich curricular content while emphasizing these skills sufficiently so that students can focus attention on them and employ them in their thinking is the challenge of this approach to teaching critical thinking. Michelle believes she can meet the challenge by structuring her lessons in ways that complement the use of these skills in the classroom with the metacognitive and transfer activities sketched earlier.

Many of the strategies Michelle uses are well documented. Costa (1985a) and Beyer (1985, 1987), for example, emphasize the importance of teaching specific thinking skills, and Perkins and Swartz (1989; Swartz 1986, 1987a, 1987b, 1989, 1991) emphasize the importance of doing this in the context of regular subject area instruction. Perkins (1987a, 1987b), Perkins and Solomon (1988), Beyer (1987), and Swartz (1986, 1989, 1991) also emphasize the importance of metacognition and teaching for transfer; and Costa (1985b) and Costa and Lowrey (1989) stress the need for "creating a classroom atmosphere . . . which promotes an open exchange of ideas and the development of important attitudes and dispositions, which are in turn manifested in our paradigms of good thinking and intelligent behavior." Finally, the root conception of the skills and attitudes of good thinking and reasoning that appears in the work of Michelle Commeyras and a number of other teachers using the same approach is consonant with work done by Ennis (1962, 1987), Glatthorn and Baron (1986), and Swartz (1987c, 1989, 1991; Swartz and Perkins 1989).

A LESSON ON CHOICE AND RESPONSIBILITY

In the course of the trial, it is revealed that Hans (who understands English better than the officers who questioned Saul) found Saul strange — in fact, he wondered at the time if Saul wasn't a bit crazy — but he did not challenge his superiors for fear of being punished. This is one of the incidents that Michelle builds a lesson around. She wants her students to think about whether Hans had a responsibility to tell his superiors about his suspicions regarding Saul. This is an easy situation for students to relate to, for Hans's choice is similar to ones they often face — it is fundamentally a choice between protecting oneself and helping another. The critical and creative thinking framework that Michelle superimposes on the incident is especially important because it involves the organized use of skills necessary in most real-life, value-oriented decision making, even when the issues are not so dramatic.

Good decision making counters tendencies to make hasty and ill-reasoned choices. It involves considering our options, ascertaining relevant facts about each, and weighing the importance of these facts in making our choice. It is a process that requires clear, careful, and systematic thought. We sometimes make poor choices because we do not consider other options or we fail to gather all the relevant facts (especially about the consequences of each option) or to prioritize the conflicting values we place on these facts.

Michelle encourages her students to focus on options, relevant facts, and values by appropriate questioning techniques. Here is part of her lesson (Swartz 1987a), which helps students to think about the consequences of Hans's options and then to value and weigh these options to make a decision:

1. *Predict and verify the consequences of Hans's intervening on behalf of Saul.* The rationale for predicting and verifying consequences is that it focuses on cause and effect relationships. Students consider all the alternatives while keeping in mind the original questions. Verification requires comparing and contrasting information and gets students thinking about chance, likelihood, necessity, or the impossibility of causal relationships.

   Strategy: Have students list proposed consequences on the blackboard. Then have them discuss the probability of these consequences by rating them from most to least likely and explaining why. For example, suppose they listed these two possible consequences: (1) the Hessians might decide that Saul isn't a spy, and (2) Hans might get kicked out of the unit. We would then consider, given the evidence in the

text, how likely each is, and compare the two in connection with Hans's thinking.
2. *List the reasons for and against Hans's intervention on behalf of Saul.* The rationale for listing the reasons for and against Hans's intervention is that it encourages looking at many possible reasons before coming to a conclusion. Both stated and unstated reasons can be identified through this process. It also provides opportunities for generalizing about values or principles, and for considering these critically.

Strategy: List the students' reasons on the blackboard under the headings *for* and *against*. Have the students vote on which reason is the best in each category. Ask the students to be advocates for their choices. In this activity students can be directed to prioritize the values and value principles that underlie the reasons, and to argue for these priorities. Finally, ask the students to make a decision on the original question: Did Hans have a responsibility to talk to his superiors about Saul Clamberham's appearing strange or crazy? Why?

Often this discussion of the pros and cons of Hans's options leads to identification and discussion of some basic patterns of moral decision making: Are the consequences for Hans the only factors to consider in deciding what he should do? Should we do things that lead to the best consequences for everyone affected? Are consequences the only factors we should consider in deciding what to do? Questions like these help students consider basic moral perspectives without prejudgment. Because students typically focus on broad issues, they tend to contrast egoistic, utilitarian, and nonutilitarian approaches to moral decision making. Michelle asks her students to choose one or another of these positions and to debate the question among themselves.

In having her students think about Hans's decision, this teacher focuses her students' attention on the different elements that go into making good decisions (generating options, making well-founded predictions, and assessing their applicability to particular options) and on prompting them to practice good thinking through appropriate questioning.

PROMOTING GOOD THINKING ABOUT CHOICES AS ESSENTIAL TO MORAL EDUCATION

Michelle does not presume that activities like this are all there is to moral education. Attitudes and character traits that promote careful, reflective choice and commitments to act are also of crucial importance. But she does believe that the kind of choice modeled in this lesson incorporates the essence of the cognitive activity that characterizes good moral reasoning. This has three basic components that can be taught to students: the use of an organizing strategy for such reasoning, the use of critical thinking skills in assessing the factual information and judgments made in such reasoning, and the reflective use of a framework of values in weighing relevant factual information to make the best choice.

These components operate on the content provided in the story of Hans and on relevant background information about the incident being considered. The result should be a well-considered choice about what Hans should do. Collaborative learning techniques involving small group work, open classroom discussion, and individual work by students can all blend to enhance these choices. Figure 6.1 represents this framework for teaching good reflective decision making.

To have a real impact on students' habits of thought and choice, the lesson must be reinforced by other lessons that help students use the same forms of organized thinking. There are ample opportunities for such reinforcing lessons both in the diverse literature read by seventh-grade students and in the novel *The Hessian* itself. Expanding teaching to consider the application of reflective decision making to situations in students' lives can and should be part of such an approach.

Equally important, however, is the reinforcement of this approach across a school curriculum. Other teachers can use reflective decision making with material from their own fields of study. Historical decisions like Lincoln's issuing the Emancipation Proclamation or Harry Truman's decision to drop the atomic bomb on Hiroshima are natural subjects around which to structure such activities. Decisions about what to serve in the school cafeteria can be the focus for similar activities in a biology course, as can more value-laden issues about the production, storage, and disposal of poison gas in a high school chemistry class. Indeed, each of these examples has been developed into a decision-making lesson using the same principles of moral reasoning that Michelle employs in *The Hessian* (Schraer & Stolze 1987; Dorin, Demmin, & Gabel 1989).

TEACHING STUDENTS WHAT IS RIGHT AND WRONG VERSUS TEACHING GOOD THINKING ABOUT WHAT IS RIGHT AND WRONG

Michelle's approach to teaching students how to make good moral choices is a thinking-skills approach; and, as in other process approaches, there is no direct instruction about what is right or wrong. This dichotomy between teaching content in moral education

FIGURE 6.1
Decision Making Flow Chart

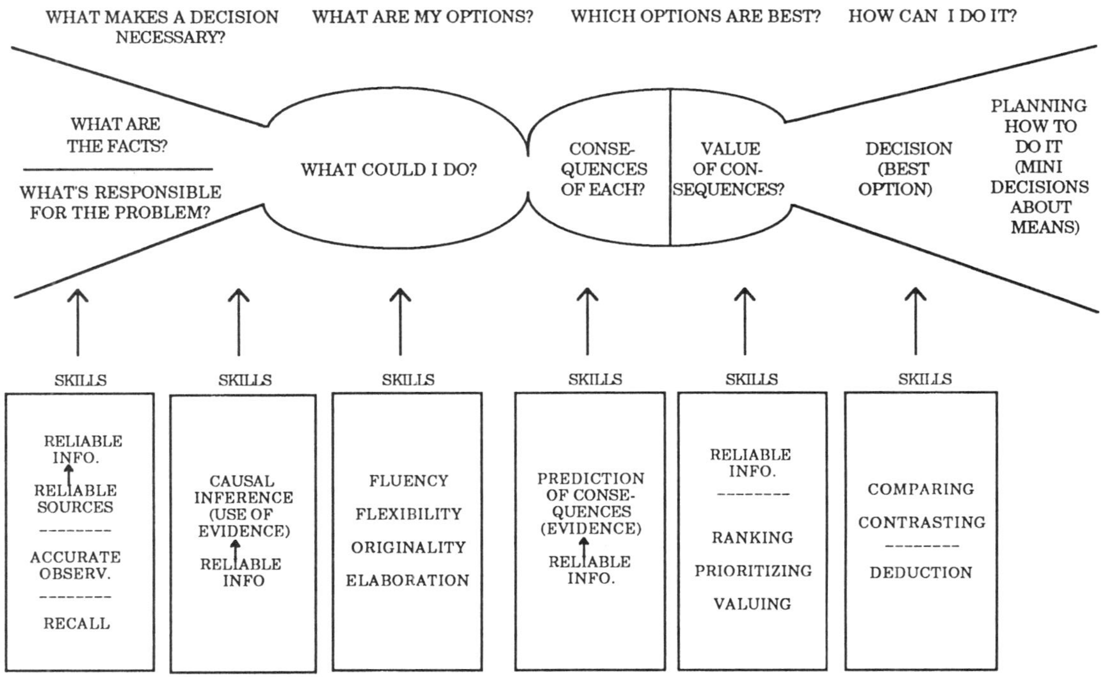
WHAT MAKES A DECISION NECESSARY?
WHAT ARE MY OPTIONS?
WHICH OPTIONS ARE BEST?
HOW CAN I DO IT?
WHAT ARE THE FACTS?
WHAT'S RESPONSIBLE FOR THE PROBLEM?
WHAT COULD I DO?
CONSE-QUENCES OF EACH?
VALUE OF CON-SEQUENCES?
DECISION (BEST OPTION)
PLANNING HOW TO DO IT (MINI DECISIONS ABOUT MEANS)
SKILLS
RELIABLE INFO.
RELIABLE SOURCES
ACCURATE OBSERV.
RECALL
SKILLS
CAUSAL INFERENCE (USE OF EVIDENCE)
RELIABLE INFO
SKILLS
FLUENCY
FLEXIBILITY
ORIGINALITY
ELABORATION
SKILLS
PREDICTION OF CONSE-QUENCES (EVIDENCE)
RELIABLE INFO.
SKILLS
RELIABLE INFO.
RANKING
PRIORITIZING
VALUING
SKILLS
COMPARING
CONTRASTING
DEDUCTION

FIGURE 6.2
A Manual of Morals for Common Schools.
Adapted also to the use of families.

A Manual of Morals for Common Schools.
Adapted also to the use of families.

"The Child is Father of the Man."
"'Tis a fond, yet a fearful thing to rule
O'er the opening mind in the village school;
Like wax ye can mould it in the form ye will,
What ye write on the tablet remains there still
And an angel's work is not more high,
Than aiding to form one's destiny."

_____

Stereotype Edition, Revised.

_____

Boston: Published by John P. Jewett
Andover: Wm. H. Wardwell, 1848

Contents

_____

114

115

and teaching processes whereby students make informed substantive moral judgments has been affirmed by countless educators of diverse persuasions, including Wilson (Wilson, Williams, & Sugarman 1967; Wilson 1972), Kohlberg (1975), Hirst (1974), Hall and Davis (1975), and Hersh, Paolitto, and Reimer (1982). In practice, many curricular materials (some of which will be discussed in this chapter) also embrace such process approaches (for instance, Association for Values Education and Research 1978; Beck 1983; Kohlberg 1974; McPhail 1976). On the face of it, this contrast seems to be a sharp one.

Figure 6.2 shows the title page and table of contents of a moral education manual published in 1848.

A. Hall, the author of this work, comments in the preface: "We cannot overrate the importance of having the children of our country thoroughly indoctrinated in the principles, and duly imbued with the spirit, of morality." Sometimes this is what is meant by moral education. The 1848 interpretation of this enterprise is not unlike interpretations that some proponents term *moral education* in more recent writings. In this view, substantive moral principles are taught to students in school just as the principles of grammar are taught, on the assumption that students can then apply the principles to situations outside the classroom.

Let us look at one of Hall's examples of a moral principle in which children should be thoroughly indoctrinated. Of obedience he says, "One of the first duties which children owe their parents is *obedience*. The proper spirit of obedience will lead them to comply at once with the wishes of their parents, without waiting to have them repeated a second time; it *does not* allow them to stop and argue the point with them, or to set their own will in opposition to that of their parents" (p. 150). There are, of course, exceptions to this principle, and Hall is quick to have students learn these as well: "Children are not obliged to obey their parents if the latter order them to do what is wrong and sinful; as, if a parent should ask a child to drink intoxicating liquors, or to do an injury to another" (p. 151). The similarity between what Hall believed children should be taught in 1848 and what many people believe today should come as no surprise; it has been a perennial theme in moral education since Plato.

USING MORAL PRINCIPLES IN MAKING CHOICES

Moral educators who adopt Hall's approach often take it for granted that becoming morally educated involves no more than learning principles of morality like obedience; but, of course, this is not the case. We must also learn to apply these principles. How do we do this?

Suppose that Hans's father was a member of the Hessian regiment and told him not to tell his superior officers what he suspected about Saul. To use Hall's principles of parental obedience, Hans would have to combine the factual information of his father's command with the injunction about obedience in an argumentative form common in the literature on practical reasoning. The factual information may not seem to be a problem, but the form of reasoning in which the information is embedded would be a little trickier. Here is a representation of it:

> My father commands me not to speak up to my commanding officers.
> If my father commands me to do something, I have the duty to obey him.
> Ergo: I have the duty not to speak up to my commanding officers.

Forms of reasoning containing general value principles that lead to a conclusion about what ought to be done (or a duty that we have) are sometimes called practical syllogisms, and constructing moral reasoning in this fashion goes back to Aristotle's *Nicomachaean Ethics*. Using practical syllogisms correctly requires skill in deductive inference — in this case not, strictly speaking, a syllogistic inference but rather a conditional one, which falls under the rule of propositional logic. Assessing the viability of such an inference requires skill in reconstructing such arguments because the general value principle is usually suppressed in ordinary discourse and has to be made explicit in much the same way that we uncover assumptions underlying other people's reasoning. Once the argument is made explicit, as it is above, recognizing it as valid or invalid requires critical thinking skills that are offshoots of the abilities we employ when drawing such conclusions ourselves.

My point is that even the most content-oriented approaches to moral education — like that found in Hall's *Manual* — do not flinch at claiming indoctrination in a set of values as one of their chief goals. These approaches cannot simply teach students what they should value. Since the use of these principles requires various critical thinking and reasoning skills, these skills should be the goals of moral education. There is no basic inconsistency in this position. And while this represents only a small part of the critical and creative thinking skills Michelle Commeyras brings to her students, the skills needed to engage the practical syllogism fall into the family of critical thinking skills.

One important moral education program emphasizes helping students to uncover hidden general value principles and to use them in practical syllogisms (or to assess the use of practical syllogisms others seem committed to). This is the Values Reasoning Series 1978) created by the Association for Values Education and Research at the University of British Columbia (AVER). This program contains booklets for high school age and older people on issues like population control and the prison system. The goal is to encourage informed decisions about these issues, and the emphasis is on forms of reasoning important in thinking through such issues. As with Michelle's approach, the program does not engage students in open-ended discussions of the issues, however interesting these might be, but it aims at helping students develop and use the skills necessary for good moral reasoning. For example, the following argument is presented in the teacher's manual:

Factual claim (premise)	Strip mining will poison many streams in the Kootenay region.
Value judgment (conclusion)	Strip mining in the Kootenays is undesirable.

The authors of the manual say about this argument:

Notice that the conclusion of this argument does not follow logically from its premises; that is, it would not be contradictory to accept the premise and reject the conclusion. Someone might think that poisoned streams are desirable. . . . To make the conclusion follow logically, we have to add another premise, and this premise must be some value standard or principle which indicates how the factual claim is relevant to the conclusion. The complete argument might look like this:

Value premise (principles)	It is undesirable to poison streams.
Factual premise	Strip mining in the Kootenays will poison streams.
Value conclusion	Strip mining in the Kootenays is undesirable. (pp. 2–3)

This, then, is the basic structure of value reasoning — reasoning by which we justify value judgments.

Since this is taken by the authors of the Values Reasoning Series as a basic form of practical reasoning, part of the strategy of the program is to teach students the skills necessary to form and evaluate such inferences. They give students a series of exercises, much like those in a logic textbook, where arguments are offered but a premise is missing, and the students have to furnish the missing premise. They also give students a number of practical syllogisms, some of which are valid and some not, and ask students to determine their validity. All of the arguments in any given curriculum book center around a theme — for example, prisons or population control.

Constructing exercises to develop skills for working through issues like the viability of the prison system is not a technique that Michelle Commeyras uses. Such excursions seem gratuitous because, in thinking about Hans's choice, students get practice in using the thinking skills necessary for good moral reasoning. Still, there may be some virtue in asking students who have a hard time focusing on the skills in question to do more detached exercises. To make these exercises effective, a connection will have to be made between the exercises and the thinking they employ when they think about a situation like Hans's. The differences between Michelle's approach and that used by AVER may be only a matter of instructional detail determined by individual classroom circumstances. (Other, more important differences between Michelle's approach to moral education and the values reasoning strategies will be discussed below.)

This is not to say that the AVER materials embrace Hall's advocacy of inculcating values and value principles — in fact, AVER rejects such an approach. But the AVER materials include strategies for building competence in moral reasoning that are compatible with Hall's stance about learning what we ought and ought not to do. Indeed, these competencies seem essential if we are to use the principles that Hall lists in his manual.

SOME COMPLEXITIES OF MORAL REASONING

Unfortunately, life is not as simple as the AVER model of practical reasoning seems to indicate. There is tacit recognition of this in Hall's inclusion of exceptions. The exception to the rule of parental obedience is but one of many exceptions, so applying these principles is not a straightforward matter. In the hypothetical situation where Hans found himself ordered by his father not to speak up to his superiors, it is not enough for Hans to identify what is happening as a parental order; he must also recognize that it is not one of the exceptions to the obedience rule. This may seem simple if we use Hall's first case as a paradigm — a parent ordering his child to drink intoxicating liquors. But is it so simple in the case where a parent orders a child to do an injury to another? There too, according to Hall, the obligation to obey a parent is overridden. Surely a clever Hans might reason as follows: My father has ordered me not to speak to my superiors. But I suspect that Saul is a bit crazy. If I don't speak up, Saul will certainly lose his life — the ultimate injury. So I don't have the obligation to obey my father in this case!

Two factors must be reckoned with if we are concerned about helping students develop the abilities they need to make well-reasoned choices even if they embrace a set of moral principles learned from Hall's *Manual*. The first is that we must have a complete list of exceptions to the moral principles we are learning or at least some way of determining what the exceptions are. The second is to make sure that our judgments about exceptional circumstances are well-founded.

THE IMPORTANCE OF THINKING CRITICALLY ABOUT THE FACTS IN MORAL REASONING

Let us assume for a moment that we have dealt with the first of these concerns. We will return to it shortly. What can be done to address the second concern? Embracing even the simpler form of the practical syllogism as a structure for moral reasoning implies that we need more than deductive logic skills to make wise choices. Deduction — indeed any form of inferential ability — is only a matter of ascertaining truth- or reasonableness-preserving relationships between information we start with (information that becomes the premise of our argument) and conclusions that may follow. Whether the conclusions are reasonable — worthy of our endorsement — depends on another factor: whether the information we start with is reasonable. This problem has long been recognized by logicians. Every logic text, for example, distinguishes between the validity of an argument and its soundness. The former refers to the internal logical relations between premises and conclusion and is certifiable by the rules of logic; the latter refers to the validity of the argument *and* to the truth (or reasonableness) of the premises. In short, Hans had better be sure he has the facts straight about both his father's order and the consequences of remaining silent before he concludes that he has no obligation to obey his father and remain silent!

Michelle, then, is quite right in insisting that students focus special attention on whether the predictions they make about the consequences of speaking up or remaining silent are well-focused. This calls for skill at distinguishing between well-founded and ill-founded predictions (including mere guesses) and for skill in basing predictions on relevant evidence and recognizing when the evidence is strong enough to support the predictions. Hence the instruction and practice Michelle gives her students in using this skill are of great importance in moral reasoning. Making well-founded predictions is a critical thinking skill that also has application in less value-laden contexts, such as predicting the weather, predicting when we are going to arrive at a destination, or predicting a chemical reaction in a laboratory. There is no reason why activities that develop well-founded predictions cannot supplement Michelle's lessons if students have trouble in thinking about the implications of what Hans could do about Saul.

We should not underestimate the richness of opportunities for constructing supportive critical thinking activities in the existing K–12 curriculum. One high school teacher, for example, has his students reflect on this passage from a U.S. history textbook:

In April 1775, General Gage, the military governor of Massachusetts, sent out a body of troops to take possession of military stores at Concord, a short distance from Boston. At Lexington, a handful of "embattled farmers," who had been tipped off by Paul Revere, barred the way. The English fired a volley of shots that killed eight patriots. It was not long before the swift-riding Paul Revere spread the news of this new atrocity to the neighboring colonies. The patriots of all of New England, although still a handful, were now ready to fight the English. Even in faraway North Carolina, patriots organized to resist them. (Steinberg 1963)

In this passage there are opportunities to distance students from the text and to sensitize them to loaded words like patriot and atrocity and the possibilities of slant, point of view, and bias. But the primary emphasis in this lesson is to help students develop skill at making informed judgments about the reliability of sources, especially eyewitness accounts of the incident (Swartz 1987a, 1987b). What factors influence such reliability? In reflecting on this, and deliberately using a set of guidelines for assessing reliability that they develop themselves, the students in this classroom arm themselves with a skill of vital importance — in history, in other fields of study, and in their lives outside the classroom.

Activities like these are important in their own context, but they also provide reinforcement for using the same skills in complex, value-laden issues, as Michelle has demonstrated with her students. For Hans to make a well-considered decision about revealing his suspicions about Saul, it is clearly crucial that he find out whether the information he uses in his deliberations is reliable. One important way to do so is to determine whether it comes from a reliable source.

The array of competencies that students must develop to apply what they have learned, even from how-to books like Hall's, looks more and more like the skills that Michelle Commeyras believes students should develop and use, especially in making good decisions. Curricular projects like the Values Reasoning Series, which focus on more traditional reasoning skills (like those involved in deductive inference), must also come to terms with this reality. When such materials are used in moral education programs, teachers can supplement the program with skill-oriented activities of their own, like those Michelle describes.

IS THERE A WAY TO ASSESS OUR VALUES CRITICALLY?

It is in how basic value commitments are certified that the approaches of Hall and Commeyras differ. This issue is related not only to what actions are right or what our duties are, as Hall would put it, but also to what exceptions there are to specific moral principles.

It is important to note that stating exceptions to general rules is a way of stating priorities among principles. For example, one of Hall's principles is that we should not injure others. Another is that children should obey their parents, but if a child's parents order him or her to do something that injures another, the child is no longer obliged to obey. This means that prevention of injury is a higher priority than obedience. Thus when obligations conflict as they do in Hall's second example, one overrides the other. In short, we need to know two things about values in considering many of the choices we are faced with: we need information about what things are important for us to do if we are to be moral and which ones are more important.

Hall's approach is clear — he believes this information should simply be given to students. As he says, they are to be inculcated with it. To be less generous, this information about values and value priorities is to be accepted on his authority, and it is inappropriate for students to raise questions about these principles. However liberal one's approach to helping students use such information in their reasoning, this approach is fundamentally a noncritical one. But here educators' worst fears about indoctrination begin to surface. Hall's frank admission that indoctrination is one of his goals provides pretty strong evidence that such fears are justified.

To those whose value system is affirmed in works like Hall's *Manual*, indoctrination is too harsh a word. For example, one of the principles Hall enunciates clearly opposes slavery. He says that every man has the right to use "one's own powers of body and mind in any way that does not interfere with the rights of others" (Hall 1848, pp. 115–16). Hall, as we have seen, excepts children from this principle, but they are the only exceptions to the principle that "slavery is seen to be entirely wrong" (p. 130). To abolitionists in the mid-nineteenth century, this book recommended itself for use in schools as Hall had hoped; Reverend Emerson Davis, a member of the Massachusetts Board of Education, says that he "cheerfully recommends it to school committees and teachers. It inculcates a system of sound morality" (p. i). Reverend James Burnham, principal of the Coney Female Academy in Augusta, Maine, says, "I shall immediately adopt it. I doubt not, that parents and teachers, on examination, will welcome it as an auxiliary in the accomplishment of their great work" (p. ii). And the Honorable Nathan Weston, LL.D., late chief justice of Maine, says that it is a book in which "the principles of moral obligation . . . are made easy to the apprehension of youth, and cannot fail to contribute greatly to their improvement" (p. i). I doubt that Hall could have found such recommendations south of the Mason-Dixon line.

The point is that even in cases in which we may believe that a practice, like slavery, is morally reprehensible, inculcating this belief in children establishes a precedent that could be used to justify inculcating values that we may not accept so readily. Suppose, for example, that Hall had included injunctions against abortion or euthanasia or statements in favor of capital punishment in his manual. Such controversial principles in our society are what many object to inculcating in children. To urge that we promote the opposite is equally fraught with problems, for it turns decisions about the values to be taught into matters of political power and control. The analogies between Hall's 1848 approach and present-day controversies about teaching values should be obvious.

In this context, Michelle's strategy for helping students come to terms with value priorities may seem a remedy. It promotes the use of critical thinking skills in considering these questions and leads to critical judgments about what things are important and how important they are. Even the principles in Hall's *Manual* can be subjected to critical scrutiny and should not be embraced simply on the basis of the writer's authority.

Many writers on the subject argue that a critical thinker does not merely apply accepted standards to make judgments and decisions; rather, the *standards* of critical thought must also be subjected to careful scrutiny. This includes standards of morality as well as more formal standards of good reasoning. Early twentieth-century promoters of critical thinking such as John Dewey (1933) embrace this view, as do more recent writers on the subject — Passmore (1972), Zevin (1978), Paul (1978), and Siegel (1980), to name but a few. The real question for proponents of critical thinking is this: What are the skills and strategies that we can teach students (without trying to teach what is right in the way that Hall attempts) that will enable them to make well-reasoned critical judgments about what things are important and how important they are?

TWO STRATEGIES FOR CRITICAL
THINKING ABOUT VALUES

In helping students reflect on the wisdom of Hans's choice not to speak up to his superiors on behalf of Saul, Michelle's students recognize that the choice pits Hans's wish to avoid punishment over his wish to help Saul — indeed, over saving Saul's life. Michelle then asks whether avoiding punishment is more important than helping someone whose life is in danger, and if so, why. This prompts students to search for reasons that support Hans's choice of priorities. It is not always easy for seventh-grade students to come up with reasons, but they do rise to the challenge. When asked to role-play Hans, they say things like this:

> Being punished will really hurt and I don't like to be hurt.
> Saul is a person even though he's retarded, and if he loses his life, he'll never get it back. Even if I'm whipped, it will stop sometime. So it's worse to let Saul die.
> I don't know. I don't like being punished, but it's not so good for someone to die unfairly either.

Open discussion of this in the classroom helps students to refine their thinking and even to change their minds. Rarely is there consensus.

What is happening here? These students are looking for reasons for preferring one choice to another, based on how they prioritize conflicting values (avoiding punishment, saving another's life). We know that seeking reasons is an important part of critical thinking, and the ability to identify a reason is a critical skill of analysis or clarification. These students are on the road to developing the ability to find reasons that support value convictions, but a more important aspect of Michelle's strategy is that this leads them to discriminating judgments about whether their reasons for preferring one value over another are good. Listening to the reasoning of other students is crucial to this process, as is Michelle's questioning about why they think their reasons are good or not.

This strategy of presenting students with value conflicts is used by a number of people in moral education to examine what they feel are natural processes of moral development. Kohlberg (1971, 1974, 1975) and Gilligan (1982) have researched different ways that such development may unfold, and Kohlberg has developed classroom strategies whereby exposure to moral dilemmas can, through proper teacher prompting, advance students to the next stage of development (Kohlberg 1975). For Michelle, bringing such situations to students and raising questions about which option they prefer (and why) is not designed to lock into such natural processes. Her approach is intended to make students think about the reasons for preferring one option over the other and to exchange ideas so that they develop skill at justifying moral preferences. It may be, of course, that these goals, joined with instruction in critical thinking, are attained through the mechanisms of the developmental processes that Kohlberg and Gilligan have drawn to our attention.

Perhaps Michelle's strategy of challenging students to defend value choices in open exchanges is all that can be done to help students develop these skills (or perhaps this is all that can be done with seventh-grade students). Michelle's practices nonetheless raise deep questions about whether more can be done in the classroom to engage students in systematic critical thinking about values. Moralists and moral philosophers since Aristotle have attempted to show how we can rationally decide about values. Among these are writers who try to show how to justify general value principles in much the same way as does the model of practical reasoning we have been considering in this chapter. Kant's categorical imperatives and the principle of utility, for example, have their primary use in justifying moral rules (Frankena 1980). Can such views provide a basis for making rational choices about general value principles?

One attempt in the moral education literature reflects this approach to values and value priorities. It appears in the teacher's notes that accompany the Values Reasoning Series mentioned earlier. Four tests for the adequacy of value principles are designed to provide criteria for accepting (or rejecting) the principles in question: role exchange, universal consequences, new cases, and subsumption (AVER 1978, p. 7). Each involves a strategy for testing an alleged moral principle.

> *Role Exchange*: Ask if you would be willing to exchange places with the most disadvantaged person in a situation. If not, then the kind of action is probably morally wrong. (For example, suppose you steal a TV set from someone else. Ask: How would you like to be the person whose TV was stolen? If you wouldn't, stealing is probably wrong.)
>
> *Universal Consequences*: Ask what would happen if everyone did what you are now doing. If that would lead to bad consequences, the type of action is wrong. (For example, suppose I go through a red light, but no one else is around. If everyone went through red lights, that would be a disaster. So I shouldn't go through red lights.)
>
> *New Cases*: Apply the value principle to a new case that you haven't thought of before. If it leads to a result you think is wrong, the principle is not an adequate moral principle. (For example, suppose you're convinced that people shouldn't lie. You wonder if this is a viable principle to live by. You test it by imagining different circumstances under which the issue of telling lies may arise. One is where, in order to save a life, you must lie about something not too important. You feel that this is okay. Hence the general principle must be modified to admit an exception.)
>
> *Subsumption Test*: See whether the value principle follows logically from another which is acceptable to us. (For example, suppose you wonder whether it is right to have restrictive rules at elementary schools that prevent children

from walking home themselves. You realize that if they did this, they would have to cross many busy streets in the town, given the location of the school, and this would probably lead to a great deal of injury and even death. Since you accept the general rule that it's not right to do things that you know will lead to a great deal of injury or death, you realize that the rule about restricting the movement of students is a moral one.)

Presumably students will be taught these tests and then given difficult situations to help them develop skills. The idea of using such tests is clear. Nonetheless, we must ask whether the skills developed in learning to apply these tests are those needed to make well-founded critical judgments about values and value priorities. The tests, unfortunately, do not do what they are supposed to do.

Subsumption may help in some cases, but not in all. In a question concerning abortion, for example, those opposed to abortion often appeal to the moral principle that it is wrong to take a human life, while those in favor of it argue that it is wrong to restrict what one can do with one's own body. The problem is that the subsumption test does not give us a way to determine value priorities when they come into conflict. Similarly, the subsumption test leaves Hans with two conflicting principles and no way to decide which is a higher priority.

The new cases test might work, since it offers a chance to construct cases where there are such value conflicts. Unfortunately, a clear response to such cases is required; if the cases are fraught with problems, the test will be too. If Hans is having trouble deciding what to do about Saul, he cannot use this test to determine whether another person's well-being takes precedence over not being punished.

The role exchange test and the universal consequences test capture more intuitive approaches to values reasoning. We often ask, How would you like that to happen to you? and What if everyone did that? The universal consequences test works well where there are a lot of negative consequences to "everyone doing it," but there is a subtlety here. In a conflict between self-interest and the interests of others, this test demonstrates only that if everyone did the same thing, the result might conflict with the self-interest of the person considering the action. If everyone went through red lights when they pleased, for example, then that person contemplating the action might be in danger someday if someone else went through a red light. If he does not care whether anyone else gets injured, this test may move him by pointing out that his own self-interest will not be served if everyone acts similarly.

This test might work for Hans if he thinks he might someday be in Saul's position. And given the way the tale works out, Hans does indeed end up in much the same position. It seems clear that he would want others to testify on his behalf, even though they might be punished for doing so. Students role-playing Hans and thinking about his priorities may well use this test as a basis for deciding that speaking up on behalf of Saul — even if it means being punished — is right because helping others overrides personal benefit.

There is a problem with this case, however, not unlike problems that others have raised about this kind of test (Frankena 1980). Suppose Hans knew in advance that, no matter what he did about Saul, not everyone would do the same. Or suppose that Hans knew that what he did about Saul would not influence his later treatment in a similar situation. Suppose, for example, that Hans recognized the possibility that he might be captured and brought to trial but that he also knew the colonists were committed to giving others a fair trial and would testify on his behalf (if warranted), even though they might be punished. Would this test then have force for Hans? It is not clear that it would.

The role exchange test fares better. Here a person asks, How would I like to be in the shoes of the person most adversely affected by what I contemplate? If there is no problem, the action is permissible; if there is a problem, the action is wrong. If we asked students role-playing Hans how they would like to be in Saul's shoes, you can be sure of their reaction. Using this test, it would then be legitimate to affirm that it isn't right to let personal benefit (freedom from punishment) override saving Saul's life.

But here, too, there are problems. The test seems too simplistic for cases where we want to allow for a plurality of views that are equally viable. With issues like capital punishment and abortion, this test has the same swift and sure results. Who would want to be in the shoes of the convicted murderer on death row? Who would want to be in the place of a fetus about to be aborted? The test does not allow latitude for legitimate moral disagreement in cases like these. It forecloses a richness of thought and feeling about controversial value issues that call for much more reflection.

Although promising, the cognitive framework for exercising critical thought and judgment about values and value priorities that appears in the Values Reasoning Series has its difficulties, which leaves us with a challenge: Is there a cognitive framework for good thinking that can help students develop the skills they need to bring the best thought to bear on these issues? Admittedly, we have not considered positions such as act-utilitarianism, which abandon the idea that substantive moral principles have a key role to play in moral reasoning. Rather, we should simply consider specific consequences of our actions as they benefit or harm those affected. But with regard to values and value priorities, we may reach the limits of the possibility of thought as sufficient for guiding values.

Many have suggested that values are a matter of the heart, not the head. As obscure and extreme as such a statement may sound, it suggests thinking about moral education as more than a purely cognitive problem. Perhaps cognitive approaches must be supplemented by attention to affective elements of the moral life like empathy, care, and commitment, as writers like Blum (1983) have suggested. In the end, Michelle may be going as far as she can to help her students apply thinking to questions of value.

This discussion has introduced a constraint on cognitive approaches to teaching moral reasoning. When we try to help students develop skills that can be used to think through matters of basic values and value priorities, we should do so in ways that avoid an "anything goes" approach. There are critical standards that we can apply to our moral choices, but at the same time, the skills and strategies to help students think through these matters should not foreclose the possibility of legitimate differences. The richness of debates about hard questions — issues such as capital punishment and abortion — has brought us the best of human thought. Any attempt to teach moral reasoning should try to equip students with the attitudes of mind and the cognitive skills they need to join this debate.

REFERENCES

Association for Values Education and Research (AVER) (1978). *Prisons: Teacher's manual*. Values Reasoning Series. Toronto: Ontario Institute for Studies in Education.

Beck, C. (1983). *Values and living: Learning materials for grades 7 and 8*. Toronto: Ontario Institute for Studies Education.

Beyer, B. (1985). Teaching critical thinking: A direct approach. *Social Education* 22: 297–303.

___. (1987). *Practical strategies for the teaching of thinking*. Newton, Mass.: Allyn & Bacon.

Blum, L. (1983). *Altruism, friendship, and morality*. London: Routledge & Kegan Paul.

Costa, A. (1985a). Teaching for, of, and about thinking. In *Developing minds*, edited by A. Costa. Arlington, Va.: Association for Supervision and Curriculum Development.

___. (1985b). Teacher behaviors that enable student thinking. In *Developing minds*, edited by A. Costa. Arlington, Va.: Association for Supervision and Curriculum Development.

Costa, A., and L. Lowrey. (1989). *Classroom techniques in teaching thinking*. Pacific Grove, Calif.: Midwest Publications.

Dewey, J. (1933). *How we think*, 2d ed. Boston: Houghton Mifflin.

Dorin, H., P. Demmin, and D. Gabel. (1989). *Chemistry: The study of matter*. Teacher's resource book. Englewood Cliffs, N.J.: Prentice-Hall.

Ennis, R. (1962). A concept of critical thinking. *Harvard Educational Review* 32: 81–111.

___. (1987). A taxonomy of critical thinking dispositions and abilities. In

Teaching thinking skills: Theory and practice, edited by J. Baron and R. Sternberg. New York: Freeman.

Frankena, W. (1980). *Ethics.* Englewood Cliffs, N.J.: Prentice-Hall.

Gilligan, C. (1982). *In a different voice.* Cambridge, Mass.: Harvard University Press.

Glatthorn, A., and J. Baron. (1986). The good thinker. In *Developing minds*, edited by A. Costa. Arlington, Va.: Association for Supervision and Curriculum Development.

Hall, A. (1866). *A manual of morals for common schools.* Boston: Taggard & Thompson.

_____. (1848). *A manual of morals for common schools adapted also to the use of families.* Boston: John P. Jewett.

Hall, R., and J. Davis. (1975). *Moral education in theory and practice.* Buffalo, N.Y.: Prometheus Books.

Hersh, R., D. Paolitto, and J. Reimer. (1982). *Promoting moral growth: From Piaget to Kohlberg.* New York: Longman.

Hirst, P. (1974). *Moral education in a secular society.* London: University of London Press.

Kohlberg, L. (1971). Development as the aim of education. *Harvard Educational Review* 42: 449–96.

_____. (1974). *The trouble with truth.* Indianapolis, Ind.: Guidance Associates.

_____. (1975). The cognitive-developmental approach to moral education. *Phi Delta Kappan* (June): 670–77.

McPhail, P., J. Ungoed-Thomas, and H. Chapman. (1976). *Lifeline.* Niles, Ill.: Argus Communications.

Passmore, J. (1972). On teaching to be critical. In *Education and the development of reason*, edited by R. Dearden, P. Hirst, and R. Peters. London: Routledge & Kegan Paul.

Paul, R. (1978). Dialogical thinking: Critical thought essential to the development of rational knowledge and passions. In *Teaching thinking skills: Theory and practice*, edited by J. Baron and R. Sternberg. New York: Freeman.

Perkins, D. (1978a). Thinking frames. In *Teaching thinking skills: Theory and practice*, edited by J. Baron and R. Sternberg. New York: Freeman.

_____. (1978b). Myth and method in teaching thinking. *Teaching Thinking and Problem Solving* 9 (2): 1–9.

Perkins, D., and G. Soloman. (1988). Teaching for transfer. *Educational Leadership* 46 (1): 22–32.

Schraer, J., and R. Stolze. (1987). *Biology: The study of life.* Teacher's resource book. Newton, Mass.: Allyn & Bacon.

Siegel, H. (1980). Critical thinking as an educational ideal. *The Educational Forum* (November): 7–23.

Steinberg, S. (1963). *The United States: Story of a free people.* Boston: Allyn & Bacon.

Swartz, R. (1987a). Teaching thinking: A developmental model for the infusion of teaching for thinking into mainstream instruction. In *Teaching thinking skills: Theory and practice*, edited by J. Baron and R. Sternberg. New York: Freeman.

_____. (1987b). Critical thinking, the curriculum, and the problem of transfer. In *Thinking: The second international conference*, edited by D. Perkins, J. Lockhead, and J. Bishop. Hillsdale, N.J.: Erlbaum.

_____. (1987c). Restructuring what we teach to teach for critical thinking. In *Teaching thinking: Concepts and techniques*, edited by M. Heiman and J. Slomnienko. Washington, D.C.: National Education Association.

_____. (1991a). Influencing the teaching of critical thinking into content instruction. In *Developing minds: A resource book for teaching thinking,* edited by A. Costa, rev. ed., Vol. 1, pp. 177–184. Alexandria, VA: Association for Supervision and Curriculum Development.

___. (1989). Making good thinking stick: The role of metacognition, extended practice, and teacher modeling in the teaching of thinking. In *Thinking across cultures: The third international conference on thinking,* edited by D. Topping et al. Hillsdale, N.J.: Erlbaum.

___. (1991b). Structured teaching for critical thinking and reasoning in standard subject area instruction. In *Informal reasoning and education,* edited by D. Perkins, J. Segal, and J. Yoss. Hillsdale, N.J.: Erlbaum.

Swartz, R., and D. Perkins. (1989). *Teaching thinking: Issues and approaches.* Pacific Grove, Calif.: Midwest Publications.

Wilson, J. (1972). *Practical methods of moral education.* London: Heinemann Educational Books.

Wilson, J., N. Williams, and B. Sugarman. (1967). *Introduction to moral education.* Harmondsworth, England: Penguin Books.

Zevin, J. (1978). Thinking critically, thinking philosophically. *The Social Studies* (November/December): 265–72.

7

Facing History and Ourselves: A Synthesis of History and Ethics in Effective History Education

Margot Stern Strom, Martin Sleeper, and Mary Johnson

In no other course was she [my daughter] exposed to real dilemmas as complex and challenging [as in Facing History]. In no other course has she been inspired to use the whole of her spiritual, moral, and intellectual resources to solve a problem. In no other course has she been so sure that the materials mattered so seriously for her development as a responsible person.
— A parent of a student in a Facing History and Ourselves[1]

Facing History and Ourselves is an educational program that encourages students to think about individual decision making and to exercise the faculty of making judgments.[2] It focuses on the history of twentieth-century genocide, on the Holocaust in particular, and presents the perspectives of perpetrators, bystanders, and victims. Since the Holocaust is the best-documented event of its type in history, an in-depth investigation of the subject provides many opportunities for probing questions about decision making and judgment in the Nazi era. Here are some of these critical questions: How did individuals decide to support or oppose the Nazi regime? What were the motivations of those who decided to help the persecuted minorities and of those who remained silent? Why did some German Jews decide to remain in Germany after Hitler came to power in 1933, while others emigrated? How did leaders of foreign nations respond to reports of Nazi persecution of minorities? Did democratic leaders show greater concern for the fate of the oppressed minorities than did their counterparts in authoritarian regimes? Addressing such issues not only enhances one's understanding of the specific events of the Holocaust, but also compels one to reflect on the universal lessons to be derived from this history: When there is a conflict between duties to the state and to an individual, how does one determine which is the more important duty? Are human rights absolute? What are the limits of authority?

Studying these unique and universal lessons of the Holocaust helps students to think morally about their own behavior and to reflect on the moral nature of the decisions they have made. They also consider the consequences of their actions and make distinctions between right and wrong and between good and bad actions. A key question that students pose as they engage in moral reasoning is, What should I do? This form of reasoning is essential in order for them to move to the stage of making judgments in which they apply the principles of moral thinking to particular circumstances. Making judgments can be an extremely complex process because in some cases no single principle can be applied. Conflicting principles may be involved, so that one must determine which one takes precedence, or one may have to balance between two or more seemingly equal principles.

The fundamental concerns of Facing History and Ourselves figure prominently in the works of the philosopher-historian Hannah Arendt. Arendt has traced her impulse to think about thinking to the Eichmann trial where, instead of ideological conviction, evil motives, or stupidity, she found thoughtlessness. Eichmann was protected from thinking by routines, clichés, conventions, standardized responses, and expressions. Arendt asked, "Could the activity of thinking as such, the habit of examining . . . be among the conditions that make men abstain from evil-doing or even condition them against it?"[3] Although she considered the activity of thinking to be vital for helping one to enter into a dialogue with the self and to break down preconceived ideas, she believed that thinking itself was productless. Judgment, she explained, is the bridge between thought and action. It is the faculty that enables one to deal with "the radical discontinuity between principle (a product of reason) and particular (in reality and not of its own making)."[4] Making judgments is not a mechanical process of applying a rule or law; it is an art that must be carried out within the realm of choice. In *Thinking and Moral Considerations*, Arendt clarified the relationship between thinking and judgment:

> The purging element in thinking, Socrates' midwifery, that brings out the implications of unexamined opinions and thereby destroys them — values, doctrines, theories, and even convictions — is political by implication. For this destruction has a liberating effect on another human faculty, the faculty of judgment, which one may call, with some justification, the most political of (our) mental abilities. It is the faculty to judge particulars without subsuming them under those general rules which can be taught and learned until they

grow into habits that can be replaced by other habits and rules.[5]

When Arendt witnessed the Eichmann trial, she became even more aware of how important it was for men to exercise judgment. Eichmann, as head of Bureau IV B 4 in charge of the deportation and extermination of Jews, acknowledged no incongruity between the laws of the criminal society of Nazis and what was right in the moral sense. Arendt had learned from personal experience that "those few who were able to tell right from wrong went really by their own judgments, and they did so freely; there were no rules to be abided by, under which the particular cases with which they were confronted could be subsumed. They had to decide each instance as it arose because no roles existed for the unprecedented."[6]

The writings of Jacob Bronowski have also influenced Facing History's underlying approach.

> There is no way of exchanging information that does not demand an act of judgment. . . . All knowledge, all information between human beings can only be exchanged within a play of tolerance. And that is true whether the exchange is in science, or in literature, or in religion, or in politics, or even in any form of thought that aspires to dogma.[7]

For Bronowski, the ability to tolerate divergent views distinguished man from all other creatures:

> Man is the only creature not locked in his environment. His imagination, his reason, his emotional subtlety and toughness make it possible for him not to accept the environment, but to change it. And that series of inventions by which man from age to age has remade his environment is a different kind of evolution — not biological, but cultural evolution.[8]

It is a central tragedy of our times, wrote Bronowski, that scientists who were developing with "the most exquisite precision the Principle of Tolerance" ignored or were unaware of the fact that tolerance was being systematically eliminated from German cultural and scientific life. The abandonment of tolerance, Bronowski lamented, stifled creativity and threatened European cultural evolution.[9]

Just as Bronowski and Arendt emphasize that judgment results from the interaction of ideas, the Facing History program stresses that students need to examine a variety of perspectives on issues, placing themselves in situations of others and learning to listen to differing, at times conflicting, points of view.[10] This method has the advantage of preventing students from becoming indoctrinated with a definitive perspective or ideology, but it also has the potential for creating discomfort since no certain answers are offered. This disease, however, does not paralyze students. The program urges them to make judgments, sifting through diverse points of view and distinguishing right from wrong. In this way, students are steered away from misguided relativism that places equal merit on all points of view and are encouraged to draw certain conclusions about the nature of moral rectitude.

A few selections from the Facing History resource book illustrate how the program moves students from thinking about issues to forming judgments. The chapter on the history of the interwar years, for instance, surveys the political choices available to Germans. While students review the main reasons that nazism attracted Germans in all walks of life, study questions for the section urge students to think of the consequences for those Germans who surrendered their freedom for jobs and security. Similarly, in the Facing History chapter on the Final Solution, students learn about the perspectives of perpetrators who viewed the brutal treatment of Jews and other minorities as beneficial for the life of the Aryan nation. As they read the testimonies of former Nazi chiefs such as Rudolf Hoess and Adolf Eichmann, they are urged to consider the tragic consequences that ensued when dogma and ideology made Germans into what Bronowski has referred to as obedient ghosts or tortured ghosts. Most disturbing for students are the readings on the Nuremberg trials in which defendants consistently denied responsibility for the deeds of the Nazi state, maintaining that their leader — Adolf Hitler — bore full responsibility for the evil of the Third Reich. Students must confront these testimonies, reflecting on which individuals and organizations bore responsibility for the genocide.

The importance of pushing students to form judgments was brought to light in the research that educator Betty Bardige conducted for her thesis entitled "Reflective Thinking and Prosocial Awareness: Students Face the Holocaust and Themselves." During the pilot phase of the program when she interviewed Facing History students and studied their journal entries, she discovered that there was a potential among some students to become mired in too much thinking; they examined different points of view as they thought seriously about a subject but lacked encouragement to form moral judgments. Based on the findings, she concluded that it was essential for teachers to help students study the consequences of the actions that people took during the Nazi era.[11]

Since 1976, Facing History and Ourselves has been translating the ideas of such thinkers as Arendt and Bronowski into an educational program that stimulates moral reasoning and intellectual growth among students and teachers in diverse educational settings throughout the United States and parts of Canada. More than 30,000 teachers have received training from the Facing History staff, and approximately 450,000 students annually use the program and its materials. Through workshops and institutes, teachers learn about the underlying theories of the program and the resources designed to introduce these ideas in the classroom. Annual conferences, follow-up workshops, and seminars enable these teachers to keep abreast of new resources and pedagogical approaches to teaching about modern racism and the capability of governments and their citizens of committing genocide. Adult education classes enable parents and interested members of the community to study the history of the Holocaust and its legacy, and in some communities parents and their children come together to preview and discuss films dealing with the Holocaust.

This chapter examines the process by which Facing History moves from theory to practice considering the pedagogical goals of the program, the content and resources of the program, the impact Facing History has had on students of all ages, and an explanation of what makes Facing History effective in diverse educational settings.

GOALS OF THE PROGRAM

Facing History's publications and accompanying audiovisual materials have four fundamental goals. Reaching each of these goals helps students to sharpen their skills in moral reasoning and critical thinking and to make judgments.

The first goal is to introduce students to the history of the Holocaust, which is frequently given only cursory attention or is even omitted entirely in conventional history texts and courses.[12] The resource book is not intended to provide a comprehensive overview and analysis of all the facets of Weimar and Nazi Germany history. Rather, readings are selected to illuminate the range of choices available and the actual choices that ordinary men, women, and children made during the Hitler era. As students become familiar with the kinds of decisions made by people who lived during the Third Reich, they begin thinking about what they would have done, trying to put themselves into the situations of the individuals. Further, they begin to wonder about their own reactions to crisis situations: What should I do when asked to compromise my values? What should I do when the laws of the state require me to act in a way that conflicts with what I believe to be the right behavior? In this way students gain sufficient familiarity with the history of the Third Reich and the experiences of real people to begin relating that history to their own lives and behavior.

The second goal is to help students recognize the complexity of making choices during the Third Reich, for there are no simple answers to the complex questions raised by the study of modern genocide. For instance, in examining why certain individuals collaborated with the Nazis in their policy of extermination while others openly resisted it, students must grapple with the ambiguity of ethical choices in the modern world. In her book *Mischling Second Degree: My Childhood in Nazi Germany*, Ilse Koehn discusses the diversity of motives and personalities found among the followers of the Nazi party. "Life is almost always more complicated than we think," she begins. "Behind the gleaming ranks of those who seem totalitarian robots stand men and women, various and diverse, complex and complicated, some brave, some cowardly, some brainwashed, some violently idiosyncratic, and all of them very human."[13]

Students also learn about the difficult choices confronted by victims of the Third Reich. In studying the situation of German Jews during the early part of the Nazi era, for instance, students frequently wonder why they didn't leave as soon as anti-Semitic legislation was enacted. But as they listen to the testimonies of those involved, they learn that a variety of factors influenced decisions of whether to emigrate or remain in the homeland. Peter Gay, for example, a Berlin Jew who attended a gymnasium between 1933 and 1938, says that his headmaster recommended him for the advanced classical track in 1935, the very year that the Nuremberg laws made Jews second-class citizens. Explains Gay,

> There are lots of incidents like this which suggest something that is extremely important in the study of the history of this period, namely how unbelievably complicated it was, or to use more popular language, how conflicting the signals were. You got all kinds of signals. Obviously, the government said you are . . . scum and you can't do this and you can't do that. On the other hand, a great many other people said: "Nonsense, I don't believe in this." It is that kind of thing that one should keep in mind.[14]

Once the Nazis began to implement the Final Solution, choices for the victims either narrowed considerably or, in many cases, disappeared. Inmates in the concentration camps and ghettos could no longer make decisions about their own freedom, and as a result they acted in ways they never would have under normal circumstances. Lawrence Langer, author of several works on Holocaust literature, observes that the victims of the Third Reich were in a situation of making choiceless choices — they lacked the necessary freedom for operating in the traditional framework of morality.[15]

A third goal (which is closely linked to the second) is that of helping students understand that the Holocaust was not inevitable. It resulted from people's making choices: choosing to vote for the Nazis; choosing not to speak out against injustice and the elimination of the democratic freedoms and protections of citizenship; choosing to collaborate with or resist the Nazi regime. While standing amid the ashes of Auschwitz, Jacob Bronowski reminded the world that modern technology and machinery had not been the cause of the Holocaust. Instead, it had been "obedient ghosts, or tortured ghosts" who had made this history.[16] Human beings had made certain decisions to use technology in a destructive manner; but by the same token, human beings also could apply modern scientific knowledge and machinery toward improving society and saving lives.

Doctors who supported and collaborated with the Nazi regime offer a particularly vivid example of how human beings, not some abstract force or modern machinery, were responsible for the Final Solution. Throughout the early Nazi era, the medical profession made no formal protests regarding the discriminatory treatment of Jews and other "inferior" peoples; rather, the profession complied with health regulations prohibiting marriages between so-called unfit peoples and requiring psychopaths and other mentally unfit individuals to undergo sterilization. From 1939 until the end of the war, members of all branches of the profession participated in a euthanasia program designed to eliminate certain categories of "useless eaters" in the mental hospitals. During the Holocaust, there were doctors involved in the killing process and in human experimentation at the concentration camps. To date, there is no evidence that members of the medical profession were coerced into working in the camps; on the contrary, the evidence suggests that greed and ambition strongly motivated doctors who served the Nazi regime.[17]

The fourth goal of Facing History is to build a sense of a community of learners, embracing the teacher and students. As Hannah Arendt observed, the activity of thinking initially requires that one engage in self-dialogue, which enables one to formulate moral principles. Once an individual has established a moral framework, he or she is prepared to make judgments when engaging in dialogue with others. The essence of being human, according to Arendt, is participating in moral discourse with others:

The world is not humane because it is made by human beings, and it does not become humane just because the human voice sounds in it, but only when it has become the object of discourse. However much we are affected by the things of the world, however deeply they may stir and stimulate us, they become human for us only when we can discuss them with our fellows. . . . We humanize what is going on in the world and in

ourselves only by speaking of it, and in the course of speaking
of it we learn to be human.[18]

In the classroom, both the teachers and students come together to
share insights and reactions to a number of complex questions. The
resource book, *Facing History and Ourselves: Holocaust and Human
Behavior*, is designed for the use of both teachers and students.
Students are thus made privy to material traditionally directed to the
teacher. In this way the resource book invites students to enter the
adult world. At the same time, it encourages teachers to learn along
with their students rather than to assume an authoritarian role by
which knowledge flows from the teacher down to the students.

The content of the resource book reinforces the idea that learning is a cooperative endeavor of both teachers and students. Inter-
spersed throughout the chapters are students' reactions to readings and audiovisual materials. These demonstrate that children
have the potential to be moral philosophers. Not only are they capable of sharing in the learning experience with adults, but at
times their insights into situations and their reflections on the
actions of people during the Nazi era bring a new perspective to the
subject.

An effective way to prepare students for entering the community
of learners is to have them maintain journals, recording their
reactions to the material. In making their entries, students are
engaging in self-dialogue, determining what their own views are and
raising questions about issues that have inspired their curiosity
during the course. Some teachers encourage students to incorporate
poems, quotations, anecdotes, and artwork that relate to their
understanding of the Holocaust; the idea is for them to draw on all
aspects of their learning experience in confronting the difficult and
often painful history of the Nazi era.[19] "The material is grim, and it
can build up inside and make you feel ugly and hopeless," wrote one
high school senior. "My journal was a confidante that no person
could have been because it was always there. My journal was a daily
reminder so that when class didn't meet or there wasn't time to
discuss something we wanted to, we held our own class with our
journals."[20]

THE MATERIALS OF THE PROGRAM

Facing History has developed publications and audiovisual
materials that help students examine the lessons of the Holocaust,
focusing particularly on the choices people made in the past and on
the choices people are making today. Each of the publications'
sections entitled "Usings" encourages students to face themselves
after facing the facts of the history.

The central publication for the program is *Facing History and Ourselves: Holocaust and Human Behavior*. A resource book with 12 chapters, it contains a broad range of readings in each chapter from which teachers may select those most appropriate and engaging for their students. Further, the Facing History Resource Center contains audiovisual materials that can enrich themes in each of the chapters. The chapter titles, with a short description of the content, are as follows:

Rationale — This chapter discusses the reasons for studying a topic that is often left out of textbooks.

Society and the Individual — The role of the individual in society and those forces in society that contribute to an individual's identity are explored.

Anti-Semitism: A Case Study of Prejudice and Discrimination — This chapter examines how the phenomenon of anti-Semitism relates to all forms of hatred in society, and discusses the unique features of anti-Semitism in twentieth-century Germany.

German History: World War I to World War II — Discussed here are general themes in German history before the Holocaust.

Nazi Philosophy and Policy — This chapter is an examination of the theories and policies of National Socialism as set forth in the 1930s.

Preparing for Obedience — This chapter studies Nazi propaganda and education that disseminated the national socialist ideology to the German people and to populations in Nazi-occupied territories.

Victims of Tyranny — An examination is made of the civilians singled out by Nazi policy for destruction independent of the war (Jews, Gypsies, homosexuals, Communists, Jehovah's Witnesses).

The Holocaust — This chapter looks at the dynamics of carrying out the Final Solution, considering the role of the perpetrators and the conditions for victims of the extermination policy.

Who Knew — Studied here is the response of individuals and nations to knowledge of the Final Solution.

Judgment — This chapter is a discussion of the Nuremberg trials and their legacy to modern concepts and practices of justice.

Armenia: A Case of a Forgotten Genocide — Do we learn from past experiences?

Choosing to Participate — Explored here is how individuals and groups can make a difference in order to prevent injustice and the abuse of human rights.

The early chapters in the resource book seek to engage students in thinking about decision making and about the vocabulary of morality in their own lives while they consider the choices people have made within a given society. The next chapters, which present the history of anti-Semitism in Europe between World War I and World War II and discuss the preparation for obedience to the Nazis, provide critical content and lessons for thinking about the choices people had for making a difference. Students encounter the actual range of human responses made to Nazi ideology during the decades of choice before the Holocaust began. Certain strongly held myths that students hope will give simple explanations for this history are dispelled when the students realize how many years the citizens of Germany had to vote for policy, to read Nazi handouts, to decide on taking an oath, or to risk speaking out for the dismissed faculty colleagues or for the Jews in their classes or in their neighborhoods. Of vital importance are the readings on the evolution of anti-Semitism from the time of the early Christian era to that of the Third Reich; they show the persistence of myths about Jews over the centuries and the manner in which modern thinkers and politicians advanced racial theories that offered spurious scientific justification for negative stereotypes and myths about Jews. In these early lessons, students develop a vocabulary for making decisions and for making judgments that will provide a foundation for sharpening their reasoning skills.

When students learn about totalitarianism, racism, and the policy of *Lebensraum* (living space), they make critical connections to the study of human rights. Questions about the protection of the law and the power of the demagogue make this history of dehumanization relevant to individual choice today. It is in reading these chapters that students begin wondering, What would I have done?

Particularly effective in helping students make these connections with the past are the descriptions of lesson plans in Nazi schools. In reading the stories of those school children, students think about the type of education that might have counteracted the indoctrination and racial biases inherent in Nazi education, and they begin thinking about the type of education that could support risk-taking in the name of justice for all citizens.

Later, as students learn about the actual war within the war and about the systematic plans for carrying out the Final Solution, they give up another strongly held myth that attributes the Holocaust to the deeds and vision of a single madman, Adolf Hitler. As they begin to read about the involvement of citizens, the military, and the bureaucracy in implementing plans for the extermination of Jews and other minorities, they are often dismayed. Once again, the simple explanations for complex history fail them.

In the next chapters, the vocabulary of reason and choice that students explored in the initial chapters fails to help them confront the facts of the Holocaust. Thinking about the policy of extermination, its victims, its victimizers, and its bystanders demands a leap of the imagination and a new vocabulary of annihilation. The choiceless choices of this extreme history of human behavior do not reflect the options between right and wrong but between one form of abnormal response and another. At this point, students learn that a confrontation with this history demands more than coping with information. As one student remarked, "This history would be much easier to learn if it weren't true."

In the "Who Knew" chapter, students investigate the range of human responses to the Holocaust as they read about individuals, groups, and nations that had a chance to make a difference. Some chose to act while others did not. Some students and teachers prefer to emphasize the acts of courage that rekindle hope in humanity; this approach, however, devalues the reality of the mass murder, human experimentation, and extermination of children, men, and women. It is easier, for example, to dwell on the subject of Denmark, a nation that saved a large percentage of its own Jewish citizens, than it is to learn about the roles of the churches, the U.S. president and public, and the collaborators in many occupied countries. To study heroes and heroines and to talk about human dignity without confronting the failure to act is to distort and distract from the painful reality of the history.

To balance the selections that focus on acts of courage (like those demonstrated by the Danes), the resource book also includes readings about people and nations that stood by without participating in rescue. For instance, there are readings about the Wagner-Rogers Bill and the SS *St. Louis* that illustrate how the U.S. Congress and public failed to assist German Jewish refugees before the war and the Final Solution. There are also readings about political and religious leaders who failed to oppose nazism even after they had ample evidence that the Nazi regime was carrying out a policy of extermination. Just as it is important for students to be aware of those individuals and nations that resisted the oppression of nazism, it is equally important that they also confront the stories of people and nations that remained silent and did nothing to oppose Nazi brutality.

Next, students read the chapter "Judgment," which provides them with an opportunity to learn about the international war crimes trials, to read the testimonies of victimizers and victims, and to think about the consequences, punishment, revenge, and retribution for individuals and nations. When students learn that one of the 12 men sentenced to death at Nuremberg was indicted for turning neighbor against neighbor and breaking the moral backbone of the citizenry, the power of words takes on a new meaning.

Journalist Bill Moyers points out that one of the most effective ways to see that students question the revisionists, who deny that the Holocaust occurred, is to introduce them to the proceedings of the Nuremberg trials. This confrontation with the evidence is necessary so that the students can begin to make distinctions between myth and reality. "We live in a world of fiction," explains Moyers:

> Prime time entertainment, fiction; so many of the books that children read, fiction. This is a world in which fable and fiction have become gospel. Unless we keep hammering home the irrefutable and indisputable facts of the human experience, history as it was experienced by people, we are going to find ourselves increasingly unable to draw distinctions between what was and what we think was.[21]

As they begin thinking about the power of denial to suppress the truth of the past, students look at the case study of the genocide of the Armenian people. Many themes from chapters on the Holocaust reappear in the Armenian case: the process whereby a nation, in this case Turkey, moves from protecting its minorities to defining them as the enemy, depriving them of the right to human dignity, and finally taking their lives; the process by which a minority is cast as an enemy; the role of technology in implementing policies of mass murder; and the power of modern nationalism. Students are outraged by the attempt to omit such history from their studies. And they remind their teachers of the ability of education to make a difference in the lives of individuals, groups, and nations. We do indeed study the past in order to think about our future.

The final chapter of the program is designed to help students make judgments about how they can make a difference in their own lives; this is a way of deepening students' awareness of what constitutes rights and responsibilities in a modern democracy. Students also consider steps they can take to oppose racism and discrimination in their own schools and communities. If they can learn how to take a stand without getting caught up in dogma, if they can learn to listen to the reasoning of someone taking a different stand, and if they can participate in an open dialogue, then perhaps they will not someday indict their teachers as have some German adults who grew up during the Nazi era. "Trust my teachers?" wrote one German, reflecting on his schooling during the Third Reich. "Who taught me nine years of Latin, six years of Greek, two years of English, philosophy, science and fine arts, and yet we're so clumsy at the fine art of teaching history?"[22]

Establishing a closure for this course can be as difficult as searching for a way to begin it. On a practical pedagogical level, the organized classroom lessons must come to an end, and we do offer some concluding activities. On the other hand, the questions and issues raised in this study are ongoing concerns. As one student put it, "This isn't the end, is it? I mean, how do you just stop studying it?" Many students begin to wonder what they can do to prevent the kind of abuse of human rights that occurred in Nazi Germany; they want to think about ways in which they can make responsible choices as citizens and become constructive members of their society.

The resource book's last chapter, "Choosing to Participate," addresses the concerns of students who are questioning where they fit in society and whether their actions can influence the present and future in a positive way. The materials help students learn about the diverse ways people can participate as citizens: in community work, in human service, in politics and social advocacy, and in other kinds of voluntary and nonprofit activity. Through this conceptual framework, students can understand the history and contemporary nature of participation and why participation is vital to strong democracy. Integrated into this chapter is the transcript of an interview with journalist Bill Moyers, who states the issue this way: "If you do not believe that you can make a difference, that you matter, you're not going to try to matter, and you will leave it to someone else who may or may not do what is in the best interest of your values or democracy's values."[23] In facing history and themselves, the students become better prepared to confront the social and ethical issues of the present and to accept responsibility for and to participate in today's challenging world. And perhaps most importantly, they preserve hope for a better future.

Some additional books supplement the resource book: *The Facing History Annotated Bibliography*; the companion manual, *Elements of Time*; and the companion resource guide, *Choosing to Participate*. The bibliography suggests additional readings for students and teachers on the major themes of the program. *Elements of Time* is designed to help teachers integrate video testimonies of Holocaust survivors and witnesses into the Facing History unit; descriptions of video portraits tell the stories of 14 survivors with different experiences during the Third Reich, and video montages include excerpts from testimonies. Like the resource book, the companion manual suggests activities that will help students to think about how they would have responded to the circumstances of Nazi Germany and to reflect on their own process of decision making. *Choosing to Participate* is a resource guide that can be used either to enhance the last chapter of the resource book or as a separate unit to focus on citizen participation and community service. The opening section explores the motivations of individuals and groups who help others; subsequent chapters trace the evolution of U.S. traditions and institutions dealing with care, charity, and philanthropy.

Other publications deal with special themes in the program. The book *Poetry* captures the experiences that Sonia Weitz had as an adolescent in five concentration and displaced persons camps at the end of the war. *Student Journals in Response to Facing History and Ourselves* is a collection of student responses to each of the chapters in the resource book; the students' concern for the issues covered in the unit is clearly evident. A number of information packets offer supplementary documents and commentary on topics included in the resource book: "Questions of Professional Ethics Raised by a Study of the Nuremberg Trials"; "Auschwitz: Crimes against Mankind"; "Rescuers: What Motivated Them?"; "The Art of Samual Bak: The Artistic Expression of a Child Survivor"; "Kristallnacht: The Precursor to the Final Solution?"; and last, the Facing History newsletter, which appears three or four times a year, keeps the network of Facing History teachers and educators abreast of current research on genocide and of the latest development in pedagogy.

RESPONSES FROM BOTH STUDENTS AND TEACHERS

Feedback from students, teachers, and parents suggests that the Facing History program is reaching its goals in a variety of educational settings. In some cases, the influence has been subtle, with students observing that they have begun to think differently about stereotypes and racial slurs and will find it harder to be passive bystanders when they witness acts or words of brutality. In other instances, the changes have been more dramatic, with students vowing to take direct steps to combat prejudice and intolerance in their communities.

Teachers often report that their students relate issues raised in this program to their own lives, and each may feel the impact at a different point. There is one point, however, at which it is virtually impossible for participants to avoid confronting issues very close to home — any discussion on racism, prejudice, or discrimination in the context of a Facing History unit almost invariably draws parallels to racism within our own society, especially within our schools and neighborhoods. In all probability, racial slurs, graffiti, and fights within the schools and neighborhoods where students have studied the Holocaust will continue. Nevertheless, program evaluations have demonstrated that students and teachers in the program gain an expanded awareness of justice issues. In one telling instance, a student taking Facing History after drawing a swastika in his notebook erased the symbol upon learning its Nazi connotations.

Students themselves are likely to mention changes in their thinking in their journals. For example, after a student read and discussed the chapter, "Anti-Semitism: A Case Study of Prejudice and Discrimination," he wrote, "I see prejudice now, in other people and in me; I'm afraid of old people, I get angry at shy people, I label (Hippie, Preppie, etc.). Prejudice grew, it was fed, watered, and given sun, transplanted. Here, choices are involved too. I make a choice to recognize my prejudices, to try to conquer them."

One teacher tells the story of an eighth grader who did not appear to be paying much attention throughout the unit, yet gave an unexpected response on the final day of class when asked to tell what he had learned in Facing History. "At least," he began, "I don't feel like a waxed car anymore. You know, after a car is waxed how the beads of water come off. Well, when I hear racial jokes I am at least aware I have heard them — they don't just roll off with no effect on me."[24]

Other issues in the program that elicit considerable concern from students are stereotyping and prejudging groups of people. Although many of the readings pertain to the discriminatory patterns in Nazi legislation and education, the students see similar mechanisms at work in their own democratic society today.

Just as many students believe the program has altered their perceptions and compelled them to think more about their behavior, teachers often remark that they will never be able to teach in the same way after working with the Facing History program. In attending workshops and institutes, teachers experience the very same materials they will later use with their students. They too must confront painful subject matter and assess the prejudices and preconceived notions they bring to their classrooms. Furthermore, they have an opportunity to exchange ideas on teaching controversial topics with other teachers and educators. "I have had a difficult time in finding the right words to describe the Facing History training," wrote a participant at a recent summer institute.

I have had difficulty, in part, because so many things took place, and on so many different levels. Alternately casting ourselves in the roles of teacher and student, we acquired information about the history itself; we explored our own feelings, beliefs, and assumptions about genocide, racism, violence, and resistance; and we became our own community while still representing diverse and separate communities back home.[25]

Follow-up work in special workshops and seminars or in one-on-one meetings with members of the staff provides teachers with information on new materials and scholarship and with ways of reviewing and assessing teaching methods.[26] For example, a tenth-grade social studies teacher at a vocational high school in western Massachusetts spoke on the phone nightly with a staff member during the first semester he offered the course. The staff member suggested approaches and possible readings and on several occasions visited the class to give lessons on German history, a topic that the teacher felt uncomfortable presenting. By the next year, that same teacher could present the history himself and helped train his colleagues to use the program.[27] Another eighth-grade social studies teacher who has worked with the program for ten years believes that the ongoing interaction with members of the staff and other teachers using the program is invaluable. "After teaching about the Holocaust for several years," he explains, "it is possible to become numb to the subject and not teach it as effectively as it can and should be taught. Working with the staff and colleagues keeps me alerted to the latest issues in scholarship and new materials to be tried."[28]

For many teachers, the sense of rejuvenation that comes from involvement with the program makes them more vital and effective in the classroom. An eighth-grade teacher from Albuquerque, New Mexico, who felt burned out and planned to leave teaching, attended a summer institute that renewed her commitment to the profession. The following year she piloted Facing History in her school and helped host a Facing History workshop for teachers in her community.[29] A professor of education in a New England college, disappointed by the student response to routine education courses, found that students were stimulated and challenged by Facing History.[30]

Parents and relatives also notice the impact the program has on their children. During dinner, for instance, they find that their sons and daughters are asking questions and talking about issues brought up in Facing History classes. Not only do students want to learn more about the Nazi era, but they also want to discuss ways they can prevent such abuses and become responsible citizens.

WHY THE PROGRAM IS EFFECTIVE

One of the principle reasons the program elicits such interest is that the content touches on themes that help students recognize the importance of critical thinking and the inherent dangers of thoughtlessness. As I. F. Stone has observed, a study of fascism is critical for educating students in the art of thinking, for in studying this phenomenon, they become aware of the techniques of indoctrination and of the technology of persuasion and propaganda that is possible in the twentieth century. The more one investigates the subject, the more aware one becomes of how important careful thought and reflection are for the preservation of freedom and justice. "Of all the forms of political organization that do not permit freedom," Stone said, "only totalitarianism consciously seeks to crowd out the ability to think. Man cannot be silenced, he can only be crowded into not speaking."[31]

The Nazi propaganda machine concentrated on suppressing thinking. Leni Riefenstahl, a celebrated cinematic artist and Hitler's filmmaker, said that "the object of propaganda has little to do with truth, its object is to make people lose their judgment."[32] Hitler himself pointed out that "propaganda consists in attracting the crowd, not in educating those who are already educated."[33] The U.S. writer Milton Mayer, who interviewed Germans from many occupations after World War II, found that the great majority had failed to object to the Nazi regime because they lacked time to think about what was taking place — they were either too busy with their day-to-day activities or too interested in protecting jobs and family to take the necessary time to consider the consequences of a dictatorial regime. A university professor who spoke with Mayer explained how the process of indoctrination made people accept new morals and principles they would not have accepted in the past. He continued:

> Suddenly, it all comes down, all at once. You see what you are, what you have done, or, more accurately, what you haven't done (for that was all that was required of most of us: that we do nothing). . . . You remember those early meetings of your department in the university when, if one had stood, others would have stood, perhaps, but no one stood. A small matter, a matter of hiring this man or that, and you hired this one rather than that. You remember everything now, and your heart breaks. Too late. You are compromised beyond repair.[34]

Highlighting the importance of moral reasoning are the readings that examine the mentality and actions of the perpetrators of the Final Solution. Nazi leaders such as Auschwitz Commandant Rudolf Hoess and Einsatzgruppen leader Otto Ohlendorff took pride in the fact that they obeyed orders and carried them out to the letter of the Nazi law. As students read the reminiscences of these men, they begin to recognize the importance of thinking for themselves and not following orders simply to follow orders. Didn't these leaders have any moral values? How could they live with their consciences after committing such atrocities? Weren't they in a position to resist or undermine orders to commit mass murder?

The Facing History approach of synthesizing history and ethics broadens the traditional definition of history, making the discipline more relevant for students.[35] For the last two centuries, the Rankian tradition of objective history has been the dominant paradigm, influencing the training of professional historians and the presentation of history in classrooms and textbooks. Emotional responses to the material, empathizing with people of earlier generations and drawing parallels between the past and present violate the criteria for the scientific study of history established by von Ranke and his colleagues. At the same time, the appointment of historians to positions in the social sciences and the specialization within the discipline has shorn the study of history of its clear relevance to contemporary human beings, who must live with the consequences of history. But individual comprehension, evaluation, and participation act as links between history and all the humanities, past and present, the personal and the public.

Facing History has revived the time-honored tradition of history as a moral science, which goes back to antiquity and peaked in the eighteenth-century works of Edward Gibbon and David Hume. From the perspective of these historians, history is a branch of moral philosophy, and its lessons serve as guidelines for prudent thinking and moral behavior. Today, this tradition offers historians a new way to view their role in society. They need not be confined to the ivory tower where they work with specialists interested in specific historical topics; instead, they have an opportunity to communicate with a much broader audience by applying their skills to helping members of the general public think critically about social and political issues and to reflect on their moral values and behavior.

Although the Rankian definition of history has dominated the profession since the nineteenth century, the earlier understanding of history as a moral science never totally disappeared. Progressive educators in the 1930s, for instance, advocated social participation for all students. Paul Hannah offered curriculum solutions for the Depression years, and he is echoed by educators today who believe that children learn to be socially responsible by practicing democracy and through experience in governing themselves. Hannah argues that "children have an obligation to contribute to the solution of the great social and economic problems of the nation, not merely by understanding them but through social participation."[36] In the 1940s, a Harvard committee of educators emphasized the study of history through philosophy and literature as necessary for bringing goodness to our society.[37]

Facing History is in the vanguard of clarifying for people, both historians and nonhistorians, the relevance that history has for contemporary thought and ethics. In addition to preparing materials for schools in hundreds of communities, the program provides teacher training services and classes for adult learners who have reached thousands since the inception of the program 14 years ago. Moreover, the program holds annual conferences on issues of human rights and justice, inviting educators, professionals, and interested members of the community to enter into dialogue about aspects of Holocaust history that are relevant to our lives today.

The broader definition of history embraced in the Facing History program excites interest among students of all ages; but it has particular attraction for adolescents. The lives of students in this age group are centered in peer groups and mutual relationships. These students are likely to be struggling with issues of trust, loyalty, and responsibility as individuals within groups. If a Holocaust program is to be an integral part of the social studies curriculum for this age group, it must support and challenge students while they are beginning to see themselves as unique individuals but who are, at the same time, boys and girls desperately needing to belong. Such a program must help students whose newly discovered ideas of subjectivity raise the problems of differing perspectives, competing truths, and the need to understand motives and to consider the intentions and abilities of themselves and others. Adolescence is a time of major developmental transitions. In their regular curriculum and in any Holocaust program that is part of that curriculum, these students need to engage in moral reasoning to become aware of their own development.

According to educational theorists, the Facing History approach includes components vital for making history a lively and meaningful discipline for adolescents. The academic and psychological framework is well suited to adolescents' levels of intellectual and emotional development, and its central themes focus on the interaction between the individual and the world in a way that, according to Piagetian theory, defines development. Growth is fostered when, as a consequence of interaction with the environment, the individual confronts new stimuli for which his or her present understanding is inadequate. In order to resolve this imbalance between the individual's internal order and the external world, an entire reorganization of cognitive structure must occur.[38]

The normative hallmark of cognitive development in adolescence is the capacity for hypothetical thought. Whereas most children tend to think of history in concrete, descriptive, and linear terms, adolescents are more capable of formulating hypotheses and of performing intellectual operations upon these hypotheses. The capacity for thinking hypothetically has three important implications for the study of history. First, students who have reached this stage of cognitive development are able to reason deductively. Unlike the concrete-thinking child, the adolescent can begin with an abstract principle and from it deduce the concrete manifestation in a particular historical context. Second, hypothetical thinking permits the adolescent to work with the point of view of an individual in the past. The adolescent can understand, more easily than can the child, that if a person lived under a certain set of circumstances, he or she might well have believed and acted on a particular set of ideas, strange as these ideas might seem by today's standards. The third and perhaps most important element of the development of hypothetical thought is the power of speculation. While the child often clings to the reality of a given situation, adolescents are more capable of speculating about what happened or did not happen in history. The adolescent can now understand that what happened did not necessarily have to happen; an event was the result of certain circumstances at a certain time. The adolescent can then imagine alternatives, construct different possibilities, and play out their outcome. This process, in turn, enables adolescents to tolerate ambiguity — they do not see issues strictly in terms of black and white but are sensitive to the nuances that complicate decision making.[39]

The content of Facing History offers ample opportunity for students to exercise their skills in thinking hypothetically. Lesson plans move from an explanation of what did happen to a consideration of what might have happened or how individuals or groups could have prevented an event from happening. Readings on the rise of the National Socialist party, for example, survey the voting patterns and party platforms of the Weimar era. Following these facts are case studies of German voters, and students are asked to speculate on which parties the subjects of the case studies might have supported. Additional exercises encourage students to consider how Germans of the early 1930s might have prevented the Hitler regime from coming to power.

Just as the content of the course encourages students to think about the should and would questions, it complicates their thinking by dispelling myths and avoiding simple explanations for complex forms of human behavior. This is clearly illustrated by the students' responses to the stories of Holocaust survivors. Their initial gut reaction to the history of the Final Solution is to ask why the victims failed to resist. As Holocaust survivor and author Primo Levi has explained, "Among the questions that are put to us [survivors in classrooms], one is never absent; indeed, as the years go by, it is formulated with ever increasing persistence, and with an ever less hidden accent of accusation. More than a simple question, it is a family of questions. Why did you not escape? Why did you not rebel? Why did you not avoid capture 'beforehand'?"[40]

However, hearing the stories of survivors in classroom appearances and in video testimonies makes students more sensitive to the circumstances that prevented resistance activities or inhibited victims from implementing plans for resistance. They also become more aware of the spectrum of resistance activities, ranging from organized armed resistance to individual acts of spiritual resistance. In their journals and class discussions, students do not blame the victims for their impotence, but they do review the specific circumstances that confronted the victims and consider the consequences of open resistance in the Nazi era.

At the same time the program challenges students to use their powers of imagination and speculation about the past, it also meets their emotional needs. A principal psychological task for adolescents is the achievement of a sense of identity, a certainty and confidence about the self. To fulfill this task, the adolescent spends a great deal of time thinking about himself: about who he is; how he came to be what he is; what he might become; how others judge him; and how, in light of that judgment, he judges himself. Thus, on an intellectual level, a student is taking the view of a person or an idea in the past; on the psychological level, the student wonders about the meaning of that point of view for himself or herself.[41]

Throughout the program, students are encouraged to relate the history to their own lives. For instance, while they are studying the chapter "Preparing for Obedience," they consider the roles that education and mass media play in shaping their attitudes and behavior. Reading about the response of foreign nations to the Holocaust, they wonder what adults in their own families and neighborhoods were doing during World War II. At the close of the course, they begin thinking about specific ways in which they can make a difference and prevent the kind of abuse of human rights that occurred during the Hitler era.

A high school teacher who has worked with Facing History since its beginning describes how the program's approach addresses the students' intellectual and emotional needs:

Facing History and Ourselves is a curriculum that honors duality: process and product, head and heart, history and ethics. Besides providing a vigorous and demanding academic experience, it offers an opportunity for students to examine and sometimes modify the values they bring to class. Much is demanded of those who participate in the course, not the least of which is the continued capacity to experience sadness, to avoid the lure of easy answers and stereotypes that can so easily distance us from human experience, from others, and even from ourselves.[42]

In this way, history, as presented in the Facing History program, appeals to students of all ages. By reviving the idea that history is a branch of moral science, the program makes the discipline relevant to present concerns and compels participants to ask what they should do when confronted with moral choices. The program has special relevance for adolescents because it fosters their intellectual growth and helps them grapple with their own questions of identity.

NOTES

1.   Letter from a parent of a Facing History student to members of the Facing History and Ourselves staff, November 1988.

2.   For an overview of the theory and practice of Facing History and Ourselves, see the article issue of Moral Education Forum, Summer 1981. On the

evolution of the program see "Facing History Has a History," *Facing History and Ourselves News* (Spring 1986).

3. Hannah Arendt, *The Life of the Mind: Thinking*, vol. 1 (New York: Harcourt Brace Jovanovich, 1971), p. 5.

4. As discussed in Elizabeth Minnich, "To Judge in Freedom: Hannah Arendt on the Relation of Thinking and Morality," unpublished paper, available at the Facing History Resource Center, p. 15.

5. As quoted in Minnich, "To Judge in Freedom," pp. 16–17.

6. Michael Denneny, "The Privilege of Ourselves: Hannah Arendt on Judgment," in *Hannah Arendt: The Recovery of the Public World*, ed. Melvyn A. Hill (New York: St. Martin's Press, 1979), p. 255.

7. Jacob Bronowski, *The Ascent of Man* (Boston: Little, Brown, 1973), p. 364.

8. Ibid., p. 19.

9. "When Hitler arrived in 1933, the tradition of scholarship in Germany was destroyed, almost overnight. Now the train to Berlin was a symbol of flight. Europe was no longer hospitable to the imagination — and not just the scientific imagination. A whole conception of culture was in retreat: the conception that human knowledge is personal and responsible, an unending adventure at the edge of certainty. Silence fell, as after the trial of Galileo." Bronowski, *Ascent of Man*, p. 367.

10. Margot Stern Strom, "Facing History from Theory to Practice in the Classroom." Keynote address, Fourth Annual Facing History Conference, Harvard Graduate School of Education, April 28, 1988; videotape of conference available at the Facing History Resource Center.

11. Betty Bardige, "Reflective Thinking and Prosocial Awareness: Students Face the Holocaust and Themselves" (Ph.D. diss., Harvard Graduate School of Education, 1983). Also, see Betty Bardige, "Things So Finely Human: Moral Sensibilities at Risk in Adolescence," in *Contributions of Women's Thinking to Psychological Theory and Education*, ed. Carol Gilligan, Janie Ward, and Jill Taylor with Betty Bardige (Cambridge, Mass.: GEHD Study Center and distributed by the Harvard University Press, 1988).

12. Margot Stern Strom and William S. Parsons, *Facing History and Ourselves: Holocaust and Human Behavior* (Watertown, Mass.: Intentional Publications, 1982).

13. Ilse Koehn, *Mischling Second Degree: My Childhood in Nazi Germany* (New York: Greenwillow Books, 1977).

14. Mary Johnson and Philip Johnson, "The Turning Point: Peter Gay Remembers," *Dimensions: A Journal for Holocaust Studies* 4 (October 1988): 23.

15. Lawrence Langer, *Versions of Survival: The Holocaust and Human Spirit* (New York: State University of New York Press, 1981).

16. Bronowski, *Ascent of Man*, p. 370.

17. For a comprehensive treatment of this subject, see Robert J. Lifton, *Nazi Doctors: Medical Killing and the Psychology of Genocide* (New York: Basic Books, 1986). See also Facing History special information packet, "Questions in Medical Ethics Raised by the Nuremberg Trials," available at the Facing History Resource Center.

18. As quoted in Margot Stern Strom, "Facing History and Ourselves: Holocaust and Human Behavior," *Moral Education Forum*, Summer 1981, p. 13.

19. As quoted in Elizabeth Colt and Fanny Connelly, "Excerpts from Student Journals," in response to the curriculum Facing History and Ourselves: Holocaust and Human Behavior, available at the Facing History Resource Center.

20. As quoted in Lisa Colt, Fanny Connelly, and John Paine, "Excerpts from Student Journals," *Moral Education Forum*, Summer 1981, p. 20.

21. Interview with Bill Moyers by Margo Stern Strom, in *Facing History and Ourselves News*, Fall 1988, pp. 6–7.

22. As quoted in Strom and Parsons, *Facing History and Ourselves*, p. 16.

23. Interview with Bill Moyers, p. 7.

24. Incident reported by William Parsons, cofounder and former program director of Facing History and Ourselves.

25. Melinda Fine, "Reflections on the 1988 Facing History Summer Institute." (Unpublished report available at the Facing History Resource Center).

26. Follow-up activities are crucial to the work of the program and enable the staff to keep track of how the program is being implemented.

27. Interview with Richard Sinkoski, 1984. Audiocassette copy available at the Facing History Resource Center.

28. Bill Miller, "Teaching Facing History," presentation at the Fourth Annual Facing History Conference "Facing History in Perspective: From Theory to the Classroom," Harvard Graduate School of Education, April 28, 1988.

29. Interviews with participants at the Facing History and Ourselves 1983 Summer Institute. Audiocassettes available at the Facing History Resource Center.

30. Mary Johnson, "College and University Students Face History," *Facing History and Ourselves News*, Spring 1984.

31. As quoted in Strom, "Facing History," p. 12.

32. Ralph Manheim, *Mein Kampf: The German Mania for Objectivity* (New York: Houghton Mifflin, 1971).

33. As quoted in Strom, "Facing History," p. 12.

34. Milton Mayer, *They Thought They Were Free: The Germans, 1933–1945* (Chicago: University of Chicago Press, 1955), pp. 166–72.

35. Leopold von Ranke was a nineteenth-century German historian who insisted that history should be confined to laying out all the facts so it would meet the criteria of being a scientific discipline. For additional discussion of the contrasts between the Rankian approach and Facing History, see Mary Johnson and Margo Stern Strom, "Facing History and Ourselves: Holocaust and Human Behavior," *Organization of American Historians Newsletter*, November 1985.

36. Diane Ravitch, "Tot Sociology: What Happened to History in the Grade Schools," *The Key Reporter of Phi Beta Kappa* (Autumn 1987): 2.

37. Paul Buck, John Finley, Raphael Demos, Leigh Hoadley, Byron S. Hollinshead, Wilbur K. Jordan, Ivor A. Richards, Phillip J. Rulon, Arthur M. Schlesinger, Robert Ulich, George Wald, and Benjamin F. Wright, *General Education in a Free Society* (Harvard University Committee, 1945).

38. Barbel Inhelder and Jean Piaget, *The Growth of Logical Thinking from Childhood to Adolescence* (New York: Basic Books, 1958).

39. Martin E. Sleeper, "A Developmental Framework for History Education in Adolescence," *School Review* 84 (November 1975): 91–107.

40. Primo Levi, *The Drowned and the Saved*, trans. from the Italian by Raymond Rosenthal (New York: Summit Books, 1988), pp. 150–51.

41. Erik Erikson, *Identity: Youth and Crisis* (New York: Norton, 1968); Lawrence Kohlberg and Carol Gilligan, "The Adolescent as a Philosopher: The Discovery of Self in a Post-Conventional World," *Daedalus* 100 (Fall 1971): 1051–86.

42. Colt, Connelly, and Paine, "Excerpts from Student Journals," p. 19.

8

Athletic Development and Personal Growth

Jeffrey Pratt Beedy

There is a popular belief that participation in organized sports builds character. Many parents want their children to take part in sports because of the inherent psychological, social, and moral experiences that encourage overall personal growth. Despite the fact that much has been written about the value of team sports in promoting important social values, very little empirical data actually support these claims; in fact, some recent studies suggest that sports often do just the opposite and promote negative characteristics such as overcompetitiveness, individualism, and low self-esteem. Do sports build character? If so, how? It is clear that sports provide the potential for encouraging character-building traits, but whether they actually do depends upon a number of factors, including how the experience is structured and what role the coach plays. Although the idea of sports influencing children's personal growth has many implications, this chapter will focus on children aged 6 to 12 engaged in team sports.

ORGANIZED YOUTH SPORTS IN THE UNITED STATES: A HISTORICAL PERSPECTIVE

Long before organized sports became popular in the United States, the idea that sports build character and promote important social values was accepted in the British public schools (which were actually private secondary schools) during the mid-nineteenth century (Sage, 1986). Students and athletes in these early games played an active role in organizing and governing games (a component often missing in adult-run youth sports programs in the United States). But equally important, the social milieu supported values such as camaraderie, fair play, and winning or losing gracefully, and sports were seen as a medium for promoting these qualities. In short, there was a clear and logical connection between cultural philosophy and game practice.

When the idea of organized sports for schoolchildren was transported to the United States at the turn of the century, educators and parents believed that sport participation would promote prosocial values. Luther Gulick founded the Public Schools Athletic League (PSAL) on the basis of this idea, and in 1903 organized sports were brought into the school system. Initially organized sports programs centered on young boys, but in 1905 girls too began to participate in a limited program of exercise and activity in conjunction with PSAL.

Sports soon became an integral part of the school curriculum, and children's participation increased in a growth that paralleled that of the United States itself. However, in the 1930s educators began to question whether the benefits of competitive sports outweighed their potential harm, and the debate evolved into the more critical view that characterized the 1970s. One response was the introduction of new games that emphasized cooperation and participation and downplayed competition and selectivity; cooperative sports offered another alternative for many children and adults. By the middle of the decade, educators and sports scientists had joined together in a more scientific examination of what was taking place on U.S. playing fields. The Youth Sports Task Force of the National Association for Sport and Physical Education developed its "Bill of Rights for Young Athletes" in 1976 to provide volunteers, whose numbers had grown by this time to 2.5 million, with guidelines for organizing and coaching young children while encouraging overall development (Wiggins 1987, p. 13).

The amount of information available about youth sports has increased considerably, but disseminating the results of research and coaching clinics has proved a problem for several reasons. First, understanding youth sports as an educational process is still a relatively new phenomenon, and many coaches are simply not up-to-date; the coaching community is, by and large, conservative. Many coaches are skeptical about new ideas, especially those coming from the research community. Second, while most coaches are willing to attend workshops, few are interested in attending the lengthy courses that lead to accreditation. A third problem arises in connecting theory to practice with models that actually work for coaches. Many researchers conduct theoretical studies independent of the sport environment, and they often have little application to performance on the field. Other studies discuss the issues of sport participation but lack the empirical validation of traditional research methods. Finally, current research and clinics are frequently geared to the volunteer coach and offer little to the professional, or they focus on techniques for improving athletes' performance rather than on understanding children. Halbert argues that "coaches of children need to know more about children. For example, how do children grow and develop? What motivates them? What are the best communication patterns to use?" (1986, p. 67).

It is worthwhile in this context to examine some of the relevant theories in developmental psychology in general — and youth sports in particular — to see how the sport environment should be structured to encourage both athletic development and personal growth. (Sport environment here means organized youth sports; structuring the sport environment means the way in which these rules and interactions are organized, implemented, and thought about, and this includes the role played by the adult coach.) Let us begin by reviewing some of the theoretical and empirical models of social and moral development to help us understand how children organize their thinking about their experiences in team sports.

UNDERSTANDING THE SOCIAL WORLD OF ORGANIZED YOUTH SPORTS: A THEORETICAL PERSPECTIVE

Organized team sports provide opportunities to encourage the development of prosocial qualities, but participation in and of itself will not necessarily promote personal growth. The discussions, observations, thinking, and interactions that occur in conjunction with personal issues (persisting in the face of difficulties, for example, or accommodating both victory and defeat) and interpersonal relations (that is, fairness to teammates, coaches, team rules, distribution of playing time and positions) ultimately lead to personal growth. So it makes sense to look at the theories behind team-related issues and the sports relationships that stimulate thinking about social and moral issues.

Team sports provide a complex social world where people with different perspectives and roles work together toward mutually inclusive goals. This social world embraces relationships among teammates, parents, and coaches; issues of team conflict and harmony; and fairness in relation to team rules (for example, distribution of playing time) that arise as children and adolescents participate in competitive team sports. How these issues are addressed and resolved determines to a large extent whether sports will be a positive experience. The success of any sport program is influenced to some degree by how well adults understand the way each child experiences the social world of sports — if we can understand how children organize and experience their thinking about the social world, we can address change and development more effectively (Damon 1977). Let us examine more closely how a team works and the role of the coach.

HOW A TEAM WORKS

Theories of social and moral development are particularly helpful in understanding how a team works toward a common goal. Turiel (1978), for example, identifies the team as a social organization consisting of participants with both similar and different roles and perspectives; working with others requires a certain understanding and coordination of these roles and perspectives. Mead (1934) suggests that a child's ability to coordinate roles develops through a series of stages that reflect an increasing ability not only to coordinate the roles and perspectives of the self in relation to others, but also ultimately to understand the point of view of the group in relation to the larger society. Participation on a team requires that the players think about their teammates in different ways. A situation might arise, for instance, where an individual must make a decision that may not advance his or her interests but will benefit the team as a whole.

Sullivan (1940) uses the terms *competition*, *compromise*, *cooperation*, and *collaboration* to describe the developmental progression of children's understanding of peer group interaction, which moves from an individualistic "I" orientation to a mutual "we." The terms are helpful in understanding how children experience the interactions that occur in the context of team sports. For instance, the child who speaks of what the team "can do for *me*" has a developmentally different notion of the team than the child who speaks of team objectives in relation to *us*. Similarly, children develop from an individualistic or egocentric notion of the rules to an understanding that the rules of the game are formed by mutual consent (Piaget 1965).

A number of recent studies have focused on children's social understanding in relation to role-taking and communication skills (Flavell et al. 1968; DeVries 1970; Selman and Byrne 1974). Even more recently, Selman (1980) has identified four interpersonal relationships — concepts of individuals, friendships, peer groups, and parents — that reflect a similar stage sequence. Many of the issues concerning peer-group relations (for example, group unity, group organization, the role and function of leadership) are similar to those that apply to organized sport teams. Both peer groups and sport teams, for example, are social organizations with internal structures and rules that require organization and leadership to accomplish tasks.

These studies suggest that children's awareness of the perspectives of other develops from an egocentric view to one that enables them to take another's perspective. Because participation on a team requires give-and-take and interpersonal perspective taking, adults need to know how children understand their roles in relation to those of other team members. Developmental models are helpful in describing how children think about issues such as teamwork and working toward common team goals.

THE TEAM AS A COMMUNITY: COLLECTIVE EXPECTATIONS AND VALUES

Players on teams often share expectations. For many children and adolescents, these friendships, goals, and ideas are very important aspects of the team experience. They contribute to the process whereby children develop beliefs about how people ought to treat one another. Kohlberg (1981) maintains that social groups such as classes, clubs, and teams are important for children and adolescents as a means to confront issues of fairness, since these issues arise naturally as part of group activities. To some extent, a sports team must share certain values if its members are to work together toward common goals; but not all groups and teams are communities with collective expectations and values: "In sociological literature the term *Gemeinschaft*, or community, is typically contrasted with the term *Gesellschaft*, society or association. Community implies an internally valued set of relations and sharings. Association suggests that social relations or groups are valued instrumentally in aiding the individual's purposes of guaranteeing his rights" (Kohlberg 1981, p. 46).

Whether the teams share common expectations or not, the sport environment offers a vehicle for the discussion of moral issues as they arise naturally within the context of group play. How do issues like the distribution of playing time and positions, the implementation of team rules, and the interaction between the coach and players affect children's understanding of fairness? These issues influence how children believe people ought to behave toward one another, and the role of the coach as a leader and role model is crucial to this process in team sports.

THE COACH AS LEADER AND ROLE MODEL

The coach often represents one of children's first role models after parents and teachers. The coach shares the fun, excitement, and disappointment of sports activities. Martens et al. (1981) point out that "successful coaches not only teach children skills of the sport, they also teach and model the skills needed for successful living in our society" (p. xiv). Equally important, the coach is responsible for establishing team policy and for the safety, education, and development of the players.

How do relationships and interactions with a coach influence the way children view themselves and the world around them? One way to address this question is to explore the way children develop their understanding of others. Research in developmental psychology indicates that children's understanding of responsibilities and roles develops with time and experience (Selman et al. 1979; Turiel 1983). Turiel suggests that:

> The youngest children do not have stable concepts of internal processes of persons and, therefore, rely on the external situations to predict behaviors. The formation of stable concepts of internal psychological processes occurs between the ages of 7 and 12 years, resulting in an overgeneralization of the influence of internal dispositions in predicting behavior. Subsequently, there is an increasing view of behavior as determined by the interaction of personal disposition and situational factors. (1983, p. 84)

This description is useful in understanding how children at different levels of development understand the adult coach. If, for example, the coach of a team of seven-year-olds, no matter how well intentioned, shouts a great deal at the players (negative external cues), the children may not understand the coach's intentions as well as older children would; coaches knowledgeable of children's developmental understanding will include encouragement and fun activities (positive external cues) in their coaching repertoire.

ENCOURAGING ATHLETIC DEVELOPMENT AND PERSONAL GROWTH

Research on moral development and sport activity is limited. However, some recent research (Bredemeier, et al. in press; Romance, Weiss, and Bockovan 1986) shows that intervention programs that stress social interaction, interdependence, and negotiation opportunities can improve young athletes' moral reasoning about sports. (This point will be discussed in more depth later in this chapter.)

Sports provide a natural environment for young people to work through important personal and interpersonal issues. If structured correctly, athletic programs can help children develop both as athletes and as people, with clear values and skills like the ability to share, to negotiate, to persevere in the face of difficulties, and to accept both defeat and victory. But philosophy and sport participation alone do not guarantee the development of prosocial values. If sports are to promote these qualities, the philosophy of the school or sport program must be carried into the locker rooms and the team van and onto the playing fields.

If we want our sports programs to promote prosocial values, we must ask several important questions. Why do we want our children to play organized sports? What do we consider important prosocial qualities? What are the goals of sports participation for children? How will their participation help them develop as people? In what ways are goals carried out within the sports experience? In other words, in what ways does playing sports contribute to the development of goals such as personal growth and character? This last question has particular significance if coaches are to be successful in connecting theory to practice. Discussed below are some of the important factors the coach needs to consider in organizing the philosophy, rules, and interactions with young athletes; but first and foremost, adults need to recognize the influence that coaches have.

THE ROLE OF THE COACH

The coach becomes part of the child's world in a way that few activities allow: forming friendships, influencing ideas about justice and caring, developing ways to work with others, and in general having a great deal of fun. The coach can help young children develop their athletic skills, friendships, sense of self-esteem, and confidence. For many children, coaches play a significant role in their developing years, for they decide who plays where and how much playing time each athlete receives. According to Horn (1987), "the behavior of the individual teacher or coach affects the psychosocial development of children above and beyond that exerted by the school, curriculum, or athletic program itself" (p. 122). If sports are to offer opportunities for personal growth, adults need to understand their responsibility for the overall development of the children involved.

SETTING CLEAR GOALS

Coaches must establish an open, fair, and objective approach to rules, distribution of playing time and positions, and discipline to support the overall philosophy of the sports program. Each school and sports program is different, but schools in general and coaches in particular must be clear on what issues and values they believe are important and what will be done if the rules are violated. Coaches and administrators need to ask what determines who will make the team and how much playing time each player will get. Skill? Hard work? Last year's performance? The questions are subtle, yet they have great impact on how children feel about themselves and the world around them. Young people need clear guidelines — ambiguity creates uncertainty, hurt feelings, and loss of self-esteem. How a coach deals with these questions will influence whether sports will contribute to the personal growth of the athletes involved. Although athletic programs vary in their objectives, it is fair to assume that athletic development and personal growth are important goals. Toward this end, the sport environment should encourage athletes to be self-confident, independent and responsible, goal oriented, caring, interpersonally competent, focused and disciplined, team oriented, understanding of diversity, and appreciative of good health and life-long fitness.

ADDRESSING IMPORTANT ISSUES

Sports do not build character unless important issues are recognized and addressed in an educational way. For example, many claim that team sports develop cooperation. This may be true, but if competitive sports are to assist in young people's understanding of cooperation, issues pertaining to the idea of working together toward a collective end (for example, bringing the equipment, cheering on the teammate who takes your place on the field, and being willing to play a position other than your favorite) need to be brought to the attention of the young athletes. Character skills and sport skills can only be developed if they are recognized, addressed, and practiced. Team sports enter the psychological, social, and moral domain by providing difficult situations that stimulate active thinking and require perspective taking by the participants. However, the coach must intervene (unless the coach offers some type of intervention, sports offer no distinct advantage for promoting personal growth in children) and must have a general knowledge of how children develop socially, morally, and psychologically.

The sport environment should be organized in a way that encourages children to consider several perspectives. For example, children under ten years old generally understand the idea of cooperation but have difficulty with what Selman et al. (1979) refer to as "mutual perspectivism" and Sullivan (1953) refers to as "collaboration." By whatever name, they are important components of team play. To encourage this type of perspective taking, discussions for eight-to-ten-year-olds should include opportunities for children to take a third person or team perspective. The coach plays the role of the mediator in these discussions, offering suggestions that require mutually oriented solutions to team issues. Yeates and Selman (1989) indicate the importance of understanding how children develop in the process of intervention:

Intervention programs are most effective when they attempt to encourage social-cognitive conceptualizations that are about one step above children's current levels. That is, children often can understand and incorporate ideas and suggestions that are "one step up" from their current stage of cognitive attainment, but are unlikely to make use of interventions that are more than one level higher. (p. 32)

What Yeates and Selman refer to as "one step above" the child's thinking means exposing the child to ideas that include a more developed understanding of the responsibility that each person has to a larger concern — for example, the team. The coach can encourage children to think about a subject from a number of perspectives.

In addition to acting as a role model, the coach needs to interact with young athletes in a way that assures that discussions are both productive and safe. If the athletes tend to focus on individual interests, the coach can help them think about their responsibility to the team. Meetings where coaches and athletes can exchange ideas in a constructive manner allow important concerns and feelings to be discussed and provide the athletes with an opportunity to think about possible solutions. In one way, this process is similar to the process of developing sports skills — children presented with tasks a little above their skill level are likely to feel challenged and excited about learning. For example, when asked to catch ground balls and fly balls, young baseball players begin to develop skills as a result of the number of attempts to catch the ball, the application of present motor (fielding) skills, the coach's explanation of how to field a grounder, and the athlete's perception of the overall situation (Beedy 1988). The same principle of interaction is necessary to stimulate psychological, social, and moral growth in children, and the sport environment should be structured to encourage thinking, discussion, and interaction between people with different roles. In the same way that sports-related skills need to be practiced, moral reasoning and interpersonal understanding require an environment that exercises thought about these issues.

CREATING OPPORTUNITIES FOR DISCUSSION

Bredemeier and Shields (1987) point out that, "Hann's research suggests that for an experience to be effective in promoting moral growth it must be interpersonal, the participants must perceive their interdependence, and there must be opportunity for dialogue and negotiation" (p. 160). The following situations provide coaches with natural opportunities to help young athletes think about and discuss issues concerning themselves and the team.

Warm-Up and Cool-Down Meetings

We are all aware of the value of stretching out before and after a strenuous workout, but the same principles can be used to help young athletes process some of the psychological aspects of competing. The coach can use a meeting before the game to discuss strategies and offer players different perspectives on the game. In this instance, the coach plays the role of an educator in providing ideas and strategies that increase the likelihood of success. Similarly, the coach can use cool-down team meetings to discuss the events that took place during the game. This is an excellent way to help young athletes understand competition as a process and a product — with process meaning persistence in the face of difficulties, working to improve the execution of plays, and helping the team, and product meaning winning, the most runs, the fastest time, or first place.

Coaches can use warm-up or cool-down meetings to help athletes understand the difference between two different conceptions of winning. Let us say, for example, that a baseball team has won (or lost) a game by a large margin, and the players are feeling elated (or very down) about the outcome. The coach can meet with the players and dissect the game into specific components (first inning, fourth inning, double plays, bunts, cut-offs, and so forth) and have the players work on executing the plays correctly. Athletes can learn to execute plays in cool-down meetings, but just as important, the coach can help the athletes to think about competition and playing in relation to skills and the execution of plays rather than in relation to the number of runs scored or the fastest time. Once the session is over and the coach has helped the players understand the win (or loss) in relation to elements that contributed to the victory (or defeat), players will leave the meeting thinking about the correct way to bunt, to make a cut-off, or to take a flush instead of focusing on the game's score. Most important, such meetings help children relate the process of development and execution of skills to the product of winning a game. Cool-down meetings can help athletes put development, competition, and winning into proper perspective.

Team Rules

Young athletes can be challenged quite effectively by discussion of rules that affect everyone. A team rule, for example, might require that players attend all practices and share in equipment cleanup in order to participate in Saturday's game. During the week before an important game, the star player misses a practice (and offers no excuse) on Tuesday and leaves practice early on Wednesday without helping with equipment cleanup. Using this example, coach and players can engage in a discussion about the rules and each player's commitment to the team as a community with shared values and expectations. Discussions that include defining the problem and thinking about solutions are an important part of the learning process. The coach can moderate and direct the discussion, and he or she is usually in the best position to make a final decision. The point is that the children have an opportunity to think about the situation and to offer solutions to the problem.

Distribution of Playing Time and Positions

An excellent way to help young children learn to negotiate with their peers and begin to understand concepts of fairness is to distribute playing time and positions in interesting ways. In one case, 18 eight-to-ten-year-olds negotiated among themselves to determine how the positions and playing time would be distributed during a six-inning baseball game (Beedy 1987). I (as coach) asked each player to give me the three positions he or she most wanted to play. Just before the game, I explained that I would name each position and the two or three players who wanted that position, and those players would then negotiate on who would play which inning. The batting order was alphabetical, so everyone would bat whether that player had been on the field the previous inning or not (in other words, the batting order was continuous). Further, the players were free to switch positions at any time, as long as they worked it out with all the players involved.

During the game, an interesting phenomenon occurred — there was no squabbling among the players, and few, if any, requests were made of me. This allowed me to concentrate on the game as the coach and freed the kids to have fun and learn. After the game, all the team members reported that they liked the fact that everyone had been treated equally and that no one was hurt or left out.

Prior to having the children negotiate positions and playing time, I had held two meetings with the players to describe what I was doing and what they had to do to make the process work. This assured the fairness and protection of feelings among children at a developmental period when they might have had difficulty establishing the structure themselves. This process could work with athletes of different ages and ability levels, provided that the rules and discussions are adapted to the needs of the children involved.

Interpersonal Conflicts and Moral Issues:
Other Opportunities for Discussion

Team sports enter the moral domain by situations that sometimes violate the rights of others or interfere with their welfare. Whether it is how playing time should be distributed or whether someone who missed practice should be allowed to play in the big game, sports provide opportunities for coaches and athletes to address issues that affect the team as a whole. A number of researchers have recently suggested that one way to encourage thinking about others is through moral dialogue (Haan 1977, 1978; Haan, Aerts, & Cooper 1985), which allows players to understand the views and feelings of their teammate and helps individual players work together. According to Haan (1987), moral dialogue is any interaction that affects the welfare of others. Four conditions must be present if a dialogue is to be moral in nature. Bredemeier and Shields describe these conditions as:

> First, a valid moral dialogue must seek consensus. All parties must accept the solution as the best that can be achieved given the limitations of the situation and the unique characteristics of the discussants. All persons hold power of veto, and any use of force to gain resolution automatically invalidates the conclusions. Second, participants must have equal opportunity to influence the conclusions. Any restrictions on the freedom to participate equally in moral exchange inevitably result in moral distortions. Third, all participants must have equal access to information. Finally, valid moral exchanges only take place when participants are mindful of their future lives together. (1987, p. 153)

Anyone involved in competitive sports realizes that it would be difficult to satisfy all of these conditions, and Haan agrees that we can rarely satisfy all of them in real life. The important point is to encourage young children to think about issues of fairness, caring, and cooperation as they relate to the individual and the team. However, according to Bredemeier and Shields (1987), it is in this very area that many youth sport programs fail to focus.

Unfortunately, it is precisely this dialogical dynamic that is progressively removed as one shifts from games to sports and from less competitive, informal sport to more elite, structured sport. Moral discussion pertinent to such issues as what should be done about rule violations, when and why participants should risk injury, who should play, and on what basis rewards should be distributed are rare, even among those involved with children's programs (p. 161).

To illustrate how team sports enter the moral domain, let me describe a theft at an all-boys New Sport Experience Camp (NSEC) that I direct in Maine. This particular case occurred within the sport environment, but the incident could have taken place in a school or club or at home. It is, however, a common moral issue within sport communities and can disrupt the sense of trust within the community.

The problem surfaced when several campers reported money missing from their rooms. One 15-year-old coach-in-training (CIT) went around the camp to find out who had had money stolen and discovered that about $47 was missing. I asked the CIT, along with two other interested campers, to present the issue at a meeting of the entire camp that night. Lawrence Kohlberg was at the camp at the time and attended the meeting, along with the camp staff (approximately ten adults). My role was to monitor the discussion. I explained to the campers, who ranged in age from 8 to 15, that they had to be called upon, and once they had the floor, they could voice their concern and their proposal. I also asked that each camper not talk unless he had the floor.

After about an hour of discussing what the act of theft does to the sense of trust, I asked the campers to offer proposals on how we might work toward resolving the situation. Initially, the focus was on blaming the thief or the victims who were careless about leaving money in the rooms; but as the meeting progressed, the campers began to move toward resolving the issue. The first proposal (from an 11-year-old) suggested that campers "shouldn't leave money around their rooms. They should instead give their money to the directors." The next proposal (from a 14-year-old) was that the directors "set up a rule so the thief will not be punished if he returns the money. There is enough justice in the shame felt through having to return the stolen money." Two campers, one 14 and the other 12, proposed that the thief "leave the money in the room with a note of apology."

At this point, an 18-year-old suggested that the money might have been spent and that, even if the thief knew he had done wrong, he would be unable to return the money. A 17-year-old counselor responded, "If he does see it's wrong and he wants to return the money, the only fair thing to do, even if he has the money, is to come to a counselor he feels comfortable with and admit he took it. If he has the money, it doesn't even have to be relayed back to the directors who it was." A third counselor (age 18) suggested that if the person who stole the money didn't have it, he could borrow it from the directors and have his parents pay it back or take it out of his allowance. At this point, Lawrence Kohlberg asked, "If the money isn't returned, does the rest of the community have any responsibility to the persons who had the money stolen?" In response to his question, it was suggested that the entire camp "chip in a dollar to show that we are a community" (an 11-year-old) "so the victims can do all the things we can do" (a 14-year-old).

The final proposal suggested that first, the thief should return the money to the directors who would not reveal his identity. If the money was not returned in 24 hours, everyone would be encouraged to chip in a dollar to the victims. The thief did not return the money, and the majority of campers (approximately 45) contributed enough money to make up the total sum missing.

The important part of this process was not what happened in the end. Rather, the most important aspect was that the campers had a chance to think about a number of important issues. Equally important, by having a group meeting, the children were exposed to a wide range of perspectives, some of them more developed than their own. The same general process can be used to address many group issues to help children widen their tolerance and understand themselves and the world in which they live. Finally, in addition to the exercise in moral thinking, the campers had an opportunity to develop their interpersonal negotiation skills. That is to say, the discussion helped the campers distinguish between making a relevant point and making one that served little purpose in moving toward a resolution. By the time we got to the final vote, most of the campers understood the difference between constructive proposals and unhelpful accusations. They also understood the importance of addressing and resolving an issue. And of course, the coach's job is to facilitate this process of moral growth.

DEVELOPMENTAL PERSPECTIVES ON YOUTH SPORTS

In most cases, the experience of playing on a team is different for an 8-year-old than it is for a 16-year-old. Experience, background, ability, and overall development all make this so. Both the philosophy and the structure (the rules, goals, interpersonal interactions, and so forth) can be organized to meet the interests and talents of children at different developmental stages.

Sports for Children under Age Eight

Cooperative games offer an environment that de-emphasizes winning and also requires cooperation to reach individual and group goals. Players must coordinate their efforts in a way that benefits the team as a whole. In this sense, cooperative games offer an appropriate introduction to team sports, since children can enjoy interacting with friends as they learn to work toward a mutual goal. The structure of cooperative games requires players to overcome obstacles such as time and objects instead of people, but an individual player can advance his position only by helping other players to advance theirs. Thus children are encouraged to develop a more team-oriented approach to games and sports.

Cooperative games provide the foundation for competitive team sports where intrateam cooperation is not required and often not encouraged. They have particular value for children under the age of nine or ten. Although many younger children enjoy playing the more competitive games offered in organized youth sport programs, many cooperative elements can be incorporated into competitive games to help them understand the value of team play.

Sports for Children Aged Eight to Ten

Learning to Cooperate in a Competitive Environment

Playing on a team requires understanding about how others think, feel, and act. To coordinate plays and get along with teammates, for example, athletes need to understand, to a certain extent, how people work together in groups for common goals. Until this notion of the team is understood, children have difficulty executing collaborative team activities (for example, sacrificing a personal shot because a teammate has a better position). Sometimes competitive team sports for children under nine or ten can result in fighting, confusion, and hurt feelings, which is why so much confusion generally surrounds youth sports at the beginning levels. Jay Coakley refers to this as beehive soccer: "Immediately following the open kick, there will be forty 9-year-old legs within 10 yards of the soccer ball, and they will follow that ball like a swarm of bees following its queen. Meanwhile, there are sideline pleas to 'stay in position' and 'get back to where you belong'" (1986, p. 62). What Coakley is referring to is the fact that most 9-year-olds have not yet developed an understanding of the team as a group of players working collaboratively toward a common goal. Research on cooperation indicates that this understanding of others (in this case, the team) develops from an individualistic (beehive soccer) to a collaborative understanding of the team (team mutual). Children's understanding of the other person's perspective within a mutual group task is a developmental phenomenon.

It is important that young children learn to work with others and realize how that relates to the concept of teamwork. Structuring competitive team sports to include some cooperative elements takes some of the emphasis off personal attainment and places it on working together. Competitive team sports, with selectivity and winning as the goals, are considerably different structurally from the cooperative games environment. Contriently interdependent is a term used to refer to a situation where an individual's successful attainment of a goal is interfered with by another's successful attainment of his or her goal. The goals in a competitive game such as soccer or basketball are contriently interdependent because only one team can win, and one team's success means another team's failure.

Competitive team sports not only encourage contriently interdependent goals between teams, but they also promote the same competitive atmosphere among team members when selectivity and winning are the major goals — that is, players often have to compete for playing time and positions with their teammates. If positions and playing time, for example, are dependent on ability (as is the case in many youth sport programs), individual players' goals (playing) are contriently interdependent with those of their teammates. By restructuring the objectives and rules to include some cooperative goals and rules (such as equal distribution of playing time and positions), competitive sports can encourage interdependent goals.

If the distribution of playing time or the making of the team is dependent upon a child's performance, then he or she is put into a position of conflict between competing with teammates and working cooperatively with them toward a mutual goal. Children often resolve this type of conflict competitively instead of cooperatively, which may be why coaches see athletes at this age (eight to ten) hogging the ball, not passing, and fighting, activities that frequently disrupt the team (Beedy 1988). In this case, the sport environment is encouraging intrateam competition (competition among individuals) instead of cooperation. Such demands are unnecessary at this age. This is not to say that competitive team sports cannot promote teamwork, but to promote the development of cooperation and collaboration, the program should include equal participation and an emphasis on collaboration and skill development rather than on selectivity and winning.

A second problem with competitive team sports for children under nine or ten is that winning and extrinsic goals (trophies, first place, play-offs, and so on) are sometimes presented to players as important goals. This places the child in a situation of conflict between pursuing a goal of personal or instrumental interest (that is, to win because it is valued by coach, parents, or peers) and collaboration (passing the ball and giving up personal success for the betterment of the team). In soccer, for example, rules might be modified for children between the ages of eight and ten to require that all players must touch the ball before a shot can be made. Thus a skilled player who tends to control the game would be required to think about other members of the team, and the final shot will be more of a team effort. Another rule could require that no player make two successive goals or that all players must have a chance to score before the player who scored first can attempt another shot. Similar modifications can be made in basketball, lacrosse, hockey, and other team sports. These changes require that all players contribute to the goal of winning; but, more important, they encourage players to think about their teammates before pursuing an individual course of action.

Using Cooperation to Develop Empathy

From a theoretical perspective, the goal of structuring competitive games cooperatively is to provide an environment that requires children to think about team play before individual effort. Research indicates that cooperatively structured environments help young children to consider other people's perspectives and to develop empathy for others. According to Johnson and Johnson,

> Cooperativeness may be increased when individuals are trained to take the affective and cognitive perspective of others. Thus, the use of cooperative goal structures within learning situations may be crucial to cognitive development of students, the education of egocentricism necessary for social development, ability to communicate effectively, empathy, and autonomous moral judgment based upon mutual reciprocity and justice. (1974, p. 22)

Altering competitive team sports to include cooperative objectives and rules can help young athletes learn to cooperate in competitive situations, and, what is more, such alterations can provide the developmental foundation for understanding collaborative play.

Exposing Young Children to a Variety of Sports and Encouraging Adults

Children should be exposed to a wide variety of sport activities, especially during the formative years of their lives. Many schools and towns offer only conventional sports (football, baseball, and soccer), and a young child better suited for running might not realize his or her potential as an athlete. And because children develop at different rates, their athletic and personal skills tend to be at different levels. According to Coakley, this early exposure to a variety of sports is especially important for girls:

> I would argue that it is *never* too early for a child to engage in expressive physical activities. In fact, the more, the better, and the more diversified, both socially and physically, the better. This is true for both boys and girls, but especially for girls, because at this point they are more likely to receive messages, subtle and otherwise, that sometimes inhibit involvement. (1986, p. 59)

Allowing children some choice avoids forcing them into a sport they do not enjoy and may eventually quit because of lack of interest. Except for specialty sports such as gymnastics, swimming, and tennis, there is no evidence that early organized competitive sports are beneficial to the later development of the child, either as an athlete or as a person (Coakley 1986; Malina 1986; Passer 1986). It is more important that sports and games at this age be fun and free of the adult-imposed constraints that can have negative effects on the child's first sport experience (Bloom 1985; Martens et al. 1981; Orlick 1982). According to recent studies (Bloom 1985; Horn 1987), the child's earliest coach or instructor should be positive, friendly, and encouraging. Parents, relatives, siblings, and friends can offer support while introducing sports to children in the early years. If the child enjoys a certain sport and feels good about himself or herself, there will be plenty of time later on to concentrate on the sport and become more intensely involved.

A Summary

My experience as a coach, together with interviews with children aged eight to ten, reveal several things about children's preferences for and understanding of sport activities. Children at this age want to play a lot, have fun, and have a coach who is encouraging and who does things with them. Long, intensive activities aimed at developing athletic skills are not likely to be appreciated or understood by children at the 8- to 10-year-old level. Young athletes can work at learning new plays and skills, but the coach must be creative in how he or she introduces technical drills, should mix in fun, and should emphasize encouragement. Here are some guidelines for coaching 8- to 10-year-olds:

1. Allow players to share equal playing time.
2. Have players rotate positions to gain the perspective of other positions and to expand potential in each area.
3. Alternate practices and workouts with activities that are fun and also provide a workout. Take a hike, play tag or capture the flag, or go roller-skating in addition to practicing and playing the regular sport.
4. Involve the team in nonsport activities as a team (picnics, games, trips, and so forth) to promote a sense of community, but not necessarily in activities related to winning or championships.
5. Give every team member a responsibility (organizing equipment or videotape, keeping score, and so on) to promote a sense of belonging and accountability.
6. Mediate conflicts quickly and firmly with a minimum of shouting. Keep conflicts under control and think of ways they can be resolved educationally.
7. Mix in a bit of humor when introducing rules, technical drills, and concepts as a way of balancing the approach and keeping the players motivated and interested.
8. Use interesting ways to distribute playing time and positions evenly (deciding batting or running order by birthdays, last names, first names, and so forth).
9. Make no verbal comparisons between players. They can hurt children's feelings and their sense of self.
10. Think up creative ways to introduce sport skills.

Sports for 11- to 12-Year-Olds

At about 11 or 12 years of age children begin to adjust to the social and psychological demands of junior high school, and organized team sports take on a new dimension. Competition, selectivity, and winning become increasingly important in school and town teams, and this is often the first time competitive interscholastic sports are offered as part of the school curriculum. In many programs, children of lesser ability must share playing time with their more talented peers, so sports become a socially prized activity. Unfortunately, many youth programs become increasingly competitive and selective, and average athletes find it difficult to stay involved.

Participation in competitive team sports ideally encourages a group perspective whereby individual members contribute different ideas and talents for the benefit of the team as a whole. At age 11 or 12 children begin to understand the idea of collaboration, recognizing that their ideas, efforts, and performance affect the team (Beedy 1988). The cooperative modifications used with younger children are not as necessary at this level. The New Sport Experience Camp (NSEC) uses the following guidelines to structure the level of play for 11- to 12-year-olds.

Distribution of Playing Time and Positions

Because of athletes' increasing differences in size, ability, and interest, the coach needs to take a more active role in distributing positions. In some cases, safety takes priority. For example, at the NSEC the wide range in ability and strength among the 11- and 12-year-old baseball players meant that a couple of the 11-year-olds posed a danger in batting against their same-aged peers. To remedy the problem, I explained the need for two teams to the players. Although some were initially disappointed at being placed on the lower team (they all knew which team was which), they reported at the end of the season that they enjoyed the opportunity to play at their ability level.

Increase Intensity of Skill Instruction

Although skill instruction is important for the 8-to-10-year-olds, the emphasis is more on enjoyment because it is initially more important to strengthen interest and motivation than skill. If children are interested, they are more likely to stay with the sport as they get older, when they can begin to develop technical mastery. Children are also less likely to burn out later on. Longer attention spans and greater motivation to learn technical aspects of the game are found in 11- and 12-year-olds, and they can appreciate practice that focuses more on learning the correct way to perform a particular maneuver and less on simply having fun.

Leadership Responsibilities and Opportunities

Sports programs can begin to introduce the role of leadership and responsibility with children in the 11-to-12-year-old range. Players can help umpire and officiate games or organize practices. Leadership roles can provide players with a sense of pride and can improve understanding of how younger players think about sports. From a theoretical perspective, leadership responsibility encourages a collaborative understanding of being a part of the team. Better athletes, for example, can learn to sacrifice extra hitting practice to help younger players develop their skills, and research suggests that peer teaching actually helps both parties learn the task at hand. Umpiring games or coaching younger players gives young athletes an opportunity to explore activities that offer new and challenging rewards. For the less skilled player, it might be an opportunity to gain skill in a sport they might not otherwise have an opportunity to play at the junior high school level. Many 11- and 12-year-olds are not ready for these opportunities, however, or may not wish to be involved, and it is important that the coach be sensitive to this.

Important Considerations for All Ages: Appreciating That All Children Are Different

Athletic teams are made up of people with diverse styles, interests, skills, and backgrounds. Although all children pass through similar stages of development, they do so at different rates and with different styles and agendas, and coaches need to be cognizant of these individual differences. Not all players will be motivated by the coach's pep talk, for example; some, in fact, may be less motivated by such tactics (Martens et al. 1981). Some athletes do not like to talk about their problems and will feel threatened should the coach want to discuss personal issues. The point is that, although there are developmental similarities at certain ages in the way children organize their thinking, there are important differences as well. Coaches need to get to know their players individually.

Coaches often arrive at a practice or a game with their own agenda in mind. Who is going to play where? Will the new slalom poles arrive on time? Who will start in Saturday's game? But athletes also come with their own agendas, which may or may not coincide with those of their coaches. Coaches can address both performance and personal growth by being in tune with athletes' personal lives. Although not all athletes want to discuss their personal lives with their coaches, many enjoy knowing that the coach is there if needed and that he or she understands. Being aware and available is most important; the athletes can take care of the rest. The coach should also bear in mind that joining an organized sport team, entering puberty, and going off to college are important events in children's lives. These may involve emotions, friends, and interests outside the sports experience, but they can have a great influence on the athletes' performance on the team. Coaches of athletes experiencing these upheavals need to be sensitive to their thoughts and feelings, both on and off the court.

It is also helpful to be aware of individual differences and to know what attracts each person to the sport. Every coach needs to ask what each child's biggest concern is. Not to be embarrassed? To please his or her parents? To be popular? To get in shape? To have fun? To get a college scholarship? Understanding what attracts the child to sports will enable the coach to assist each athlete in reaching his or her goals, and with this kind of understanding and support, the child is more likely to develop a lifelong interest in sports.

SUMMARY

Sports represent an important lens through which young people view the world and begin to understand how people of different perspectives interact with one another and work toward common goals. Learning to work, play, and interact with others develops important lifetime skills and will help children in their future roles. Team sports provide coaches with opportunities to help children understand these values and relations as they interact with their peers. Sports not only help children develop; sports can also be a powerful means for addressing important childhood issues and for improving relationships. It is our responsibility as athletes, teachers, role models, and friends to make sure this is a valuable experience.

REFERENCES

Beedy, J. (1987). Children's conceptions of team sports: A socio-moral perspective. Unpublished qualifying paper, Graduate School of Education, Harvard University.

____. (1988). *Understanding the interpersonal world of youth sports*. Unpublished doctoral dissertation, Harvard University, Cambridge.

Bloom, B., ed. (1985). *Developing talent in young people*. New York: Ballantine Books.

Bredemeier, B. J., and D. L. Shields. (1987). Moral growth through physical activity: A structural/developmental approach. In *Advances in pediatric sports sciences*. Vol. 2, *Behavioral issues*, edited by D. Gould and M. R. Weiss. Champaign, Ill.: Human Kinetics Publishers, Inc.

Bredemeier, B. J., M. R. Weiss, D. L. Shields, and R. M. Schewchuk. Promoting moral growth in a summer camp. Unpublished manuscript.

Coakley, J. (1986). When should children begin competing? A sociological perspective. In *The 1984 olympic scientific congress proceedings*. Vol. 10, *Sport for children and youths*, edited by M. R. Weiss and D. Gould. Champaign, Ill.: Human Kinetics Publishers, Inc.

Damon, W. (1977). *The social world of the child*. San Francisco: Jossey-Bass.

DeVries, R. (1970). The development of role taking as reflected by the behavior of bright, average, and retarded children in a social guessing game. *Child Development* 41:759–70.

Flavell, J. H., C. Fry, J. Wright, and P. Javis. (1968). *The development of role-taking and communication skills in children*. New York: John Wiley.

Haan, N. (1977). A manual for interaction morality. Unpublished manuscript, University of California, Berkeley.

_____. (1978). Two moralities in action contexts: Relationships to thought, ego regulation, and development. *Journal of Personality and Social Psychology* 36: 286–305.

_____. (1987). Moral growth through physical activity: A structural/developmental approach. In *Advances in pediatric sport sciences*. Vol. 2, *Behavioral issues*, edited by D. Gould and M. R. Weiss. Champaign, Ill: Human Kinetics Publishers, Inc.

Haan, N., E. Aerts, and B. Cooper. (1985). *On moral grounds*. New York: University Press.

Halbert, J. A. (1986). When should children begin competing? A coach's perspective. In *The 1984 olympic scientific congress proceedings*. Vol. 10, *Sport for children and youths*, edited by M. R. Weiss and D. Gould. Champaign, Ill.: Human Kinetics Publishers, Inc.

Horn, T. S. (1987). The influence of teacher-coach behavior on the psychological development of children. In *Advances in pediatric sports sciences*. Vol. 2, *Behavioral issues*, edited by D. Gould and M. R. Weiss. Champaign, Ill.: Human Kinetics Publishers, Inc.

Johnson, D. W., and R. T. Johnson. (1974). Instructional goal structure: Cooperative, competitive, or individualistic. *Review of Educational Research* 44: 213–40.

Kohlberg, L. (1981). *The meaning and measurement of moral development*. Heinz Werner Lecture Series, Vol. 13. Worcester, Mass.: Clark University Press.

Malina, R. M. (1986). When should children begin competing? Readiness for competitive sport. In *The 1984 olympic scientific congress proceedings*. Vol. 10, *Sport for children and youths*, edited by M. R. Weiss and D. Gould. Champaign, Ill.: Human Kinetics Publishers, Inc.

Martens, R., R. W. Christina, J. S. Harvey, and B. J. Sharkey. (1981). *Coaching young athletes*. Champaign, Ill.: Human Kinetics Publishers, Inc.

Mead, G. H. (1934). *Mind, self, and society*. Chicago: University of Chicago Press.

Orlick, T. (1982). *Cooperative sports and games book*. New York: Pantheon Books.

Passer, M. W. (1986). When should children begin competing? A psychological perspective. In *The 1984 olympic scientific congress proceedings*. Vol. 10, *Sport for children and youths*, edited by M. R. Weiss and D. Gould. Champaign, Ill.: Human Kinetics Publishers, Inc.

Piaget, J. (1932). *The moral judgment of the child*. New York: The Free Press. Reprinted 1965.

Romance, T., M. Weiss, and J. Bockovan. (1986) A program to promote moral development through elementary school physical education. *Journal of Teachers of Physical Education* 5 (2): 126–36.

Sage, G. H. (1986). The effects of physical activity on the social development of children. In *Academy papers: The effects of physical activity on children*. Champaign, Ill.: Human Kinetics Publishers, Inc.

Selman, R. L. (1980). *The growth of interpersonal understanding: Developmental and clinical analyses*. New York: Academic Press.

Selman, R. L., and D. F. Byrne. (1974). A structural-developmental analysis of levels of role-taking in middle childhood. *Child Development* 45 (2): 803–6.

Selman, R. L., D. Lavin, E. Cooney, N. Jacobs, and S. Brion-Beisels. (1979). *Assessing interpersonal understanding.* Unpublished manuscript.

Sullivan, H. S. (1940). *Conceptions of modern psychiatry.* New York: W. W. Norton and Company, Inc.

____. (1953). *The interpersonal theory of psychiatry.* New York: W. W. Norton and Company, Inc.

Turiel, E. (1978). The development of concepts of social structure: A social convention. In *Development of social understanding,* edited by J. Glick and A. Clarke-Stewart. New York: Gardner Press.

____. (1983). Domains and categories in social-cognitive development. In *The relationship between social and cognitive development,* edited by W. F. Overton. Hillsdale, N. J.: Lawrence Erlbaum Associates.

Wiggins, D. K. (1987). A history of organized play and highly competitive sports for American children. In *Advances in pediatric sport sciences.* Vol. 2, *Behavioral issues,* edited by D. Gould and M. R. Weiss. Champaign, Ill: Human Kinetics Publishers, Inc.

Yeates, K. O., and R. Selman. (1989). Social competence in the schools: Toward an integrative developmental model for intervention. *Developmental Review* 9: 64–100.

III

MORAL EDUCATION
AND DEMOCRACY

9

The Adolescent as a Citizen

Ralph Mosher

A democratic high school in which adolescents have a serious role in governance and adjudication? What kind of quixotic oxymoron is that? For a comprehensive description and analysis of what we have learned from 15 years of applied research in three such democratic high schools, see Mosher, Kenny, and Garrod (under review). One of our findings is that there are prior questions. Just as it is premature to describe how to educate for democracy before having dealt with why public schools should do that, so too are democratic understandings and competencies inextricably tied to the broader cognitive, socio-moral, and political development of U.S. youth. This discussion will examine what we know generally about these developments in adolescents, especially as they bear on adolescents' ability to think and act democratically.

INTRODUCTION

Adolescence is often experienced by the young person and his parents and teachers as the worst of times. It is, however, one of the many paradoxes in coming of age that adolescence can be one of the best times in which to educate. Rowher has described it as a prime time for education. The reason is that fully abstract thought is for the first time possible. Piaget has described this critical transition and increment in human intelligence as the shift from reality-bound, concrete, "what you see is what is" thinking to that of formal operations. By this he means the intellectual capacity to deal with abstraction, to think about thinking and other things that never were or will be concrete, such as, the distributive principle, formal operations, love, justice, democracy, rights, responsibilities, one's self, identity (Who do I want to be in the future?), and so on.

We shall turn later to a detailed examination of the development of adolescents' political thinking. But first let us briefly illustrate concrete and abstract thinking in the political realm and the dramatic difference of understanding involved.

THE DEVELOPMENT OF MORAL REASONING

Concrete and Abstract Thinking

Children in the fifth grade at Sacajawea School in Portland, Oregon, were asked to define what the law is. Some of their answers follow:

> Law is a jail. Law is a court.
> The Law says: "Don't go through a red light and don't go through a stop sign."
> If you do not follow the Law, you can get put in jail by policemen. You can get bailed out by someone else.
> Law means to obey what people say and to obey our parents and to obey traffic signals.
> Law means that you cannot do something like skipping school. And skipping school is wrong.
> Law is two men in a black and white car with lights that make noise.
> They have a Law in basketball that if you hit someone's arm six times, you're fouled out!

By comparison, a group of teachers offered the following definitions of the law:

> Law is the set of rules by which we govern ourselves and which are subject to change as needed by society.
> A complex system of rules that maintain justice within a social system.
> A system of rules and regulations evolved to insure the rights of individuals and groups within society and to define the justice structure of that society.
> Law is a way of applying measures of safety, protecting human rights, and defining acceptable and appropriate behavior within a society at large.

The fifth graders' thinking is classically concrete — that is, it is limited to concrete objects (two men in a black and white car with lights that make noise) and situations (skipping school is wrong). Further, it is thought focused on the child's own perspective (if you hit somebody's arm six times, you're fouled out!) and limited to the here-and-now (skipping school, playing basketball, obeying a red light, and so forth). But that it is a partial understanding of the meaning of the law allowing only partial citizenship (for example, acting lawfully) to the children is also clear. Art Linkletter made a fortune out of adult laughter at kids "saying the darndest things." The important thing for their parents and teachers to understand is that children express themselves concretely not because of obtuseness or stubbornness but because of a pervasive concretism that characterizes their developing intelligence during the elementary school years. Unfortunately, however, many of the problems that people and society face are not concrete. So concrete thinking represents a transitional stage in human intelligence — although it may in fact be the predominant way of thinking for many adults as well.

For the teachers asked the same question as the fifth graders, abstraction was the order of the day. As noted, their thinking is expanded to ideas (justice, the rights of individuals, a complex system of rules, and the justice structure of society), to possibilities (insuring the rights of individuals and groups within society, or subject to change as needed by society), and to the perspective of others (defining acceptable and appropriate behavior as deemed important and necessary by the society at large). Being able to think in these ways enlarges one's ability to understand the law as well as to accommodate oneself to it (that is, to obey). That seems self-evident.

Formal operations is the highest stage of thinking in Piaget's study of the evolution of human intelligence. Theoretically achievable by everyone, it is in fact achieved by considerably fewer than half of U.S. adolescents and adults. The fortunate minority become capable of abstraction — the capacity for thinking about the many things that might be, could be, and should be in the adolescent's physical, social, and personal worlds. Reality, the concretism that preoccupies and bounds the thinking of younger children, begins to shift to the background, and possibility comes to the forefront — a more comprehensive, logically exhaustive, systematic, and abstract way of understanding. The formally operational adolescent can think about thoughts, words, ideas, and hypotheses, and she can do so with regard to a wide range of phenomena, from the physical world to real and ideal concepts of the self. The adolescent can consider, for example, weightlessness, the surface of the moon or Mars, or, in the personal realm, sexual intercourse, love and intimacy, who to be when she grows up, the values by which she will live, and so on.

Recall, however, that the fully developed formal operations stage is the exception, not the rule, among normal adolescents. Probably only one-fourth to one-third of U.S. high school students are capable of mature abstract thought. Troublesome sex differences in formal operations, in the sense that many more boys than girls evidence this capacity, are reported by Dulit (1979) although not by Piaget. Formal operations may not be commonplace or characteristic because it is not pervasively in demand, whereas concrete thinking is.

> In summary, then, fully developed formal stage thinking appears to be a kind of "cognitive maturity." It integrates all that has gone before. It is far from commonplace. . . . In that sense, it is more ideal than typical, more potential than actual . . . a potentiality only partially attained by most and fully attained by some. (Dulit 1979, p. 39)

Whether formal operations or scientific thought really constitutes humanity's crowning intellectual achievement is subject to sharp disagreement. Broughton has argued that Piaget confused the mathematical thinking practiced by the gnomes of Zurich or the scientific or high technological thought of Silicone Valley or Route 128 outside Boston with the highest form of human intelligence. For example, what about a Beethoven symphony or the Declaration of Independence? It seems to be stretching things to say that these master works are simply formal operations or scientific thought expressed in a different content.

Unquestionably, the intellectual capacity for abstract thinking is essential to success in much of the high school's program. And academic achievement is traditionally the first responsibility of good citizenship in secondary school. Yet as has been noted, there is substantial evidence that fewer than half of U.S. adolescents can think this way. This seems to be especially the case for many poor black and Hispanic adolescents in the cities. They may be streetwise beyond their years, but such practical intelligence is purchased at the price of the development of their abstract intelligence. As noted already, many — indeed, most — adolescent girls fail tests of formal operations. And, I suspect, working-class white adolescents do too.

Many of the adolescents we teach are unable to think abstractly. Their experience of trying to learn or comprehend algebra or the U.S. Constitution must be similar to the partial comprehension and total frustration that I, as a non-Italian speaker, would feel watching a John Wayne movie on Italian television with Italian voices dubbed in. The anxiety that many educators feel when presented with statistics may be a better analogy. Typically, the concretely operational adolescent really is trying to understand a foreign language and is being judged as personally worthy and as socially or economically useful (as a citizen) by how well he or she does. What's more, U.S. industry has concluded that the ability to think mathematically, scientifically and technically is the most valuable type of human competence or knowledge. As one black woman executive at a major corporation in Chicago told me,

What's really important in corporate culture is being able to say the right thing, mastery of the English language, social polish, and willingness to work. Skills aren't that important. Corporations select people who already are at these modes. If you don't look right and speak right, you don't fit in. But those who come in with these particular attitudes get reinforced, get ahead.

That is how one gets ahead. We admire certain kinds of intellect. Abstract, reflective, and critical thinking are three species that come quickly to mind. And many are excluded. Nor is it hard to infer what the effects would be of being unable to think this way on someone's motivation to go on trying in school.

Writing in *Social Education* (November/December 1985), David Matthews addresses the issue of "how to educate a socially responsible, civically competent person" (p. 679). He identifies at least four distinct approaches. The first is designed "to insure civic literacy — knowledge . . . about what governments do, how powers are divided among the branches, how legislatures work, how bills are passed. The result is usually a course called 'Civics' or 'American government'" (p. 679). A second approach to civic education has emphasized teaching values. A third approach emphasizes civic skills such as leadership. The fourth way to develop civic competence "may be the most influential of all, even though it is passive" (p. 679). Matthews describes this as

Civics by "indirectionists." . . . Indirectionists admit that there is such a thing as civic virtue but, like Socrates, they doubt that anyone is qualified to teach it. They place their faith in their subjects and in the efficacy of intellectual discipline itself. They argue . . . persuasively that the development of the mind, of the capacity to reason, is the best guarantor of any kind of competence, civic or otherwise. They approach the issue of civic competence indirectly, that is, through the mastery of a discipline. (p. 679)

The point is not an overview of approaches to civic education, although that is certainly pertinent. What is most germane to the argument here is that all four roads to Athens — in particular, civics by indirection — assume a capacity for formal operations on the part of the adolescent. As we have seen, that is simply not an assumption we can make about a majority of high schoolers.

ABSTRACT THINKING AND ADOLESCENCE

The emergence of abstract thought at adolescence also makes other ways of understanding and behaving possible — for example, moral understanding of right and wrong, good or bad, or personal and social understanding of one's self and of one's social and civic world. Adolescents whose growth is on target or normal are balanced between two very different views of morality and society. One is essentially selfish, the other social. Let us examine them briefly and then consider some of their consequences for the individual, for his academic and civic learning, and for society.

I will use moral understanding as a primary window for viewing, or as a way of illustrating, these two states of mind in adolescence. Its core is the meaning of right and wrong, what one's rights and obligations are, what one owes to oneself and others, and what is good and bad. Why moral understanding? I know it best. And as Pericles said, "Politics is character." Elsewhere I have talked about adolescent growth as a nine-fold helix (Mosher 1979). Adolescents come of age with regard to at least nine broad, interrelated human competencies: intellectual, moral, personal, social-civic, vocational, physical, spiritual, emotional, and aesthetic. Growth is more holistic than particularistic. Thus, in describing moral development in adolescence, we foreshadow other elements of growth.

STAGE-TWO THINKING

Me First or We First?

Piaget and, more particularly, Kohlberg have described (not very imaginatively, by the way) these two moralities that coexist uneasily or compete for the minds of teenagers as stages two and three. Stage-two thinking Kohlberg termed "instrumental hedonism and concrete reciprocity." Although it is most characteristic or typical of children in middle school, stage two is also readily recognizable as the basic ethic of many adult transactions. Consider the examples of the Bible salesman played by Ryan O'Neal in the motion picture *Paper Moon*, Ferdinand Marcos' looting of the Philippine treasury, the price increases of the Organization of Petroleum Exporting Countries oil cartel, or the role played by Michael Douglas in the movie *Wall Street*. These examples demonstrate the essential selfishness and manipulation characteristic of this view of right and wrong.

The adolescent's fundamental goal at stage two is to maximize his own gain or profit and to minimize his losses in any interaction with others. Greed, self-protectiveness, and opportunism are part of this way of thinking. That, combined with the hard core of self-interest, can make stage-two thinking decidedly unappealing in our teenagers or associates. Other people's rights or feelings matter very little except as factors to be manipulated in making the best deal for oneself. Pretty much anything is fair in love, war, or business so long as that person gets his way. Instrumental hedonism means that you do what is necessary to please yourself. The adolescent looks to maximize his own pleasure, gain, or advantage.

At the same time, the absence of any developed sense of obligation to other people or their rights or the idea that one's principal moral responsibility is to oneself, *numero uno*, is what gives stage-two thinking its fundamental appeal and power. It is "me first." A rash of recent popular books have argued essentially this point of view. What one does owe to others is understood in very concrete terms: You scratch my back and I'll scratch yours. You get what you give.

People at stage two in moral reasoning conform in order to be rewarded, have favors returned, and so forth. They go along in order to get something in return: tickets to a Led Zeppelin concert, a promotion or a pay rise, or a vicuña coat. My university dean, for instance, bragged with evident relish about dangling "eighty deals" before his faculty members in order to get the votes he needed on a critical policy matter. In my case, the price, the release of grant monies to appoint a research associate, was not right. On principle, my vote was not for sale. Had it been, at stage two, the price would have been much higher. But the point is clear — human relations are viewed in terms of the marketplace. Conformity, doing what others want, what teachers or public officials say is right, is for sale at stage two. Only the price has to be right for the deal to be cut.

STAGE-THREE THINKING

The competing views of right and wrong in the minds of teenagers is what Kohlberg described as stage three, the "good boy/good girl morality." The typical adolescent begins to think about right and wrong as people around him do. Almost literally, in others' words, his thinking becomes conventional. For the adolescent who thinks this way, what his or her friends regard as right and wrong assumes great force because to belong, to be accepted, one goes along loyally with the values and norms of the peer group. Parents can be painfully aware of this shift in their children's allegiance to friends. And if the company the teenager keeps is "bad," there are real vulnerabilities and victimizations. Other adults — for example, a favorite teacher or coach, a parent, or an old brother or sister — may be the source of the code of conduct. The adolescent wants the recognition and respect of other people; to be affirmed by them and to please them, he will try to be as much like them as possible.

The power for good of this identification is movingly described by a reporter (J. Foreman 1980) interviewing Jim Craig, Olympic ice hockey gold medalist in 1980:

The scene is etched in the hearts of millions of Americans who sat, that day in February, transfixed in front of their televisions in stunned delight: at the moment of greatest gold-medal glory, the camera zoomed in on the face of Jim Craig, the young goalie from Massachusetts, as he searched the crowd with his eyes, saying, "Where's my father?'

The father-and-son imagery of that moment was electric — a boy/man who not only still spoke to his father but actually wanted to share his own highest moment with him.

Foreman tells us that Jim's father, Don Craig, made their children the center of his life even when his wife was alive. He adds:

> Even then, the center of his being, like his wife's, was the children. The mere suggestion that life might, for other people, hold other priorities seems to strike him as simply untrue to his experience, idiotic, unthinkable. His answer is short and to the point: "What else is there?"
>
> Jim echoes that simplicity of feeling: "It's not a big, complex thing. Just two little words which mean a lot. Love and respect."

In essence, it is across this bridge of love and respect that the highly self-centered individual at stage two becomes a social being, a citizen, and joins the human race. Uncertainty about sexuality and about who one is or will become plus a need to be connected to others are part of the shift. Selman says that another aspect of growth makes the moral transition possible — the ability to see the world through the eyes of another means that one has matured. And it is clear for the stage-three adolescent that who matters has changed dramatically from the "me-firstism" of stage-two thinking. There is now a very concrete sense of "we": the "Point kids," "jocks," "greasers," and so on. The viewpoint of what is right and wrong and of what obligations the individual has is finely tuned to what his or her particular group believes.

Kohlberg says of stage-three thinking, good behavior is that which pleases or helps others and is approved by them. There is much conformity to stereotypical images of what is majority or natural behavior. Behavior is often judged by intention; "he means well" becomes important for the first time and is overused. One seeks approval by being nice.

Most parents and teachers regard stage-three moral thinking as a great leap forward from stage-two me-firstism. And it is. But before concluding that the aim of citizenship education with adolescents is to promote this stage-three, "we first," social understanding and to educate for conventional morality, good sons and daughters, team players, friends, citizens, or workers, we need to add a bit more to our picture of the two predominant mindsets of adolescents.

STAGE-FOUR THINKING

A more mature stage of moral understanding (Kohlberg's stage four) is within reach of some adolescents. Let me introduce it briefly with a personal anecdote about adolescence and the law that demonstrates why moral judgment and action are not one and the same. My oldest daughter, then 16, was driving me across town. She ran a traffic light, which changed from yellow to red when we were in the intersection. I pointed that out to her. She replied, "I'm sorry, but everyone does it." In best (or worst) "heavy" father tone, I said that that was no excuse for her to do so. Again, the reply was, "But I see people doing it every day" (which, in Massachusetts, is true). Three minutes later she failed to stop at a stop sign. I blew up. Her reply was, "But I could see in both directions and there were no cars." I said (in strained tones, I'm sure), "We'll talk later."

We did. I said to Rebecca that I had considered her a responsible driver; my experience had been that she was very careful. For that reason, I had trusted her to drive friends for a month in winter to a hospital internship that had involved a 40-mile round trip over icy roads each day. Thus I was taken aback by the two traffic violations in the space of a few minutes, and I felt she had let down both herself and me. Rebecca argued that she was tired and was not paying attention as well as she should have or as she did during the daily round trip to the hospital. She insisted that the light was yellow and did not turn red until she was virtually through the intersection. Further, she was worried about slamming on the brakes and being hit by the car behind us. She said she simply did not see the stop sign — it was on a dark, infrequently traveled street. Finally, she said that I was overreacting, at least slightly.

I pointed out that, had a police car been present, the reaction probably would not have been slight. Indeed, I considered it likely that she would have been ticketed and charged with a loss of points. She thought that the police did not care about such violations, for she saw them take place every day and no police enforcement followed. I pointed out that laws depended on individual drivers, not the police, for their observance and enforcement — that when the police were not present, there was a special need for drivers to obey traffic laws. Otherwise, the safety of everyone — drivers and pedestrians — was imperiled. This she termed my idealism. I also expressed my concern for her life (and that of her friends) and noted that accidents can happen as often near home, on infrequently traveled side streets, as they can going to work, Monday through Friday. The point is that we talked. My stage-two arguments — "you'll be fined" — she rejected as unlikely: "Everyone does it and gets away with it." The police do not seem to care; implicitly, why should she? My stage-four arguments — that laws depend upon responsible drivers, not the police, for their observance and that when the police are not present, every driver has a special obligation to contribute to public safety and to orderly driving — she regarded as lofty idealism. But my stage-three arguments about personal trust she heard and responded to. In retrospect, I think I should have made that theme clearer: my trust in her maturity and responsibility as a good driver had been the basis on which I had allowed her to make the daily trip to the hospital.

The point of this anecdote is not so much to illustrate how natural moral discussions with adolescents may occur. Rather, it is to introduce Kohlberg's stage four in moral thought. Variously referred to as a law-and-order or social-system-and-conscience conception of morality, it is the highest or most complex form of moral thinking we are likely to encounter or can realistically expect from our children or teenagers. Indeed, most adults, at their best, will only partially articulate this legal point of view. Thus getting children and especially adolescents to a beginning understanding and use of stage-four thinking is a goal and benchmark of civic education in the values and moral cognitions that underlie democratic thinking and action.

Remember that at stage three the person takes his or her cues as to what is right from spouse, family, and friends. But at stage four one's thinking about who and what may be right has expanded significantly in outlook and perspective. Now the person is concerned about how the various groups in his or her society define right and wrong and how the law incorporates a common view. Or if the perspective is still personalized (shades of stage three), what does the president, the Supreme Court, the senior senator, or the cardinal say about desegregated public housing, busing, or AIDS victims, for example? A generalized social view of right and wrong, as expressed in civil, criminal, religious, medical, military, or other codes, becomes central to the individual's thinking and behavior about what is right and wrong.

In this framework, the reason for obeying the law is that rules have the purpose of holding one's society together, of giving it solidity and cohesion. Order is a very important value. Norms are the cement that establish what is kosher and what is not; what is allowable, proper, and fair and what is not; and who, by maintaining the laws, has full privileges and rights as a citizen. Laws and their equal application give a predictability, an order, and a fairness to social, economic, and political interactions. Rules require people to cooperate, which they must do if society is to survive and the trains are to run on time.

For example, steel-belted radial tires are warranted to go 30,000 miles and not to blow out at 5,000. The law can and does require manufacturers to replace defective tires. Warranties as well as payment are part of the mutual obligation between buyer and seller and must have force. Similarly, the obligations (for example, paying taxes or registering for the draft) that go with the general benefits of membership in a society are made binding on all through enactment into law. They then must be respected. Basic security for the individual, his property, and his civil rights are embedded in a set of laws guaranteeing the same rights, obligations, and treatment for all citizens. Only if everyone is mutually bound by a law can it genuinely protect my rights. And punishment is necessary to enforce the law. The alternative is disorder, inequity, an à la carte society in which people pick and choose which laws they will obey.

Now this is a pretty sophisticated understanding of the reasons for laws. That is why so few children, adolescents, or adults fully get hold of it. Again, getting high school students to at least a beginning comprehension of the rule of law is a criterion of the civic education we pursue. Let us next look at an example of adolescent moral understanding within the school setting.

POLITICS CAN BE CHARACTER: ISSUES IN SCHOOL GOVERNANCE

How moral reasoning may be engaged in school governance was illustrated in a remarkable town meeting debate I listened to at Brookline High School on November 7, 1984. The proximity to Veterans' Day was an unintended coincidence. A social studies teacher raised the issue of whether Brookline High School should participate in a national scholarship competition supported by the Veterans of Foreign Wars (VFW) that was restricted to U.S. citizens. Her point, not immediately clear to the group, was that the competition discriminated against the 10 percent to 15 percent of Brookline High School students who are foreign born and not, as yet, U.S. citizens. The student chairman initially limited discussion to five speakers, then to ten, then accepted a motion from the head-master that the town meeting of Brookline High School write a letter to the VFW asking that the citizenship clause be deleted in future years and stating Brookline High School's intention not to participate if a citizenship test were to be continued. The effect of the motion was not to penalize current applicants but to request clarification and a policy change from the VFW and to take a moral stand in the future in opposition to any citizenship test.

A seriously physically handicapped student then made a very moving speech in support of the proposal, reporting his nomination by the headmaster for a special summer camp awarded by the VFW, the withdrawal of the award by the VFW when it learned of his disability, and the boy's feeling of outrage and belittlement. A second student spoke in support of the proposal. The social studies teacher, obviously dissatisfied, asserted that the motion and the group were failing to address the immediate and profound issue of discrimination against the approximately 15 percent of the Brookline High School students who are foreign born and not, as yet, U.S. citizens. Her position was for an immediate boycott of the contest by Brookline High School on the ethical principle of opposition to discrimination. Another student asserted that this would penalize many applicants who badly needed the financial aid.

The handicapped student spoke again, this time in support of the stronger motion. He said the United States was founded by people who stood up for their rights, that some people may have to be inconvenienced in order to make a point, and that something may have to be sacrificed for a principle. Yet another student argued that U.S. citizens are specially privileged and that they take a better life for granted, enjoying the best economy and best sense of moving forward. By accepting a contest that discriminates, he said, we do a disservice to the bounty and sense of fair play in the United States. He personally would not feel right about taking money not available to all students. The question was called, and the straw vote on the headmaster's motion was defeated 20 to 14.

According to the rules of town meeting, three speakers for the minority position (in this case those favoring the headmaster's motion) and two for the majority position argued that to shut off scholarship eligibility for everyone was wrong, that this would infringe on the equal rights of both the majority and the individual, that the town meeting needed to know whether the stipulation was because of malicious intent or a policy not considered by the VFW, and that private groups and institutions have the right to stipulate the criteria for scholarship awards as long as they do not violate the Bill of Rights (for example, limiting scholarship awards to students of Brookline High School only).

Two speakers supporting the headmaster's motion pointed out that the Daughters of the American Revolution had been quick to change a similar clause in its scholarship policy. The headmaster said that Brookline High School has, as a community, a powerful moral voice, that the VFW is not a private institution, and that there is no citizenship test for joining the military. He added that he had never felt better about being on the losing side of a vote; indeed, the response of the students was the most encouraging moment of his five years at the school, and "everyone should remember that to discriminate against one is to discriminate against all." The final vote was 26 opposed, 8 in favor; the motion was defeated.

This is a report of who said what to the best of one participant-observer's notes and recollection. The precise form or order of the arguments is not the point. What is clear is that *democratic school governance does touch naturally on some of the many moral issues that confront students and teachers daily* and that the discussion and, I submit, the *action* on such matters (and not their particular resolution) are what is critical to the moral development of students and the community.

But let us return to the town meeting a week later. The commander of the Brookline VFW post spoke to the town meeting upon its invitation. He pointed out that the prior vote of the town meeting had the effect of denying 90 percent of the students the opportunity to win a $14,000 scholarship. He asked the town meeting to reconsider its vote, saying that "foreign nationals one day will become citizens, or their brothers and sisters will, and be eligible to win the scholarship." He did not see the VFW as discriminatory and expressed the concern that "someone may win the scholarship and not stay in the country. It boils down to that."

A student asked what kind of effect a letter to the VFW might have:

Student: You spoke to the national headquarters and couldn't budge them.

VFW Commander: It's a step in the right direction. They'll certainly consider a letter.

Student: Can the VFW give this contest and not go through the school?

VFW Commander: Yes, but we'd rather go through the school.

Student: It's a fact that 10 percent of our students are not citizens. And I gather it has happened that people have taken the test and gone abroad to hurt the nation. Do we take the greater chance of hurting someone in the 90 percent who might win or hurting someone in the 10 percent by excluding them? I don't hear that the VFW is singling out BHS. If the VFW has no problem with their policy that the scholarship winner should remain in America, why should we?

Student: My pledge to the United States is more moving because it is to one nation, indivisible, with liberty ad justice for *all*. The rights of all should not be denied to some. It's not true that this policy discriminates against only 10 percent; it discriminates against all.

Student: We're dealing with a lot of "what ifs" here. We shouldn't divide Brookline High School into 90 percent citizens, 10 percent noncitizens. If 10 percent are excluded, we all should boycott the contest.

Student: The issue is drawing arbitrary moral lines between 90 percent and 10 percent of the students. There's no law broken here. Foreign citizens are subject to different laws than American citizens. It's a moral law that matters here.

Student: A lot of kids need the money, a chance to get that scholarship. Some of our seniors don't have enough money. There are other contests for the excluded kids.

Student: The VFW says, "All youth should partake in an essay on the benefits of America," yet they exclude non-Americans. A person is a person and should have equal rights to compete. Someone of another country may be more apt to appreciate our government and country. Immigrants, by immigrating, are acting on their views about America.

VFW Commander: The members of the VFW have given dearly and believe in giving to their own whether right or wrong.

Student: The 10 percent shouldn't be looked at. We shouldn't boycott the contest on their behalf. We should make our feeling well known, contact other schools and encourage them to write letters to the VFW. But if we boycott, a lot of people who need scholarship money are hurt.

VFW Commander: Non–United States citizens can serve in our armed forces. My great-great-grandfather got off the boat in New York and put on a blue uniform. That's how he became a citizen.

Student: It's unfortunate that money has to come into it. It would be easier to decide if it wasn't such a large scholarship.

Student: By Mr. S [the VFW commander] coming, it shows that the Veterans of Foreign Wars have heard us. They care about us; they came to value our belief. And all scholarships discriminate in some way, even those at Brookline High School. Scholarships for black students, Italo-American students, and so on. And isn't it a freedom of Americans to leave the country, the right to travel?

Student (minority, black American): There are only three major scholarships at Brookline for which I could apply. This is one of them; it's very broad. Most of our scholarships are highly restrictive.

Student (immigrant, Chinese): As an immigrant, this discussion has really made me feel like a member of the school, of the country. I haven't heard any persuasive, clear reasons for us being excluded. It's not easier for us now in America than it was for other immigrants before us.

VFW Commander: I'm grateful that you see the scholarship as being very broad. It's unfortunate that it restricts. If you work on this, perhaps the VFW will change, for example, to include legal residents.

Student (physically handicapped): I move we let the original motion (that Brookline High School not participate so long as a citizenship test is continued) stand.

The motion was seconded and passed, with 25 in favor of letting the motion stand, 13 opposed, and 2 abstaining.

As Pericles said, "Politics is [or can be] character." Issues in school governance that may not be formally understood by all as moral, nonetheless are. And when they occur in such a natural way and lead to actions affecting the quality of life in the school, I believe they are especially powerful. How they arise spontaneously in the governance of a large high school, how they stimulate debate (in which several stages of moral reasoning interact and in that way gradually prompt the adoption of higher stage thinking by more students), and how students may, in fact, construe the issues in more complex terms than VFW commanders are illustrated. Some readers may question whether elite student leaders, to whom all Ivy League scholarship doors may be open, are taking the moral high ground at the expense of a needy majority. But the principles at issue are clearly engaged and operative: that where one is discriminated against, all are; that a concept of justice is needed to correct a utilitarian view of the greatest good for the greatest number; and that the majority in a democracy is obligated to go the extra mile to protect the interests and rights of disenfranchised or dispossessed minorities. These are not hypothetical dilemmas. Rather, the debate is about real, imminent dilemmas, and the decisions lead to actions affecting the school. It is here that civic education, defined as the teaching of values, and the democratic governance of the school make common cause.

THE IMPORTANCE OF THE SOCIAL GROUP IN ADOLESCENCE

A rising tide of cognitive development in adolescence lifts many boats. George Mead believed that social reasoning — that is, how we understand others such as family, friends, peers, and institutions in relation to ourselves — is the core of human intelligence. Asserting what particular knowledge is of most worth to the person is a gutsy stance. Yet how the individual understands and relates to the purposes and activities of her social group seems key to civic literacy and civic skills. Several theorists, among them Loevinger, Erikson, and Selman, offer useful insights into this domain of adolescent thinking and, in particular, its potential for a strong antidemocratic undertow.

THEORETICAL VIEWS

Probably the most contemporary and scientific theory of ego development is that advanced by Jane Loevinger. Her research tells us much about how the adolescent's character and social and interpersonal thinking develop. The personal points of view of the thousands of adolescents she has studied, their egos or selves, plus the meanings they make of their social world have much in common with their moral perspectives.

For example, Loevinger (1979) describes one of the ego lenses of adolescence as the self-protective stage:

> Self-control is fragile, and there is a corresponding vulnerability and guardedness, hence we term the stage Self-Protective. The person at this stage understands that there are rules. . . . His main rule is, however, "Don't get caught." . . . He uses rules for his own satisfaction and advantage. . . . The Self-Protective person has the notion of blame, but he externalizes it to other people or to circumstances. Somebody "gets into trouble" because he runs around with the "wrong people." Self-criticism is not characteristic. . . . Getting caught defines an action as wrong. . . . An older child or adult who remains here may become opportunistic, deceptive, and preoccupied with control and advantage in his relations with other people. For such a person, life is a zero-sum game; what one person gains, someone else has to lose. There is more or less opportunistic hedonism. Work is perceived as onerous. The good life is the easy life with lots of money and nice things. (p. 113)

Loevinger's description reminds us of adolescents we have known, maybe even were. Certainly its moral perspective sounds very much like Kohlberg's stage two, particularly in the description of people, who, lacking trust, take the malignant version of the self-protective course — that is, opportunism, exploitativeness, deception, and ridicule of others. Perhaps that is one route to a more or less permanent identification with the aggressor.

Probably an equal number of adolescents are at the next, conformist, stage of ego development. These adolescents typically conform to external rules and express shame or guilt for breaking them. In their social and dating world, they are concerned about belonging and about being approved and validated by peers, and they display a superficial niceness to friends. Classically other-directed, they are consciously preoccupied with their appearance ("she's so stuck-up, she thinks she's so pretty"), social acceptance ("she says, 'Jeff only dates her because he couldn't get me'"), and with what adults often consider banal feelings and behavior (such as endless telephone discussions concerning friends of both sexes, buying and listening to rock music or videos, going to rock concerts, sports, and so on). The conformist adolescent tends, conceptually, to simplifications. He uses many stereotypes about adolescents different from himself ("he hangs around with rich snobs from Chestnut Hill"; "they're jocks, they only drink milk") and clichés ("that's cool," "you know," "blow it off").

The adolescent understanding himself and his social world through the conformist lens recognizes group differences but not individual differences. There are "nerds," "freaks," "jocks," "greasers," "animals," freshmen, or seniors at Brookline High School. Or there are blacks, Jews, or "Point kids" (Irish Catholics). At a select Ivy League college, a junior referred casually to "the Eurofags who have the best-looking women at their parties." ("Eurofags," I learned, were the graduates of exclusive preparatory high schools in Europe with affected British accents.) Within these groups everyone is considered to be the same. And the only kids the conformist adolescent really likes and trusts are those like himself, other jocks, freaks, JAPs, and so on. It's my social world and welcome to it, but no out-groupers: no Irish, blacks, or nerds need apply.

Loevinger's conformist stage of ego development is, as she says, a momentous step forward because the adolescent for the first time identifies his own welfare with that of the group. But it is also clear that the conforming adolescent understands his society in a very narrow, exclusive — one might say, tribal — sense. If understanding one's self in relation to others is, as Mead said, the core of human intelligence, the other-directed adolescent has taken a momentous, but only a first, step. His social and civic education still has miles to go before Main Street can sleep peacefully.

One other developmental theorist adds importantly to our understanding of the tension and conflict within and between adolescents that results from these two broad ways of understanding being. He is Erik Erikson, the man who gave U.S. adolescents an identity crisis. And it is important to mention his work with that of the modern cognitive developmentalists such as Piaget, Kohlberg, and Loevinger, since adolescence is not solely a state of mind. Or if it is, its equilibrium is subject to strong and various perturbations: the buffeting, even anarchy, of sexual drives and such powerful emotions as anger, lust, intolerance, a need to be free, and anxiety about the future. The emotional volatility of adolescence is well-chronicled and stereotyped, and educators and parents attempt to deal with it in the most effective ways possible. And yet this emotional, existential intensity of adolescence is not captured in the otherwise extremely valuable descriptions of formal operations, Kohlberg's stage three, or even Loevinger's self-protective stage. Erikson does focus on the emotions, the ambivalence of a time when

> Deep down you are not quite sure that you are a man (or a woman), that you will ever grow together again and be attractive, that you will be able to master your drives, that you really know who you are . . . that you know what you want to be, that you know what you look like to others and that you will know how to make the right decisions without, once and for all, committing yourself to the wrong friend, sexual partner, leader or career. (Erikson [1959] 1979, p. 93)

Erikson also is describing the unconscious side of adolescent development or, to state it more accurately, the interrelationship between adolescent thinking about school problems, morality, work, the self and the impelling demands of one's body, genitals, and feelings. That these many strands of the developmental helix interact dynamically and holistically is evident in the disequilibrium of adolescents' lives. Only Erikson has discussed the effect of the unconscious drama on the developmental stages. For example, Erikson explains many of the adolescent behaviors described by Loevinger or by Kohlberg as conventional or stage three as an unconscious defense:

> They [adolescents] become remarkably clannish, intolerant and cruel in their exclusion of others who are "different," in skin color or culture or background, in tastes and gifts, and often in entirely petty aspects of dress and gesture arbitrarily selected as the signs of an ingrouper or outgrouper. It is important to understand (which does not mean condone or participate in) such intolerance as the necessary defense against a sense of identity diffusion, which is unavoidable at . . . [this] time of life. (Erikson [1959] 1979, p. 92)

What Erikson is saying is that even if you do not know who you are or whether you will ever get it together, you can be damn sure who you are not: a freak, an animal, a doper, or a greaser. And you will feel better about yourself: If I am in trouble, they really are bad news. Erikson is describing both the new barbarian — the violent or the totalitarian character that this stage can take on — and the adolescent unconscious and emotional part of its explanation.

Efforts to educate adolescents to be democratic by having them govern their own schools or participate in social and political action in their communities might be expected to encounter heavy turbulence because of such largely unconscious resistance and unreadiness on the part of many teenagers. According to Erikson:

Democracy in a country like America poses special problems in that it insists on *self-made identities* ready to grasp many chances and ready to adjust to changing necessities of booms and busts, of peace and war, of migration and determined sedentary life. Our democracy, furthermore, must present the adolescent with ideals which can be shared by youths of many backgrounds and which emphasize autonomy in the form of independence and initiative in the form of enterprise. These promises, in turn, are not easy to fulfill in increasingly complex and centralized systems of economic and political organization. . . . This is hard on many young Americans because their whole upbringing, and therefore the development of a healthy personality, depends on a certain degree of choice, a certain hope for an individual chance and a certain conviction in freedom of self-determination. (Erikson [1959] 1979, p. 93)

These words, especially about intolerance, were written 30 years ago. Yet they are prophetic of the white-black youth violence of Jones Beach or of Palestinian 15-year-olds in Gaza and on the West Bank throwing rocks at Israeli soldiers slightly older than themselves who, in their turn, enforce law and order with tear gas, beatings, and live ammunition. Adolescents are often the shock troops of political change (as in South Africa, Northern Ireland, or Iran). Whether they are ideologues, cruelly violent (consider the "necklaces" of Soweto or the broken kneecaps of Londonderry), fascist and racist (like the Ku Klux Klan), freedom riders in the bus stations of Montgomery with eyes on the prize, or Samantha Smith in a child's crusade for peace depends enormously on the civic participation models offered them by the adult society.

PRACTICAL EXPERIENCE: A SCHOOL CONFRONTS RACISM

Rock throwing, tear gas, youth violence, and police brutality in Seoul or Gaza; days of rage in Chicago; or racial fights on the playing fields of Brookline High School come with the territory of adolescence. What adult society does in response is critical. That simply reasoning together can offer a partial alternative was illustrated in a town meeting of December 8, 1985. The meeting had been announced as "a discussion about racism and the treatment of minorities at Brookline High School. Everyone is welcome to attend and to speak. Please come with specific ideas about what can be done to improve the situation." The town meeting moderator opened the session straightforwardly by saying that the only agenda was "first, the treatment of minorities at Brookline High School, the opportunity for any and all to air their thoughts and feelings about this problem; second, to address how we can be better."

Student: I'm very shocked and aghast by this happening. The way we treat minorities is coming back to a time when people are not safe because of racial difficulties. But I honestly don't know how to deal with it; I just feel strongly that we must avoid the barbarians taking over.

Student: I'm raising a point of information. Apparently there have been major incidents; will someone please describe them?

Student: Someone in Mr. L's class said, "If I have to work much harder I'll feel like a slave; all I need is a black face." And outside the Distributive Education store there was a sign "Niggers Suck."

Student: I'm a new student at Brookline High School. I just moved here from Arizona to what I thought was a very ideal, open, caring community. I was very shocked by these incidents.

Student: The real problem is that there is a lot of separation between blacks and whites in this school. It's not intentional. We need to create more interracial opportunities. For example, I'm a Jewish kid who spends much of his time in drama club. I don't meet blacks there. We need a structure where people can get to know one another better.

Student: My feeling is that the overall community is very positive, that Brookline High School is great. Incidents like these occur. A sign like that is horrible. But I think there is a very good feeling toward all groups in the school. Most people are not like this.

Student (minority): I want to say that the general feeling among minorities is one of a complete sense of anger. There was a fight too. The Black Students Association is trying to cool fights. But we feel slapped in the face.

Student: I've been at Brookline High School four years. In that time I've done little mixing and have few black friends. In the past two years there is a group of people who are mixing. Why is it that there are so few blacks and Hispanics in my classes?

Student: I'm shocked at what has happened here at Brookline High School. I feel this body needs to do something. Have there been any further developments?

Teacher: We still don't know who's responsible for the sign.

Headmaster: An individual student has offered us assistance in identifying the responsible person.

Student: Clearly something has to be done. But we can't generalize that Brookline High School is racist. Whether we're talking about one kid or ten kids, it's still a very small percentage. The headmaster has announced: "If we catch those students responsible, they're out of school." I agree, but no one will turn them in. By stating the penalty ahead, we blew the chance of the person giving himself up.

Headmaster: We've had several offers of assistance from students. We're relying on the schoolwide assembly, this meeting, and good citizenship to help. And we've had several offers to identify those responsible.

Student: As younger kids we thought of Brookline High School as a scary place. But I've seen very little tension since coming here. Why are we experiencing tension now? As a partial solution, how can we have this discussion at the classroom level throughout the school?

Student: If there is a problem and tension is felt, the way both the minority and the majority conduct themselves is critical. You should say you're upset, not angry, and cool it. Like at the dance following Friday night's game a lot of black kids not at Brookline High School came — there was pushing and a mugging. But I understand how everyone is feeling.

Student: I favor immediate expulsion for anyone doing these things. And I oppose violent retaliation by any group.

Student: Innocent kids feel a fear that they'll be beaten up by friends of the kids who put the sign up. The thought crossed my mind: take the sign down; it's against black kids and myself. But I felt fear. We have to attack a problem such as this as a group.

Student: Perhaps we can't all be buddies. But every group should be secure and not discriminated against. [The headmaster's] speech was excellent: anyone who is a racist will be expelled. Yet there is always a minority who will be racist. We can't stamp out racism per se, but we can say it won't be tolerated. I thought we were heading toward a better and brighter future, but I'm appalled by this.

Student: Once before we took a day off and addressed the issue of racism. And I believe we are troubled by a small minority.

Student: I want to say it wasn't just black kids retaliating.

Student: Rather than talk about specific incidents, we need to create a climate, a day of dialogue, as we did about South Africa and as we celebrated Martin Luther King Day. That made me, at least, feel great. I felt racial unity.

Student: Why did this happen? When we came to Brookline High School, there were a lot of separate groups. I see a lot more mixture now. The incidents may have been a reaction to that mixing. But why did this happen?

A House Teacher: I'd like to support the suggestion that we plan an educational session that will reach the entire student body. A special day or a series of sessions in which we stop the usual business of school and focus on racism.

Student: When at first I heard about these incidents, I felt angry. The headmaster also felt angry. But if we pound some kid, he'll still be prejudiced! How do you get rid of prejudice? How do you get rid of ignorance? It took events like this to make me see there are racial problems. How to get rid of prejudice first? Then get rid of one or two kids.

Student: I've been in Metco [a voluntary program busing black students from Boston to cooperating school systems] since the fourth grade. Sometimes I'd be the only black kid in class. Prejudice comes from the parents. I know some black girls have been getting a lot of hassles, and we're proposing a teacher's day for racism in the public schools. Racism is not just something which is a high school problem; it's a town problem!

(applause)

Student: If we attack a minority then we can attack majorities. It gets worse and worse, builds up steam.

Student: I think what has been expressed is admirable. Now we need, at minimum, a formal proposal for an extended homeroom schoolwide or a day of dialogue.

Student: I favor taking positive action. But I hope in so doing we don't restrict the freedom of speech of anyone.

Teacher: Saying "Niggers Suck" is like crying "Fire" in a crowded theater when there's no fire. The issue isn't free speech.

Student: But racism is a lot deeper. We can't solve it by a meeting, we have to speak personally to those students who are racist.

Student: And we need to make attendance mandatory. The people who are here aren't the ones we really want to be here.

Student: I attended a Jewish day school and was excited to come to Brookline High School. I went out of my way to make friends with all different people. The greatest thing about Brookline High School is the diversity here: Jews, Christians, blacks. It is important that we are buddies, that we reach out and take other people by the hand, that we be friends.

The town meeting moderator called for practical proposals.

Student: I propose an extended homeroom discussion of racism. The town meeting moderator and a committee of the whole are to prepare a specific plan and agenda for the homeroom discussions. A keynote speaker should be considered.

Teacher: I propose a standing committee with one member of every academic department and house and one representative from every minority group. The committee will have two functions: to honor and celebrate minorities — for example, Martin Luther King day, Polish Independence day, Saint Patrick's day; and to monitor the school's racial climate and to air and discuss racial grievances. White kids at BHS are not aware of prejudice; black kids are saying, "We have felt it more." We don't hear one another; all parties need to talk about how we feel.

Headmaster: I want to say that Brookline High School confronts problems. Town meeting can be proud of today's initiative. Most institutions in this country do not confront racism, sexism. You should feel very proud.

Student (minority): We need action right now. There is a lot of tension between black kids and Point kids [housing projects, working-class white section of Brookline].

Town meeting moderator: Do you have a specific proposal to make?

Student (minority): That the administration take action.

Headmaster: I want to say that the administration has taken strong, unequivocal action right along. This special town meeting is part of the action. I'm concerned about the belief that the administration hasn't taken action. Those students involved in violent incidents have been suspended. The area where the graffiti appeared has been rigorously patrolled. There has been a general assembly of all students and teachers.

Teacher (minority): I agree that the administration is doing everything it can possibly do. The black students want a little bit more communication from the administration. This meeting is not as open as it could be — too organized, too procedural. I suggest we hold a second general meeting next week to continue the discussion we've begun today.

The allotted time being used up, the town meeting moderator called for a continuation of discussion and the submission of concrete proposals for the following week.

In my participant-observer notes at the end of this special meeting are two comments: "White guilt; black anger — the wells of both seem full to overflowing" and "The process of democracy is sometimes indistinguishable from the process of frustration." Like the black teacher, I was struck by the short-term potential for the formal, procedural, stage-four process of democracy to refract the anger and frustration of the black and other minority students present. The reader may see classic liberal talk on the part of the white majority — put crudely, sitting on the edge of the bed talking about how great it is going to be. Perhaps the differences were those of developmental level and class (and I am sensitive to the racism or classism implicit in the very terms) in the contrast between Why does the administration not take decisive action (that is, stop racism now) by an exercise of power and sanctions? and the wimpy proposal for a standing committee to celebrate minorities and to act as a forum in which to air racial grievances.

Depending on whether one sees democracy as half-empty or half-full, the town meeting was either an arid debating forum removed from the "Niggers Suck" reality of racial incidents, where upper-class white kids can wring (and wash) their hands publicly and piously about the racism of their working-class and black peers; or it is one context in which genuinely concerned representative students, teachers, and administrators can struggle with the real nature and complexity of racial and other prejudice, its obduracy, and what various constituencies in a high school (including the traditional power structure, the administration) can and cannot do to ameliorate the situation. Recall Dewey's "faith in human intelligence and in the power of pooled and cooperative experience [which], . . . if given a show, . . . will grow and be able to generate progressively the knowledge and wisdom needed to guide collective action" (Dewey 1968, p. 59). That is the essential bet that the democratic educator makes. The social and political learnings can show how cooperation makes the wager even worth taking.

Racism, after all, is a congenital defect with which the Constitution was born. It is an issue that vexed the nation's founders in Philadelphia. Myrdahl has called it "the American Dilemma"; Allport insightfully analyzed the psychology of it nearly a half century ago. It has martyred Martin Luther King and John F. Kennedy. Nevertheless, U.S. society (as documented in the Public Broadcasting Service's *Eyes on the Prize* series) has made discernible racial progress politically and socially, if not economically. Brookline High School and "Niggers Suck," in one sense, is a pale carbon copy of Birmingham, Alabama, and these students sound politically trite in comparison with the freedom riders of the prior generation who faced mobs screaming "kill the niggers," beatings, and arrest to "arouse the conscience of the community over injustice." But the opportunity and the structures to confront real injustice, to act to right it, and to be good citizens are as immanent, we contend, in the everyday, trivial events and interactions of Brookline High School in 1985 as in the large, sweeping events in Philadelphia in 1776 or Birmingham in 1963.

POLITICAL THINKING IN ADOLESCENCE

Let us conclude with an analysis of the social-civic competence most directly pertinent to our discussion, what Joseph Adelson has called "the political imagination" of the adolescent.

Adelson's characterizations of teenagers are refreshingly pungent and incisive; they truly reflect the reality of this time in life:

The years of adolescence, twelve to sixteen, are a watershed era in the emergence of political thought. Ordinarily the youngster begins adolescence incapable of complex political discourse, that is, mute on many issues, and when not mute, then simplistic, primitive, subject to fancies, unable to enter fully the realm of political ideas. By the time this period is at an end, a dramatic change is evident; the youngster's grasp of the political world is now recognizably adult. His mind moves with some agility within the terrain of political concepts; he has achieved abstractness, complexity, and even some delicacy in his sense of political textures; he is on the threshhold of ideology, struggling to formulate a morally coherent view of how society is and might and should be arranged. (Adelson 1971, pp. 1014–15)

Adelson studied the thinking of 450 adolescents ranging in age from 11 to 18 of both sexes, of "normal to extremely high intelligence, of . . . [all] social classes and in three nations, the United States, West Germany, and Great Britain" (1971, 1014–15). A longitudinal sample was formed of 50 of these youngsters. They were asked a series of questions concerning a thousand people who move to an island in the Pacific who must compose a political order, devise a legal system, and confront the myriad problems of government.

Adelson summarized his findings briefly:

Surprisingly, it appears that neither sex nor intelligence nor social class counts for much in the growth of political concepts. There are simply no sex differences, and while there are some expectable differences associated with intelligence and social class, . . . these differences are, on the whole, minor. What does count and count heavily is age. There is a profound shift in the character of political thought, one which seems to begin at the onset of adolescence, twelve to thirteen, and which is essentially completed by the time the child is fifteen or sixteen. The shift is evident in three ways: first, in a change of cognitive mode; secondly, in a sharp decline of authoritarian views of the political system; and finally, in the achievement of a capacity for ideology. National differences in political thought, though present, are by no means as strong as age effects. A twelve-year-old German youngster's ideas of politics are closer to those of a twelve-year-old American than to those of his fifteen-year-old brother. (Adelson 1971, pp. 1014–15)

According to Adelson, "The most important change that we find in the transition from early to middle adolescence is the achievement of abstractness" (p. 1015). He makes many of the same points about the consequences of this enhanced intellectual competence that were made earlier in this chapter in the discussion of Piaget. Indeed, Adelson appears to apply, rather uncritically, a Piagetian model to the development of political thought in adolescence. Thus he finds early adolescents to have a partial, fragmented, highly personal understanding of politics: "Like a magpie, the child's mind picks up bits and pieces of data: . . . the tripartite division of the federal system . . . and the capital of North Dakota. But without the integumental function that concepts and principles provide, that data remain fragmented, random, disorganized" (p. 1030). For the younger adolescent, the processes and institutions of society are personalized. His concretism makes it difficult for him to conceive of society. He gives few signs of a sense of community and has only the weakest sense of political constitutions. There is also an extension of his perspective of time. The early adolescent is locked into the present with little sense of the past (that is, history) or of the future. It is now, baby! As he passes through the early years of adolescence, a far more powerful imagining of the future becomes possible. "What we have here, of course, is that leap from concrete to formal operations that Piaget and his associates have posited to be the key cognitive advances in the transition from childhood to adolescence" (p. 1020). Regarding human motivation, the youngster is "a naïve behaviorist." A man is selfish, period, or a criminal, period. Character is destiny.

One hesitates to say boldly that the young adolescent cannot reason about political problems, and yet one hesitates equally to say that he can. . . . At the beginning of adolescence, discourse is often so stark, so naked of embellishment, qualification, or nuance that the listener cannot tune in. (p. 1020)

Adelson argues that the significant transition in reasoning involves the acquisition of a hypothetic-deductive capacity. He cites as an example cost-benefit modes of reasoning — that is, what are the costs to each party of a proposed policy, and what are the gains?

A second major change in political thinking in adolescence was found to be the decline of authoritarianism. "Until one has spoken at some length to young adolescents, one is not likely to appreciate just how bloodthirsty they can be. . . . They propose Draconian measures even for innocuous misdeeds. . . . To a large and various set of questions on crime and punishment, they consistently propose one solution: punish, and if that does not suffice, punish harder" (pp. 1022–23). A similar habit of mind dominates the child's perception of social and political institutions. One of Adelson's most interesting findings is that the young adolescent does not spontaneously entertain the concept of amendment. "To sum up, the young adolescent's authoritarianism is omnipresent. He has only a dim appreciation of democratic forms (for example, he is indifferent to the claims of personal freedom; he is harsh and punitive toward miscreants; his morality is externalized and absolutistic). The decline and fall of the authoritarian spirit is, along with the rapid growth in abstractness (to which it is related), the most dramatic developmental event in adolescent political thought" (p. 1026).

The third change in adolescents' political thinking is the achievement of the capacity for ideology. Adelson debunks the allegedly romantic notion of adolescents as political idealists, preoccupied with the utopian reconstruction of society and the development of ideologies. Not only are utopian ideals uncommon in adolescence, the mood of most youngsters is firmly antiutopian. "We had expected to find more idealism among the young than we did; what we were totally unprepared for was the prevalence of anti-utopian views and the fierce strength with which they were held" (p. 1036). "Idealism, though it is present, is by no means modal, and is less common than skepticism, sobriety, and caution as a characteristic political affect" (p. 1027). At the onset of adolescence, the youngster's grasp of principle is dim, erratic, and shifting. "Much of the time, of course, he is simply unaware of the principles that might govern a political decision. . . . We see examples of this in the early adolescent's penchant for political catch phrases and slogans which . . . serve as a substitute for the general principles he senses are relevant but does not truly grasp" (p. 1027). (Writing at the height of the media blitz in the 1988 New Hampshire primary, one could not help but note a parallel reliance on and reduction of presidential campaigning to catch phrases and slogans.) Yet the steady advance of principle is one of the most impressive phenomena of adolescent political thought. Once acquired, it puts an end to the sentimentality that so often governs young adolescents' approaches to political issues; it allows the child to resist the appeal of the obvious and the attractive, particularly when individual and communal rights are concerned.

The acquisition of ideology also feeds on the child's rapid acquisition of political knowledge (p. 1028). Adelson defines knowledge as more than "the dreary facts" that the child learns in the typical ninth-grade civics class or information on current political realities (who won the 1988 Republican primary in Iowa or Minnesota). Adelson particularly means "the common conventions of the system, of what is and is not customarily done and why" (p. 1029). And he is cautious, skeptical of how large a part increased political knowledge (in the abstract) plays in the emergence of ideology. It is here that he uses his magpie analogy: bright, scattered pieces of knowledge, without ordering principles or coherence, remain fragmented and disordered thinking.

Adelson also examined whether politics "turns on" adolescents. He believes the typical young adolescent to be essentially indifferent to the political world. By middle adolescence, this indifference has given way, in some children, to a more keenly felt connection to the political. But although some youngsters of 15 are deeply involved in politics, most are not. And it appears that democracy begins at home; those adolescents who are intense about politics come from families that are politically active and for whom politics are "normally passionate." Whether a John Bircher, a Pat Robinson evangelical, or a Jesse Jackson supporter, the child, not surprisingly perhaps, takes the direction of his or her political thought and its intensity from the parents. Especially important is this finding: "In the great majority of instances, the child merely soaks up the tacit assumptions of the milieu" (p. 1036). We shall return to this point.

In summary, the appearance of a political ideology, defined as a coherent set of political attitudes and principles, is an unusual event in adolescence. Adelson believes that few teenagers give serious thought to the radical revision of society. Where it does happen, three themes dominate: a law-and-order or serenity concern, an abundance motif, and a preoccupation with equality. "On the whole, the mood of our youngsters is conservative; the inclination to utopia is a matter of class/social position, not fundamentally a youth phenomenon" (p. 1037).

Adelson appears to argue that citizenship — or the development of political imagination, at least — comes with the calendar of adolescence — that is, over time. The explicit model of development of political thinking, ostensibly Piagetian, is really more akin to Erikson's epigenetic assumptions. The argument is that the broad advances in political understanding (greater abstractness, less authoritarianism, and the beginnings of ideology) depend on age (as for Erikson) rather than experiences (as for Piaget). Adelson implies that, given time, these broad normative gains occur in all adolescents. Perhaps Adelson was primarily concerned to describe the optimal progress of the political imagination, not the frequency of its occurrence in adolescence. But his data seem to be ordered by a too credulous and literal translation of Piaget: "The most important change [in political thinking] is the achievement of abstractness," and "what does count and count heavily is age" (p. 1038). There seems to be no acknowledgment of the finding that 50 percent to 60 percent of U.S. adolescents do not make it to formal operations. Perhaps this, in part, resulted from the choice of subjects in Adelson's study, those of normal to extremely high intelligence.

Adelson sees the family as the real crucible of political commitment and ideology among U.S. youth. He gives little discussion or implied importance to the place of formal education in the political development of the young. Most political learning seems to result from the child's absorption of the tacit assumptions of his environment. This seems to confirm the importance given by Dewey and Piaget to the social-civic environment in which the adolescent lives at home and at school. Indeed, it leads logically to an argument for democratizing both the U.S. family and the school if the objective is to bring about democratic understanding and practice in the young.

Interestingly, Adelson found little idealism among the U.S. adolescents he studied but strong antiutopian sentiments and a pessimistic view of human nature. These adolescents were not inclined to revise U.S. society radically; their mood was conservative. Yet all this was reported in an article published in 1971, a time of turmoil on the U.S. campuses, the days of rage in Chicago, civil rights and anti-Vietnam protests, and so on. Somehow, the tacit assumptions of the sociopolitical environment seem not to have been absorbed by these young people, and that is puzzling.

But let us give credit where credit is due. Adelson describes in very detailed, colorful terms an evolving imagination in adolescence. His findings fit with the broad cognitive-developmental view of adolescence taken here and with the associated educational research. Ways of measuring this growth of political thinking seem available (the California F scale, Piagetian measures of formal operations, and so on). His cross-cultural findings (that is, of marked parallels in the basic structural characteristics of young people's thinking, plus distinctive content by culture) are important per se. Adelson may be saying, if you do not like the political climate of the young adolescent world, wait four years. Clearly he has little confidence in traditional citizenship education. But counter to this is his emphasis on the importance of the tacit curriculum of the home and school environment in shaping citizenship. The critical impact of undemocratic or democratic schools on the political development of America's children is perhaps the most important research finding of all.

CONCLUSION

What I have described, in part, are the two world views and ways of being that broadly characterize most U.S. adolescents. Whether we use stage descriptions such as concrete or formal thinking; moral stage two, three, or four; the ego stages of self-protection and conformist; whether we talk about the adolescent just before he joins the human race or just after he does, as selfish and egocentric or social, or as a member and citizen of a small fraternity; or whether we use the terms *preadolescent* and *adolescent*, these two predominant ways of thinking and being coexist uneasily in most adolescents. Certainly they do so in any adolescent society, such as a junior, senior, or alternative high school, or an *Eight is Enough* family with teenagers.

Take together (and they have to be understood as a continuum), these two world views begin to describe the characteristic competencies and boundaries of the preadolescent and what he or she will be like when he really stands up. Adolescence is better understood, not so much as a time in life (13 to 19, for example), but as two states of mind and two ways of being: two predominant and qualitatively different ways of thinking about school subjects, oneself, other people, what is right and wrong, and a selfish or social way of being. One follows the other like the day the night, but neither so fast nor so automatically. So many of the writers cited here, from Dewey to Adelson, note how crucial the everyday social environment is to the formation of the person's political and civic thought. The kind and quality of the social experience we have in the home, at school, in the street have everything to do with the individual's progress or development or lack of it. Many young people have yet to make this critical developmental passage; others are at midpoint; and too many never make it at all.

I have already mentioned the obvious. Most parents, teachers, and societies prefer stages three and four for their adolescents. Why? Because the natural progression for growth is toward more complex logic, moral understanding, and greater human competence. Because the stage three or stage four person sees her welfare as tied to that of others, she is social and civic first, selfish second. Because the adolescent at a higher stage is a lot easier to live with, she wants the approval of others and is much better able to get it. Because, if given a chance or a choice, the normal person will choose to grow. Because the costs, to the individual and his society, of staying at lower stages of development are so devastating, our jails are full of people at moral stages one and two.

So, in every sense, we are describing a critical developmental passage. People for the first time can be civic (that is, able to understand, respond to, and cooperate with the needs and norms of their group). At best, in high school, they will do so partially, with small steps and a slowly enlarging field of vision and caring with the opportunity to make friends, to know one "chum" and a few other people well, to share and cooperate in common activities, and to be accepted and affirmed by key others. This is the heart of the matter. Developmentally, to care and to cooperate come before being fair. Or, à la Gilligan, this may be a separate and equal female morality. Why, in light of what has just been described as the social center of the adolescent's gravity and concern, we would try to educate concurrently for a fuller conception and practice of democracy and justice (that is, Kohlberg's just-community school) may well be questioned. Are not these more complex ways of understanding and being in one's world too much, too soon for most teenagers, especially when adolescents' grasp of stage three, conformism, is still in formation? Would the effort to create caring communities not make better sense developmentally and educationally? For answers, this book now turns to the analysis of moral and democratic education practices in the U.S. public school.

REFERENCES

Adelson, Joseph, (1971). The political imagination of the young adolescent. *Daedalus* 100 (4): 1013–49.

Dewey, John. (1968). *Problems of men.* New York: Greenwood Press.

Dulit, Everett. (1979). Adolescent thinking à la Piaget: The formal stage. *Journal of Youth and Adolescence* 1 (4).

Erikson, Erik H. ([1959] 1979). Growth and crisis of the healthy personality. In *Adolescents' development and education: A Janus knot,* edited by Ralph Mosher. Berkeley, Calif.: McCutchan.

Foreman, J. (1980). *Boston Globe,* June 15.

Kohlberg, Lawrence, and Carol Gilligan. (1979). The adolescent as a philosopher: The discovery of the self in a postconventional world. In *Adolescents' development and education: A Janus knot,* edited by Ralph Mosher. Berkeley, Calif.: McCutchan.

Loevinger, Jane. (1979). Stages of ego development. In *Adolescents' development and education: A Janus knot,* edited by Ralph Mosher. Berkeley, Calif.: McCutchan.

Matthews, David. (1985). *Social Education* (November/December).

Mosher, Ralph, ed. (1979). *Adolescents' development and education: A Janus knot.* Berkeley, Calif.: McCutchan.

Mosher, Ralph, Robert Kenny, and Andrew Garrod. (Under review). *Preparing for citizenship: The democratic high school.*

10

Education for Democracy: Promoting Citizenship and Critical Reasoning through School Governance

Robert Howard and Robert Kenny

Participation in the political process of the United States has reached a crisis stage. Too few of those eligible actually register, and an unacceptably small percentage of registered voters actually exercise their right to cast a ballot. George Bush was elected president in 1988 by just 26.77 percent of those eligible to vote.[1] For national elections, the figures are alarming. In the past seven presidential elections, the percentage of those eligible who actually voted has declined from over 60 percent in 1960 to 50 percent in 1988 (Figure 10.1). The statistics are even more shocking for local elections run during years without a presidential contest. For voters between the ages of 18 and 24 there is even greater reason for concern. In 1984, only 16 percent of this group voted in the presidential election, a rate lower than that of any other group.[2] This pattern was repeated in 1988. "Three-quarters of the nonvoters were under the age of 45 and two-fifths were under 30."[3] Voter turnout in the United States ranks twenty-sixth out of 27 in a recent study of voting in democracies.[4] Citizens who run for political office are drawn primarily from a small minority of the population.[5] Few people participate in the political and governance process in any capacity or at any level — local or national. This crisis is represented in other measures of citizenship. For example, a recent survey commission by the American Bar Association found that only one-third of U.S. adults can correctly identify the Bill of Rights and fewer than 10 percent know it was adopted to protect them against abuses by the federal government.

What can schools do to reverse this trend? What is the mandate for schools in a democracy? Educating students to become responsible citizens in a democratic society is included as a primary goal in the statement of purpose or philosophy of most schools. An educated populace and its participation are necessary conditions for

FIGURE 10.1
Percent of Voter Participation

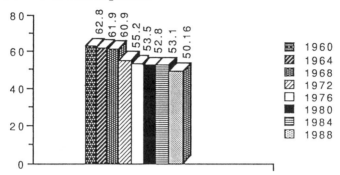

Source: Committee for the Study of the American Electorate. Figures for election years 1960 through 1984 cited in the New York *Times*, November 13, 1988; figure for election year 1988 cited in the New York *Times*, December 18, 1988. See also F. F. Piven and R. A. Cloward, *Why Americans Don't Vote* (New York: Pantheon Books, 1988).

democracy. Given the current crisis of participation, how can schools better meet that goal? Schools can provide students with the opportunity to participate in a hands-on political process. This means making schools democratic. It means not just teaching about democracy, but democratically making and enforcing policies.

We have experience with the democratic governance of schools at the elementary, middle, and high school levels, but we will limit the discussion here to democratic governance at the high school level. However, we believe the reader will be able to make the connections and applications easily to the middle and elementary school levels.[6]

Our aims for students who attend and participate in democratic schools include:

creating a positive school climate and culture by involving those affected by school policies — faculty, students, and administrators — in the creation and enforcement of those policies;

preparing students to participate fully in the major institutions of society (full participation includes, in John Dewey's terms, the "intelligent reconstruction" or change of society when required for moral or practical reasons[7]);

promoting the intellectual, social, and moral reasoning of participants — both adolescent and adult; and

promoting writing, listening, public speaking, and problem-solving skills and abilities of participants.

DEFINITION OF A DEMOCRATIC SCHOOL

A democratic school teaches democratic political participation by providing faculty, students, and administrators an opportunity to discuss and resolve issues that face the entire school community. Through this open and public process, the principal shares his or her decision-making power with the school community. With the guidance and leadership of the adults in the school, students learn the complicated process of making decisions in the context of a political setting.[8]

Providing students with hands-on experience in the physical sciences takes the students' learning beyond the theoretical and into the experiential. The best way to teach biology, chemistry, and physics is by providing students with knowledgeable, professional science teachers and with the opportunity to use well-equipped laboratories. In other words, students learn by doing in a safe environment. The same is true for the social sciences. Students need opportunities to extend political experiences beyond the theoretical or the "almost real" to the real. Allowing students to be involved in making school policies helps them understand that even relatively simple decisions can be complicated when many people are involved and when the needs and rights of different minority groups need to be considered. The placement of the bike racks, what snacks are available in the candy machines, or whether bells will ring at the end of classes — these are examples of such decisions and policies. Furthermore, getting students involved in decisions that concern smoking in school, cheating, or school vandalism increases students' awareness of the entire school community and of their responsibility to the community at large. This type of understanding lays the foundation for responsible, democratic citizenship.

WHY ARE ADMINISTRATORS INTERESTED IN DEMOCRATIC SCHOOLS?

Administrators find that involving many members of the school community in the decision-making process creates decisions and policies that, in the long run, are more completely accepted by the school community. In short, democracy is an efficient method of school administration. People involved in developing a new policy have an investment in seeing that the policy is carried out.

The shared decision-making process allows people to focus on the issues and needs of the school and to help create policies to address those needs. In this environment, participants are more likely to focus on the issues and less likely to focus on personalities. A proposal is less likely to be ignored or attacked on an *ad hominen* basis — that is, because it originated with a single administrator or with what is seen as a small group of like-minded people.

In a democratic school, the democratic processes create internal safeguards that help the community members resolve conflicts internally, rather than forcing them to seek external solutions. The most ominous of these external solutions (because of the time and resources required) is the court system. Democratic schools can help administrators, students, and parents stay out of the courts. For example, we believe the Hazelwood censorship case decided by the U.S. Supreme Court in 1988 would never have gone to court had Hazelwood East High School been a democratic school.[9]

Democratic schools do not force administrators to assume a John Wayne style of leadership and management. In democratic schools, power is not exclusively concentrated in the office of the principal. The principal is not compelled both to symbolize and to defend the base of power. As a result, there is no need for administrators to resort to dramatic and extreme measures, such as carrying bullhorns and baseball bats.[10]

Shared decision making also leads to better solutions. Quality circles and other models of participatory decision making have become important in the private sector because managers have found that those on the assembly line (or its equivalent) are in a better position to understand the implications of a policy than are those who are removed from the line. The same is true in schools.

Frequently, faculty and students have a better understanding of the impact of school policies and procedures than do administrators or school board members. We ran into such a case in one urban school while creating a program designed, in part, to improve the communication between students and educators on policy questions. This school's attendance policy required students to be in their seats when the bell rang for the first period; otherwise, they would be considered absent for the day and not allowed to attend any of their classes. The goal of the policy was to force students to take the responsibility to attend school and to send a strong message that attendance was important. During a meeting with administrators, faculty, and students, we — unaware of the school policy — asked the students what they thought of the school rules. One student spoke up, generally praising her teachers, the school administrators, and the overall climate of the school. This young woman, an adolescent mother, described her desire to graduate from this high school and attend college. She continued, however, declaring that one rule was creating difficulties for her. Each day she would get out of bed before 5:00 A.M., dress and feed her child, and then have the child at the door of the day care center when it opened at 7:00 A.M. Usually she could walk from the day care center to the school without problems. However, on snowy days in this southern New England city, she found it impossible to make it to her first class by the time the bell rang. It upset her that the school's attendance policy punished her when she was trying to be responsible.

At this meeting the educators looked at each other for a moment, and then one asked, "Why don't students sit on the attendance committee?" They recognized that the policy had had an unintended negative effect on this young woman and perhaps on other students as well. Near the end of the meeting, a better policy was being developed. The educators were reexamining the rule and working on ways to provide this young woman with transportation from the day care center to the school.

WHY ARE FACULTY INTERESTED IN DEMOCRATIC SCHOOLS?

Having discussed a democratic school from both the students' and the administrators' perspectives, let us now turn to the faculty. In addition to providing students with the opportunity to learn in an experiential way how to become involved in the political process, a democratic school restructures the school environment. It provides teachers with the opportunity to teach in different ways. As teachers and students work together in the formation and enforcement of school policies, the traditional teacher-student roles and relationships are transformed. In democratic schools, teachers are able to engage in more open-ended and Socratic discussions with students. Often these are opportunities they would not have otherwise. For example, chemistry teachers rarely have the chance to talk to students concerning First Amendment rights. These discussions can be invigorating and enjoyable for both faculty and students. They promote both student and adult development, providing an opportunity for each to consider and explore new ideas in a context not always available in a classroom setting.

An individual's reasoning about political and moral issues develops over time. The authors' orientation to moral reasoning is based on a developmental approach.[11] Developmental theory asserts that there is a pattern to an individual's moral reasoning, that is, there are stages of moral reasoning — each stage of moral reasoning has its own internal logic. Developmental theory also asserts that schools and other institutions can promote mature moral reasoning by raising moral issues and discussing them within a just and caring environment. These discussions can focus on hypothetical dilemmas (found in fairy tales, literature, movies, and so forth) and on current moral dilemmas found either in the school or the outside community. During these discussions of moral issues, individuals have their reasoning clarified, supported, and challenged. Most educators are capable of higher stages of reasoning than are their students. Individuals benefit by being exposed to more mature moral reasoning that can be a catalyst to development.[12]

Educators also benefit from the discussion. They too have their reasoning clarified, supported, and challenged. These discussions also provide educators with a valuable window into what can sometimes appear to be idiosyncratic internal logic of their students' moral reasoning. Educators can discover meaning and method in what had appeared to be adolescent madness. For example, a guidance counselor at one democratic school attended a schoolwide discussion about how truancy should be handled. During the discussion, several students recommended extreme punishment for offenders. The guidance counselor, with 15 years of experience in schools, was amazed by the harshness of the recommendations, by the primitive nature of the students' punitive logic, and by the fact that none of the students thought this reasoning to be strange or harsh. Afterward the counselor explained, "I participated in this discussion thinking I was going to be helping kids. What surprised me was how much I learned about kids whom I thought I knew pretty well, and how much I learned about the way they think. It was quite enlightening."

PROFESSIONALISM AND EMPOWERMENT

Empowering teachers is a central issue in current educational dialogue. In a democratic school, empowering students requires first sharing decision-making power with the faculty. In *A Nation Prepared*, the widely respected Carnegie Forum on Education and the Economy, it is recommended that teachers work in a professional environment in which they are able to exercise professional autonomy.[13] The forum also recommends that schools be run by committees of teachers in place of the traditional model of a nonteaching principal serving as head of the school. The structure of a democratic school realizes many of the goals advocated by the forum.

Empowering teachers in a democratic school is accomplished by involving faculty in the school's democratic forum (called by various names, such as the town meeting, the house meeting, the community meeting, the council, the senate, and so forth), that deals with issues affecting the lives of all of the school members and by creating a faculty senate (also called by different names in different schools and districts) where issues that involve the faculty alone, or the faculty and administration, are addressed. This body replicates the functions and procedures of the school's democratic forum. The difference is in its makeup and in the issues it addresses.[14]

Faculty members have four crucial roles in a democratic school government. First, faculty members need to be strong advocates of their own positions. This is, of course, the first requirement to empowerment in any setting. Second, faculty members, because they have a perspective on the school and its needs and issues that extends beyond the three- or four-year time period of students in the school, need to be strong advocates for the good of both the school community and the community at large. Third, the faculty needs to provide students with reasoning at a higher stage than the students' own, which helps the students to develop more mature reasoning. Fourth, the faculty need to understand that, because students have only a three- or four-year life at the school, some issues need to be re-solved by each school generation.

THE DEMOCRATIC OPPORTUNITIES TO
TEACH IN A DIFFERENT SETTING

During a meeting of one school democratic forum, a white, middle-class student naïvely made a series of racist statements. The issue was whether students should be permitted to listen to walkman radios in the hallway. The student said that, with walkman radios, students were cutting themselves off from social contact. The minority students argued that the radios provided them comfort in an alien environment — no one was talking to them anyway. As the discussion continued, the racist thinking became more crystallized. An African-American teacher, however, was able to challenge successfully the thinking based on racial stereotypes that some of the students were using in their complaints about radios. At one point during the discussion he said, "When you are talking about black people, you are talking about me." This kind of personal involvement in teaching is an opportunity that the teacher in the classroom does not often get. Witnessing and confronting this stereotyping is a more powerful learning experience than reading about it in a psychology or sociology textbook.

In another case, a teacher, who in every other setting works only with special needs students, had the opportunity in the democratic forum to teach both students and her colleagues about special needs students. A proposal abolishing traditional homeroom was under discussion. In place of the existing homeroom period, the first 15 minutes of the first academic period would serve as homeroom. A straw vote had been taken, and the change had received over-whelming support. Speaking against the change and in support of mainstreaming her students, the special needs teacher argued forcefully that the traditional homeroom was virtually the only remaining scheduled time in the school day when special needs students were mainstreamed with other students. She pointed out that changing the traditional homeroom would have little, if any, effect on the lives of the majority of the school community, but the change would make a significant impact on a small and powerless minority. For her students, the change would be isolating and painful. After this teacher's presentation, a final vote was taken, and the democratic forum unanimously voted to reject the change, supporting the special needs teacher and her students, even though they were a small minority of the school population.

In this example, we see that many things were taught to both students and educators that would have been impossible for this teacher to teach in her classroom setting. The special needs instructor was able to teach the rest of the school community about her students and their needs. Students who were members of a majority were provided with the opportunity to take the perspective of a minority.

DEVELOPING CRITICAL THINKING

Participation in democratic schools also encourages students to learn and develop a variety of critical thinking skills. Students must investigate and research issues as well as create arguments for their position. Participants must be able to build coalitions, speak and write convincingly, make other points of view, and listen to and consider the positions of others.

To illustrate this, let us examine one case study. Smoking on campus is a problem that autocratically imposed policies historically have a difficult time solving. A democratic high school in northern New England, like many high schools, had an outside smoking circle for students and an indoor smoking room for the faculty. It was proposed to this school's democratic forum that, because of the long and harsh New England winters, an indoor smoking room be provided for student smokers.

The proposal was brought to the democratic forum and approved by a majority vote but was summarily vetoed by the principal. In his veto explanation, the principal claimed the lack of space in the school precluded creating a student smoking room. He also believed that encouraging or supporting smoking in the school was not educationally justifiable.

This democratic forum — composed of the elected representatives of teachers, students, administrators, parents, and community members — held a schoolwide hearing on the issue. Some members proposed a schoolwide ban on smoking. Other members argued forcefully that if there was not enough space for students and faculty to smoke inside the building, then fairness dictated that no smoking take place. The health hazard smoking caused to both smokers and nonsmokers was cited as another reason for banning smoking on school grounds. In this context, smoking was no longer just an issue to be dealt with on an individual basis in the vice principal's office. It was now everyone's problem and a topic of hot debate. The principal had long wanted to ban smoking in the school but realized that such an administrative directive would be powerfully protested and ineffectively enforced. He had spent many frustrating hours trying to defend the present policy to students when they were suspended for smoking in the building. Following a second schoolwide hearing, the democratic forum voted to ban all smoking from the grounds of the school. There would be no smoking inside or outside the school by students, faculty, staff, or visitors.

The smoking issue helped to clarify the role of the democratic forum to the school. The democratic forum was seen as the major institution within school government — not just a student government. It could and did deal with issues that affected the entire school. But the smoking issue did more than clarify the role of the school government. It alleviated the smoking problem at the school by addressing the issue publicly and by involving much of the school in the creation and enforcement of the policy. For a brief time, some challenged the smoking rule, but after a few months there was no smoking in the school. The school created the policy in 1978; in 1988 the policy remained in effect, and the high school is a smoke-free environment.

By using a democratic process, the school community was able to address and effectively resolve this difficult issue. In the process the participants learned how to address a complex social and health issue that affected the school, how to lobby others and develop persuasive arguments for their position, how to compromise and build consensus, and how to use problem-solving techniques that served the good of the entire school community.

In some situations, democratic decision making might seem inefficient and long-winded, given the immediacy of the problem. However, in the long-term development of the school, it is actually far more efficient. Resolving the smoking issue at this school took a few months; but once it was resolved, the school became a smoke-free environment. Smoking was no longer a constant source of irritation for the administration, faculty, or students. For more than ten years, smoking in the school has not been an issue.

PROMOTING MORAL REASONING

During the discussion of the truancy issue mentioned earlier, we noted that individuals' reasoning about social and moral issues develops progressively. For instance, the guidance counselor was surprised at student suggestions that students face a lengthy expulsion after skipping class three times. The rationale of the students was strictly punishment oriented, with a very clear quid pro quo. They did not take into account extenuating circumstances, or the long-term results of the punishment. The teacher had a more elaborate system of reasoning about truancy that allowed for adjustment to individual cases.

In other chapters in this book, different theories of moral development are presented and discussed at length.[15] Lawrence Kohlberg claimed that "development is the aim of education" and argued that participation in democratic processes facilitates moral development. Democratic schools promote moral development by placing members of the community in situations where they have to confront and resolve social and moral issues and dilemmas facing the school community. Encouraging individuals to take the perspective of others and exposing them to reasoning at higher stages than their own, Kohlberg argues, stimulates moral development. Democratic schools provide an environment in which issues of justice are a schoolwide concern.

THE ORGANIZATION OF A DEMOCRATIC SCHOOL

The structure of a democratic school has three components: the legislative, the executive, and the judiciary. In this respect, democratic schools mirror the organization presented in the U.S. Constitution. (These institutions, however, are called by different names in different schools.) The democratic forum creates school policy, the executive body administers the decisions, and the judicial body hears complaints and addresses the issues of fairness and equity in making, implementing, and enforcing school policy. Unlike the president, who is excluded by the Constitution from legislative debate, the principal plays an important part in the school's legislative process and is often called on to explain policies and to make recommendations.

Direct and Representative Democracy

Any school creating a democratic governance structure must address certain issues. For example, there are two types of democracy: direct democracy and representative democracy. The choice for a given school is, at least in part, dictated by its size. In direct democracies, each student and faculty member has one vote; hence, every member of the community is a legislator. Unfortunately, in school settings direct democracies become ineffective and unwieldy in groups of more than one hundred members. Thus, direct democracies are practical only in alternative schools, in programs in very small schools, or where house structures within a larger school allow for such grouping. In representative democracies, legislators are elected from identified constituencies. This has obvious limitations. The election process tends to smother the minority voice.

Safeguards need to be provided to ensure that minority groups are represented and that their concerns are heard.

The Executive and the Democratic Forum

The chief executive in democratic schools is the principal. For a democratic school to exist, all levels of the administration of the school must be supportive of the process. Many democratic schools eventually have their governance system officially approved and endorsed by the board of education.

Members of the community who want to participate in the government have the opportunity to be elected as representatives to the democratic forum or to the fairness committee.

The largest governing institution in a democratic school is the democratic forum. It is a group comprising either the entire school (a direct democracy) or representatives of the students, faculty, administration, and, in some schools, the wider community. This democratic forum meets on a regular basis (weekly or biweekly) to propose and enact policies for the school.

One of the major issues facing representative democracy is how to ensure that the entire community will be represented. We know traditional elections by grade level do not do this. Alienated and minority students are not likely to run, let alone be elected. Therefore, one of the questions each school must answer is how best to conduct elections. In some schools, elections are based on homeroom or grade divisions for students and by department for faculty. Other schools hold general elections with a specific number of seats designated for faculty, students, and members of the local community. Provisions are made for groups that fail to gain representation through the regular election process by holding several seats at large to be filled by petition if the need arises.

Representation is not an issue in the direct democracy. The entire school community is immediately involved in the decision-making process. The challenge of a representative democracy is to reach out and involve those members of the community not represented in the democratic forum. This is accomplished in three ways: through the at large process, by holding open forums where members of the school community are invited to address the democratic forum, and by creating ad hoc committees as part of the legislative process. For example, in creating the smoking policy at one school, a smoking committee was created with a requirement that half of the members be legislators and half be from the larger school community. Another method of involving the entire community is to require that any major change in school policy be subjected to a schoolwide referendum before becoming effective.

The proportional makeup of the democratic forum is another important question to be addressed. That is, how many seats will be given to student, faculty, and community representatives? Although each democratic school differs in the number of total participants and in the proportional representation, our general advice is to structure the democratic forum in such a way that no one group can override a veto by itself. Our experience in democratic schools suggests that issues are decided on their merits, not by block voting. However, in building a consensus for a democratic governance structure within a school, it may be necessary, as a practical matter, to reassure some cautious members of the faculty and the wider school community that the student votes alone will not be enough to implement a policy.

Fairness or Discipline Committee — the Judiciary

In a democratic school, a judicial body (referred to as the fairness committee, discipline committee, J board, and so forth) is created to hear cases that involve a violation of school policy or some other issue involving fairness or equity. One of the issues schools must address in creating such a committee is whether its decisions are binding or advisory. In one school, the committee is made up of a group of approximately 12 people and includes students, faculty, and an administrator. Each school must also consider, in both this body and the democratic forum, how to provide both continuity and opportunity for everyone to become involved. Whether these positions in the judicial body will be elected, appointed, or some combination of the two is another issue to be considered. For example, in one school half of the committee is elected, half is appointed, and student representatives hold their seats for the duration of their schooling. Faculty members typically serve a three-year term. Any member of the school community can bring an issue to the fairness committee. In most respects, issues of discipline in a democratic school are handled in virtually the same manner as in a nondemocratic school. The fairness committee provides an avenue of appeal for those who believe they have been treated unfairly. It also provides administrators with an opportunity to create a consensus before implementing a new policy; the fairness committee can also make a decision when an administrator prefers not to make the initial decision.

Jurisdiction

Jurisdiction is a central question that any democratic body must face. The scope of each body's jurisdiction must be determined and recognized. No democratic group is all-powerful but rather is constrained by checks and balances. Any school government must operate within the laws and ordinances of the country, state, and city. It must also function within the contract negotiated between the teachers' union or association and the board of education. The potential scope of authority for a democratic school government is virtually identical to the scope of the principal's authority in a traditional school. For example, the school government may decide policies of smoking and wearing walkman radios, but not whether to smoke marijuana, increase teacher salaries, or shorten the school year.

Even though the school government cannot act in all cases, it does have the ability to pass resolutions reflecting the judgment of the school. These resolutions can have a persuasive political impact. To illustrate, in one school, the democratic forum decided to boycott a national speech contest whose sponsoring organization required that participants be U.S. citizens. This regulation unfairly excluded some members of the school community, the democratic forum concluded. This policy decision was followed by a resolution recommending that a national association of school administrators stop endorsing this speech contest. The democratic forum has the power to act on policies within the school and to recommend courses of action for bodies outside of the school.

The Veto

Another central issue is the administrator's ability to veto the policies made by the democratic forum. In all democratic schools in which we have worked, the administrator has the ability to veto, but this veto can take different forms. Veto power can be strong or weak, as the policies in the following two cases illustrate. In school A, the principal has ten days in which to sign a piece of legislation or veto it. The veto is final unless the democratic forum, with a two-thirds vote, requests that the board of education override the principal's vote. In school B, by contrast, the democratic forum itself can override the principal's veto with a two-thirds vote. It is then up to the principal to make an appeal to the board of education to change the policy. In both schools, the veto is rarely used.

The Meetings: The Place and the Time

Two other questions for democratic schools to address are when and where to hold meetings. Formal legislative meetings should be held at least every other week and preferably weekly. Fairness committee meetings should be held as needed. (When dealing with an individual's violation of a policy, the fairness committee should meet in executive session.) We think it best for most democratic schools to hold their meetings during an activity period, a time when students and faculty are freed from their regular academic classes. Alternately, one school schedules school government meetings once a week during a class period, incorporating it into the regular class schedule. The advantage of holding meetings during an activity period is that more people are free to get involved or to observe. It is important to recognize that committee meetings are crucial to the process. Given the constraints of the school schedule, much of the governing takes place in regular or ad hoc committees.

Students' ability to observe and participate in a meeting is also affected by the meeting's location. For example, school A holds its meetings in the school auditorium; its sessions are usually witnessed by several hundred members of the larger school community. While this opens up the process to the public, the size of the audience and its reactions can intimidate members of the democratic forum. Intimidation is less of a problem in school B, where the legislative meeting is held in a faculty cafeteria. Here, the size of the room and its inconvenient location greatly restrict the number of outside observers, thus making the legislative process more exclusive. Meeting in the faculty cafeteria also creates some tension between the democratic forum and the faculty it displaces from this meeting area.

Constitution

Many of the issues raised in the preceding section can be addressed in a democratic school's constitution. Most democratic schools draft their constitutions before implementing their decision-making structures. This process serves as a method of resolving some of the potential problems before they occur. The U.S. Constitution and the constitutions of other democratic schools can serve as important models to the school's drafting committee. By involving representatives from the various constituencies in the school in the drafting committee and by publishing and distributing drafts of the constitution as the writing process is under way, the school can move toward consensus and build support for the new governmental structure before it is implemented. It is also possible, although we have seen it succeed only in direct democracies in schools, to operate with an unwritten constitution, with these issues being resolved by precedent.

Leadership and Procedures

Other issues to be decided by democratic schools include the procedures they will use in their meetings and the method by which the leadership will be selected. We have found too many students and adults ready to adopt *Robert's Rules of Order* without question. Adopting *Robert's Rules of Order* gives an unfair advantage to those who know the procedures and who want to manipulate the legislative process rather than focus on the issue at hand. Our advice is to have each group develop and publish its own set of procedures and refine them as many times as necessary to make them work for the governing body.

Experience tells us that legislative and judicial bodies in democratic schools should select their own leaders. We recommend that democratic forums be moderated by comoderators (one student and one faculty member) elected on a semester or annual basis. We also suggest that an underclass moderator be selected as an alternative. This helps create continuity and allows people with sufficient experience to develop procedural skills necessary to effective leadership.

The Coordinator

The effective function of a school government requires communication and organization. We strongly recommend that an educator serve as the logistical coordinator of the democratic forum. The role of the coordinator is to assist both the legislators and the school administration in using the democratic forum. This role should be seen as that of an executive secretary. His or her duty is to facilitate the committee meetings, ensure proper communication between the democratic forum and the school administration, and provide training to the moderators of the forum. The role of the coordinator is not to provide leadership; rather, it is to ensure that the leadership of the forum gets the assistance that it needs. This person should have approximately two hours per day to work on governmental issues and procedures, depending on the size of the school and the governing body.

Agenda Committee

An agenda committee for the democratic forum needs to be established. Because most school schedules do not allow for open-ended meetings, a premium is placed on being well-prepared for legislative sessions. This committee is made up of an administrator and a small group of legislators (students and faculty). The agenda committee meets prior to the legislative meeting to rank proposals in order of their importance and to discuss what is likely to occur in the upcoming meeting. These discussions help prepare the moderators to conduct a productive session. Working with a small group of moderators helps provide continuity and leadership over the course of a year. In its ability to organize the legislative process, the agenda committee has a great deal of authority, but its power is held in check by the democratic forum's ability to change the agenda after a discussion and vote. The importance of the agenda committee cannot be overemphasized.

Elections

Providing continuity in the legislative body from one year to the next is an important matter to be considered. Holding elections early in the spring is important to ensure a smooth transition. Early elections allow newly elected representatives to join the democratic forum and judiciary after a short initiation, before the end of the school year. This allows representatives to make plans for the upcoming school year. Representatives can begin to implement these plans during the summer months, rather than starting anew each September.

Jurisdiction Committee

Periodically, issues of jurisdiction will be raised in a democratic school. To resolve these issues, a jurisdiction committee composed of representatives of the faculty senate, the school legislature, the judiciary, and an administrator meets and makes procedural decisions and recommendations. These decisions can be appealed to the school board.

CONCLUSION

Schools teach through both the formal curriculum of the school and through what has been called the hidden curriculum.[16] Through the formal curriculum, students are taught facts and academic and vocational skills. According to Philip Jackson,[17] the key words introducing what is learned indirectly or concomitantly through one's experiences in educational institution are crowds, praise, and power. Through the hidden curriculum, students learn about social relationships with individuals and institutions. Students learn they are to be evaluated and that they are subject to institutional policies. Moral education takes place in both the formal and the hidden curriculum. We believe the governance of the school, one of the most important components of the hidden curriculum, provides educators with their most powerful opportunity to promote both citizenship skills and critical reasoning. We have, throughout this chapter, described the learning that takes place and the skills that are developed by those who participate (both students and educators) in the democratic governance of their schools. We strongly advocate democratic schools for educational, psychological, and philosophical reasons.

NOTES

The authors acknowledge and thank Mayra Besosa, Susan deGersdorff, Peter Giacoma, and Cheryl Howard for their critical comments and editorial suggestions of an earlier draft of this chapter.

1. "Council for the Advancement of Citizenship," New York *Times*, December 18, 1988.

2. *Education Week*, April 27, 1988.

3. New York *Times*, November 21, 1988.

4. *Education Week*, April 27, 1988.

5. For example, compared with their numbers in the general population, wealthy white males are overrepresented in the U.S. Congress.

6. For example see T. Lickona, "Four Strategies for Fostering Character Development in Children," *Phi Delta Kappan*, February 1988; R. Weintraub, "A School Where Everyone Shares Power," *Principal* 64 (January 1985); and R. Weintraub, "City Magnet School, Lowell," *Equity and Choice*, May 1986.

7. John Dewey, *Democracy and Education* (New York: Macmillan, 1916).

8. A. Bastian, N. Fruchter, M. Gittell, C. Greer, and K. Haskins, *Choosing Equality: The Case for Democratic Schooling* (Philadelphia: Temple University Press, 1986); R. M. Baltiston, *Public Schooling and the Education of Democratic Citizens* (Jackson: University Press of Mississippi, 1985); A. Gutmann, *Democratic Education* (Princeton, N.J.: Princeton University Press, 1987); B. Honig, "Character Education in Public Schools," *Values, Pluralism and Public Education* (1987), available from People for the American Way, 1424 16th Street, Washington, D.C. 20036; M. K. Jennings and R. G. Niemi, *The Political Character of Adolescence: The Influence of Families and Schools* (Princeton, N.J.: Princeton University Press, 1974); C. Power, A. Higgins, and L. Kohlberg, *Lawrence Kohlberg's Developmental Approach to Moral Education* (New York: Columbia University Press, 1988).

9. In Hazelwood School District Kuhlmeier, the U.S. Supreme Court authorized educators to supervise and censor the content of official school newspapers.

10. For example see "Getting Tough: New Jersey Principal Joe Clark Kicks up a Storm about Discipline in City Schools," *Time*, February 1, 1988; and G. J. McKenna III, "Methodology of Oppression is Unacceptable," *Education Week*, February 17, 1988.

11. This theory is based on the work of James Mark Baldwin, Jean Piaget, Lawrence Kohlberg, Carol Gilligan, and others.

12. We would like to note that a developmental orientation to moral development is not a necessary condition for supporting democratic education. Whether or not one believes stage theories adequately capture moral development, moral reasoning is inherently a matter of communication and understanding other individuals. In that way, moral communication as institutionalized by democratic processes in school promotes reasoning about justice and caring independent of the psychological theory employed to describe that growth.

13. Carnegie Forum on Education and Economy, *A Nation Prepared: Teachers for the 21st Century.* (New York: Carnegie Forum, 1987). Available from the Carnegie Forum, P.O. Box 157, Hyattsville, Md. 20781.

14. Some impressive restructuring programs that promote professional decision making and autonomy are in place in Dade County, Florida, Hammond, Indiana, and Rochester, New York. See M. Cohen, "A Pioneering Miami School, the Control Shifts," *Boston Globe*, May 30, 1988; P. Gutis, "Rochester Asks Teacher for Extra Mile," New York *Times*, February 18, 1988; "Shared Decision Making at the School Site: Toward a Professional Model. An Interview with Patrick O'Rourke," *American Educator*, Spring 1987; A. Shanker, "Teachers Take Charge," New York *Times*, January 31, 1988; and A. Urbanski, "Restructuring the Teaching Profession," *Education Week*, October 28, 1987.

15. See also R. Coles, *The Moral Life of Children* (Boston: Atlantic Monthly Press, 1986); R. Coles, *The Political Life of Children* (Boston: Atlantic Monthly

Press, 1986); W. Damon, *The Moral Child: Nurturing Children's Natural Moral Growth* (New York: The Free Press, 1988); C. Gilligan, *In a Different Voice* (Cambridge, Mass.: Harvard University Press, 1982); L. Kohlberg, *The Philosophy of Moral Development: Essays on Moral Development*, vol. 1 (San Francisco: Harper & Row, 1981); L. Kohlberg, *The Psychology of Moral Development: Essays on Moral Development*, vol. 2 (San Francisco: Harper & Row, 1984); T. Lickona, *Raising Good Children* (New York: Bantam, 1983); R. Mosher, *Moral Education: A First Generation of Research and Development* (New York: Praeger, 1980); N. Noddings, *Caring: A Feminine Approach to Ethics and Moral Education* (Berkeley: University of California Press, 1984).

    16. See, for example, H. Giroux and D. Purpel, *The Hidden Curriculum and Moral Education: Deception or Discovery* (Berkeley, Calif.: McCutchan Publishing, 1983); P. W. Jackson, *Life in Classrooms* (New York: Holt, Rinehart and Winston, 1968); L. Kohlberg, "The Moral Atmosphere of the School," in *The Unstudied Curriculum: Its Impact on Children*, edited by N. Overly (Washington, D.C.: Association for Supervision and Curriculum Development, 1970); D. Purpel and S. Shapiro, eds., *Schools and Meaning: Essays on the Moral Nature of Schooling* (Lanham, Md.: University Press of America, 1985); M. Rutter, R. Maughar, P. Mortimore, and J. Ouston, *Fifteen Thousand Hours: Secondary Schools and Their Effects on Children* (Cambridge, Mass.: Harvard University Press, 1979).

    17. Philip Jackson, *Life in Classrooms* (New York: Holt, Rinehart and Winston, 1968).

11

The Just Community Approach to Classroom Participation

F. Clark Power and Ann Higgins

The high school moral atmosphere has an effect on the education process, and although we will focus on schools, we see the moral atmosphere construct as relevant to other institutions, such as the family and the workplace. Following the ideas of education provided by Dewey (1933), Peters (1966) and Kohlberg and Mayer (1972), we maintain that any serious inquiry into education involves fundamental ethical questions about both its aims or ends (what is worthwhile learning) and its means (what moral principles should govern the learning process). Sociologists such as Durkheim (1961) and Jackson (1968) have called attention to the fact that the educational process is more than the individual activity of the self-educated person or the interpersonal interactions between a teacher and student or between student and student. Education, in their view, also involves an interaction between the school, understood as a social institution reflecting the values of the wider society, and the students. In analyzing moral atmosphere we will focus on the school as a social environment with a particular system of organizational structures and a culture that subtly but persuasively influences the student.

Unfortunately, as Jackson (1968) and Kohlberg (1970) note, the social environment of the school is largely a hidden curriculum. Generally, educators fail to examine whether the ends and means of this curriculum are truly worthwhile and morally just.

This chapter is based on research funded by the Ford Foundation's W. T. Grant and done in collaboration with Lawrence Kohlberg as part of a study of the effects of democratic governance on the development of high school moral climates and student moral judgment.

Furthermore, because they are not critically aware of the nature and impact of the school's hidden curriculum, educators are powerless to change it, make it more just, and integrate it with their explicit classroom curriculum. For example, educators often espouse such values as justice, democracy, freedom of inquiry, and community in schools that have very limited student participation in disciplinary procedures and decision making, unequal educational opportunities, and an alienated student subculture. Issues that are vital to defining the moral atmosphere, including classroom management, discipline, relations between students and staff, and the distribution of educational rewards such as grading and admissions to specialized courses are all too often regarded simply as management concerns that have little or no moral or educational import. In our view, such concerns in fact make up a curriculum for moral education and frame the context for classroom learning. We will elaborate this position first by considering the moral atmosphere in relationship to moral development and then by investigating the relationship of the moral atmosphere to other educational aims and processes.

In making a distinction between moral education and intellectual education, we do not wish to imply that education should be divided into independent moral and nonmoral or value-free spheres. Those who advocate such a division often relegate moral education to the institutions of the family and religion, which then leaves the school free for the value-neutral pursuit of knowledge. This division is, however, unwarranted if we accept Peters's (1966) analysis of education as the moral communication of that which is worthwhile and if we acknowledge the existence of the hidden curriculum. Thus, moral and ethical principles must be the first concern of educators because these principles will determine what is worth communicating and how that communication is conducted. Philosophers, going back to Socrates, have claimed that the central goal of education must be character development — that is, the child's capacity for making free, reasonable, and morally responsible choices. This analysis of education implies that teaching facts or developing scientific or technological reasoning alone is not sufficient.

Furthermore, if students are to become full participants in a democratic society, competent to evaluate and determine the purposes of technology and science, then a concern for moral development must be at the core of civic education. We base our understanding of moral development on Kohlberg's (1984) cognitive developmental theory. This approach is relevant to both the aims and means of education because it brings into relationship philosophically derived moral principles and an empirically derived theory of human development. In a well-known longitudinal study, Colby et al. (1987) identified and validated the stages of moral judgment; they found that individuals reason about moral problems in a structured way and that these structures develop in an invariant hierarchical sequence.

TWO APPROACHES TO MORAL EDUCATION

Moral Development through Moral Discussion

There are at present two major approaches to moral education that have arisen historically out of the research of Kohlberg and his colleagues. The first, the moral discussion approach, began as a result of the efforts of Moshe Blatt, a doctoral student of Kohlberg's, who attempted to stimulate development through the discussion of hypothetical dilemmas in his Sunday school class (Blatt and Kohlberg 1975). The second, the just community approach, originated in a women's correctional institution and was later applied to high school settings (Hickey and Scharf 1980). When Blatt first started leading moral discussions, Kohlberg admitted that he was quite skeptical about the effectiveness of such a brief intervention to produce a cognitive structural change. Fortunately, Blatt was stubborn enough to persist, and he succeeded in showing that moral discussion could in fact influence development. A host of studies, reviewed by Enright, Lapsley, and Levy (1983) and Higgins (1980), have further substantiated Blatt's claims, and the moral discussion approach is now becoming a widely accepted method of moral education.

Part of the appeal of this approach is that it can be either indoctrinative or relativistic. The role of the discussion leader is modeled after that of Socrates. He or she engages students in a moral dialogue in which conflicting points of view are examined and a resolution is attempted. According to this approach, the leader never simply presents ready made solutions to be accepted on the basis of his or her adult authority but rather stimulates the students' search for the solution. This Socratic method assumes that the students are intrinsically oriented toward moral inquiry and seeks to provide the best condition for that inquiry. Necessary to the success of the moral discussion approach is the stimulation of cognitive conflict in which students must reconstruct their moral judgments in a more morally adequate way. However, this approach does not indoctrinate students into a particular set of moral or religious values or beliefs. Instead, it promotes the natural development of universal structures of moral reasoning.

The Prelude to the Just Community Approach:
The Prison and the Kibbutz

In spite of the success of the moral discussion approach, its limitations became evident when Kohlberg and his colleagues began leading discussions in correctional institutions. In those institutions, a tension arose between the ideals of fairness and community being talked about in the discussion groups and the actual injustices and hostilities perpetuated by the correctional system (Hickey and Scharf 1980). Feeling that their efforts at moral education were being undermined by the prison environment, Kohlberg, Hickey, and Scharf (1972) focused their attention on analyzing that environment. They found that custodial-type prisons encouraged low-stage (generally stages one and two) resolution of conflicts and frustrated those individuals who attempted to operate at conventional stages of reasoning (Scharf 1973). For example, inmates who demonstrated that they were capable of stage-three reasoning on the hypothetical moral dilemmas responded at stage two in real-life dilemmas related to a typical prison situation. These researchers blamed this failure of inmates to make moral judgments at the highest stage of their competence on the prison's stage-one or stage-two moral atmosphere. They showed that the prison's organizational structure, which deprived inmates of basic rights, and its punitive, custodial ideology combined to produce this low-stage moral atmosphere.

This study brought out the negative influence of the prison's hidden curriculum and led to the formulation of a new approach to moral education directed at institutional reform, the just community approach. The model for the just community approach developed partially out of a visit by Kohlberg in 1969 to an Israeli kibbutz. In contrast to the moral atmosphere of the prison, which typically inhibited moral development, the moral atmosphere within the kibbutz school, Kohlberg discovered, promoted moral development. In a cross-sectional study comparing adolescents living on a kibbutz with those living in the city, Kohlberg (1971) found that the kibbutz young people were generally at a higher stage of moral reasoning. Furthermore, he observed that disadvantaged adolescents who moved from the city to the kibbutz developed to a higher stage than did their peers who remained in the city. In a longitudinal follow-up study of these same adolescents, Reimer (1977) found that the city-born youth living on the kibbutz reached the same stage of moral reasoning by the end of high school as did their kibbutz-born counterparts.

This and follow-up research on the kibbutz demonstrated that the social environment can have a powerful positive influence on moral judgment development (Snarey 1987). Kohlberg explained that the genius of the kibbutz approach was its use of the social influence of the peer to promote intellectual learning and moral development. Crucial to this approach is the role of the adult leader, called the *madrich*.

The *madrich's* authority does not come from that individual's being an adult or having an office, but rather, it comes from the group itself. The *madrich's* influence derives from his or her under-standing of the power of the hidden curriculum and from his or her ability to use it as an educational resource through the democratic process. It is up to the *madrich* to work within the group to foster its cohesiveness and to guide the formation of norms and values that are in harmony with those of the wider kibbutz society.

Although Kohlberg was fascinated by the practice of moral education in the kibbutz, he rejected the collectivist theory of sociali-zation as the internationalization of value-relative group standards. Addressing kibbutz educators, Kohlberg wrote, "You have a practice better than your theory. . . . [It] seems better than anything we can derive from our theory . . . but we have a theory which can inform your practice and make it even better" (1971, p. 370).

The Just Community Approach

Kohlberg had the opportunity to heed his own advice to the kibbutz educators when he helped to establish an experimental democratic community program ("just community") in a women's prison and later in an alternative high school, the Cluster School. We will focus on the Cluster School experience to describe the just community approach and to show how it fostered a moral atmosphere that promoted both moral and intellectual development.

The Cluster School was composed of approximately 65 students from grades 9 to 12 (senior high) and 6 staff members. It was housed in a large urban high school. The student body represented the racial and social class diversity of the city. Cluster classes in English and social studies were held for two 50-minute periods each day. In addition, Cluster students took elective courses from Cluster teachers. They spent the other half of their school day taking required courses in the large high school. Once a week, everyone in the Cluster gathered in a community meeting to discuss issues and to make decisions about matters of discipline and governance.

The Cluster School staff, in consultation with Kohlberg, prepared for the community meeting by highlighting the moral dimensions of the issues that they expected would emerge. Their role was in many respects similar to that of the kibbutz *madrich* in that they attempted to build a community by advocating shared norms and collective responsibility. They spoke as community members on behalf of the shared ideals of justice and caring rather than espousing their personal political or value beliefs. A Cluster student summed it up this way: "They try to communicate to other people . . . to get them to see why a community, why it is best for everybody if the community benefits. [Even though] they assume that role, there isn't any real authority thing. I think they feel as equal members of the community." Informed by Kohlberg's stage theory as applied to the group, the staff members saw their advocacy in the service of building community at a higher stage of justice. As members of a democracy, they chose as the method of advocacy an open, rational persuasion. Moreover, as cognitive developmentalists, they thought of their persuasion in terms of stimulating cognitive conflict and encouraging higher stage reasoning. Note, however, that they focused on group, not individual, development.

MORAL ATMOSPHERE RESEARCH

Our research on the moral atmosphere of the school grew out of an interest in evaluating the Cluster experience and in identifying those aspects of its social institution that influenced moral development and moral action (Power, Higgins, & Kohlberg 1989). In focusing on the school's moral atmosphere, we distinguished the following parts of an environmental system, according to the scheme provided by Moos (1979) and Taiguri (1968): the physical or ecological setting, the social system, the human aggregate, and the culture. The physical setting refers to such factors as school size and the design of the school buildings and classrooms. The social system comprises fixed program components such as the faculty-student ratio, the form of governance, pedagogical methods, and so on. In Cluster, these included the democratic community meetings and the staff method of advocacy. The human aggregate is defined by the sum of the characteristics of the individuals in the school — for example, the age, sex, social class, IQ, and stage of moral judgment of students and teachers. The culture arises out of these three parts of the environmental system and mediates their influence. It is the dynamic part of the environmental system that depends upon the interactions among the other more stable parts over time. In specifying what composes school culture, we speak more particularly of the moral culture, defining as moral those norms and values that become obligatory.

In our analysis of moral culture we have identified two distinct but related dimensions: the group's collective norms and the valuing of community. These dimensions correspond to two of Durkheim's elements of morality: the spirit of discipline and the spirit of altruism or attachment to the group. Durkheim ([1925] 1973) argued that moral character develops in a context in which individuals must limit their behavior for the sake of the group. The collective norms represent the constraining force of discipline, while the sense of community represents the attractive force of belonging to a group about which one cares.

The collective norm is the central unit of our analysis. We define it as a generally agreed upon norm that obligates a group member *qua* group member. Not all schools develop truly collective norms, shared by faculty and students. In many, students circumvent or ignore the rules and follow peer group norms that originate and are maintained through a desire to conform to a student clique's behavioral standards. The existence of separate sets of norms originating within staff and student subgroups creates two problems. First, the effectiveness of the teachers' norms is limited by opposing norms held by student cliques. This in turn restricts the possibility of developing common or shared norms that then can have a strong positive influence on individual students' moral judgment and action.

Part of the just community's educational strategy is to develop norms, which are shared by both teachers and students, through democratic discussion and decision making. We have traced the development of these democratically established collective norms in terms of their degrees of collectiveness and phases. The degrees of collectiveness chart a progression in which the normative consciousness of group norms becomes more shared. The phases represent both the extent to which norms become institutionalized in a group through the democratic process and the extent to which individual members of the group commit themselves to upholding their norms. The phases also give us an indication of the strength of the group's norms as an influence on both moral behavior and reasoning.

The fact that a group might have norms at a high phase does not, in itself, guarantee that those norms will have a positive influence on individual moral reasoning. In order to assess this influence of group norms, it is necessary to analyze their moral structures. We have used Kohlberg's stages of moral development to assess the moral adequacy of the shared meanings and values represented in the collective norms.

THE MORAL ATMOSPHERE AND MORAL DEVELOPMENT

We hypothesize that the degree of collectiveness, the phase, and the stage of the norms composing the moral culture have an influence on moral development not because individuals at a lower stage internalize higher-stage collective norms and values but because these norms and values encourage group perspective taking and create cognitive conflict for individuals at lower stages. Democratic moral discussion in the just community context requires that students participate in a shared decision-making process about matters of concern to themselves, other group members, and the group as a whole. This process encourages students to take the perspective of the group into account in their deliberations. Belonging to a cohesive group with strong norms provides a powerful motivation for students to consider the perspective of the group even when that perspective conflicts with the individual student's self-interest. Because high school students typically experience that conflict as one between preconventional and conventional moral concerns, their membership in a community that has shared conventional norms can provide a strong impetus for the cognitive reorganization necessary for development.

The following community meeting discussion illustrates how such conflicts occur. During Cluster's second year, a community meeting was held to discuss a stealing incident. By that time, a stage-three collective norm of caring had been established, according to which community members should be willing to sacrifice to help another member in need. Because the thief was not known, a motion was made to make restitution collectively to the victim by having each student chip in 15 cents. One student, Bob, objected that since he did not steal the money, he should not have to pay. This provoked another student to reply, "I think if Bob feels so strongly about giving his 15 cents, that he shouldn't belong to this community." Yet another student asked Bob, "Don't you think of Cluster as a community?" He replied affirmatively; but when pressed to define what he meant by community, he qualified thus: "My definition is that people can help one another, but I didn't say nothing about giving money out." In this exchange, Bob's stage-two reasoning that the duty of helping is contingent upon the wishes of the helper is brought into conflict with the community's stage-three expectation that "everybody should care that she got her money stolen whether you stole it or not." The students who challenged Bob did not react simply as individuals speaking from a personal moral viewpoint, but as representatives of the community, speaking on behalf of its shared norms and values.

We know from subsequent group meetings and interviews that Bob later developed to stage three. In fact, he advocated a proposal for collective restitution the following year. Looking at the Cluster population as a whole, we found that significant moral judgment development did occur, especially among students who, like Bob, reasoned at stage two when they entered the school (Power, Higgins, & Kohlberg 1989).

THE MORAL ATMOSPHERE AND CLASSROOM LEARNING

We have argued that the moral atmosphere of the school constitutes a curriculum for moral development insofar as it embodies norms and values that influence moral reasoning and action. Although the most direct educational impact of the moral atmosphere is on moral development, the learning environment and, indirectly, intellectual development are also influenced. Adopting the developmental position of Dewey, Piaget, and Kohlberg, we maintain that classroom learning is most likely to occur in a moral culture in which there are many opportunities for cooperative problem solving

and in which the developmental needs of each child are acknowledged and provided for.

Before one can attempt to create such an ideal setting, particularly in an urban high school such as Cluster School, one must address
a number of problems. Student disaffection with school is one
problem. Another is the great disparity among the educational and
career goals of students, which in part corresponds to social class
differences. A third is the tension between the teacher's role as an
expert in determining the classroom curriculum and the teacher's
responsibility to respect the autonomy of the student. Although
developmental theory and research can help the teacher to interpret
better the students' educational needs even if these do not always
coincide with students' expressed wishes, there remains a gap
between teacher and student interpretations of needs that is based on
such differences as social class, sex, age, and social role. Furthermore, this gap will increase when a climate of student-teacher
mistrust exists because students do not feel understood.

In our view, the just community approach and moral atmosphere
analysis provide ways of dealing with these problems and facilitating
the classroom learning process. We will illustrate this by relating
some of our research on Cluster's history and moral atmosphere
development. This research was based on the analysis of two sets of
data: individual, open-ended interviews, and community meeting
transcripts.

THE DEVELOPMENT OF A COLLECTIVE NORM OF
ACADEMIC PARTICIPATION: THE CLUSTER SCHOOL

Cluster School began in a virtual state of chaos, without rules or
even a shared vision of what the school should be. As Cluster
members assembled for their first community meeting, there was
little cause for optimism. The black students drifted to one corner of
the room while a group of white, hippie students sat on one side and
a group of white, working-class students sat on the other. They came
from all over the city for reasons as varied as their neighborhoods. A
few were attracted by the promise of democracy, but most were
drawn by the hope of finding a more permissive and friendly
atmosphere, an alternative to the impersonal, authoritarian high
school. About 40 percent of these students had a history of truancy and other disciplinary problems. For a number of them,
Cluster was the last chance to complete high school. As we shall see,
not only did these students graduate, but most of them went on to
college.

In the din of laughter, shouting and conversation, the faculty
chairperson struggled to bring that first community meeting to
order. The agenda was the curriculum. On the blackboard was a

tentative list of elective courses which students were asked to approve or amend. Kohlberg described what took place:

> A student said he would not vote for any of the electives; he didn't like any and proposed that students would not have to attend classes. Before the faculty quite knew what was happening, a vote was taken, compulsory afternoon school was abolished, and the bell rang. I yelled that that was only a straw vote, and the next day the teachers explained that the school could not vote to violate a state law. (1980, p. 40)

Four years later, a very similar group of students gathered in the same classroom. They were noisy as ever, but the chairperson, a student, had little difficulty getting attention. Black and white students were intermingled around the room. The agenda was again the curriculum, but a very different meeting followed. The community was considering a participation rule to make classes responsible for a higher level of participation and learning. The proposal called for uniform academic standards across all classes. The discussion was heated because the autonomy of each class is important to both teachers and students. The conflict between the recognition of each class's autonomy and the desire for common academic standards was resolved by specifying that four categories (attendance, homework, tests, and class discussion) were to be included in each contract but that the weight assigned to each would be determined by each individual class.

What took place in the years between these two meetings that might explain these very different outcomes? In the fall of the first year, the Cluster staff realized it was too early to involve students in the planning of the curriculum, for the group had yet to develop effective rules about coming to class and paying attention. Staff members were aware that they had to define the issues in ways that most students would understand. The students thought that the only real rules were those that carried enforceable punishments. Some argued against an attendance rule for stage-two reasons saying, for example, "I don't understand why people would create a rule which would screw them over. Right now we can cut as much as we want." However, the majority favored a rule for reasons we judged to be stage two to three. As one student put it, "You don't have any school this way if everybody can cut anytime they like. . . . You have a school of classes where nobody shows up, where nobody does anything." After an agreement that there should be a rule, staff and students negotiated about how strict it should be. A liberal compromise was reached, allowing students ten cuts (missed classes) per half-year before they were liable for expulsion from the school.

The limitations of this liberal rule became apparent when several students were brought to the community meeting for cutting class more than ten times. One case involved a student, Sam. During the community meeting discussion, no students expressed any disappointment over Sam's violation of the rule. Instead, they argued that a lot of people had broken the rule so "why pick on Sam?" Some excused Sam's cuts by blaming the faculty for not keeping a more careful record and for not giving him the proper warning stipulated by the rule. Faculty members responded that students were preoccupied with the letter of the law rather than with its spirit and should be more concerned with upholding the attendance policy. One teacher said,

When you stop and think about it, there is a thing called spirit and a thing called letter when you talk about the law. And the spirit of the law means that you understand the law and you get a feel for it and you want to apply it generally. . . . Now the spirit of the law would say in this case . . . [that] it is not getting caught [that is important] . . . but [that] we should attend class.

Although Cluster had democratically made a rule about attendance, our analysis showed that little progress had been made toward the development of a shared norm of participation. Most students thought in a stage-two way, that class cutting was all right "as long as you don't get caught." In their view, rule enforcement was the faculty's responsibility and a matter of concern only for the student cutting and for his or her teachers. The faculty tried to counter this stage-two understanding with appeals at stages three and four that students and staff collectively should accept responsibility for being a part of what is meant to be a democratic school. "If we are supposed to have a democratic school, why is it that the teachers always end up keeping track of things. . . . I think that people in our community should be helping one another."

In terms of our scheme for classifying collective norms, the teachers were trying to raise the stage of this norm to at least the stage-three idea that a good community member had a duty to follow the community's rules for the sake of the community and not because of the threat of punishment. A second staff member said, "The point is, we are trying to develop a community. We have to have some rules in order to have a community and we have to work with those rules."

Although success was not immediate, by the second year some students began echoing the faculty's dismay at the widespread disregard for the cutting rule. Throughout that year, 16 students came before the community meeting for expulsion. Five of those students were actually expelled after violating subsequent probations without excuse. The stage of the norm remained at three because the majority still did not assume personal responsibility for seeing that others attend class. However, the stage of the norm developed from between two and three the previous year to three in this year. In the meeting dealing with expulsion, students insisted upon reciprocity between the community's obligations to help its members and the members' obligations to help the community. One student said, "It [a student's cutting class] is hurting us because we have to try to help him, but you also realize he has to meet us halfway."

In spite of such appeals, class cutting remained a major problem until the third year, the year of Cluster's first big graduating class. That year, two important decisions were made: the passage of a "no-cut" rule, and a revision of the history and English curriculum to include greater emphasis on basic skills, such as grammar and writing. Those decisions represented a dramatic shift of student concern about and involvement in Cluster's academic program.

The proposal to have a no-cut rule grew out of frustration with the permissive attitude toward cutting encouraged by the ten-cut rule. As one graduating senior psychologized, "If you have a certain amount of cuts [allowed] it gives you excuses. . . . But if you have an obligation to fulfill, then you have to face up to it and if you don't after a certain amount of time, then I guess you don't belong here. It's a question of when you want the discipline to start."

The major objection to the no-cut rule was that it did not solve the problem of boring classes. While some students conceded that classes could be boring, they rejected that excuse for cutting: "If we want to have this school, we really have to get off our cans and really help it." The rationale for upholding the no-cut rule was linked to a stage-three valuing of community. The rule against cutting had been seen by most students as a disciplinary measure, necessary for the school to function as an organization. Now cutting was seen as a form of nonparticipation and an offense against the community. The passage of the no-cut rule symbolized a commitment to attending class and to encouraging others to do so. We code this commitment to the norm as phase six, a significant change from phase three the previous year. In an open-ended interview, one student explained the benefits of the no-cut rule in terms of both moral development and academic achievement:

> I go to classes because of the no cut rule. It has to do with morals, I think. Like they have been teaching us over the years how to make good moral decisions and how to think about it before we do it. . . . If you think about the morals, there is no reason to really cut. . . . For one, you are going to miss a class and that might change your whole way of thinking about something. [Also] kids have been really questioning themselves, questioning like "how good a member of the

community am I?" I think that people feel better in their conscience if they follow their rules because they can say I am a better student than I used to be. I am a better community member.

In addition to toughening up the attendance rule, Cluster students proposed strengthening the curriculum by adding fundamentals — drills in grammar, reading, and writing — for students who needed them. Although the fundamentals were more tedious than other parts of the curriculum, a coalition of Cluster's highest and lowest academic achievers championed this proposal. It won nearly unanimous approval. This represented progress in bringing about greater student involvement in and responsibility for the academic program and the community. For many of Cluster's academically successful students, the emphasis on fundamentals would have had little benefit. Nevertheless, they supported those who they knew needed the remedial work.

One indicator of Cluster's success in developing an atmosphere conducive to academic achievement was the fact that over 90 percent of its graduates went on to college. This is a remarkably high percentage, considering the social class composition of the Cluster School and the high proportion of students with a history of severe learning and disciplinary problems. From our perspective, it was the Cluster democracy, with its emphasis on equality and student participation, that created the collective norms of integration and academic involvement that, in turn, laid the groundwork for the shared value of higher education.

Reflecting upon Cluster School's moral atmosphere development over four years, we see that a disorganized group of individuals who had difficulty agreeing about any restrictions on their behavior became a community with shared goals of learning and academic achievement. The ten-cut rule in the first two years was intended simply to limit negative behavior. It was replaced by the no-cut rule and later by the participation rule, which obligated students to make positive contributions to the community. The basis for student compliance with the norm changed from fear or avoidance of punishment to a self-consciously chosen commitment to live up to responsibilities as a community member.

The extension of the democratic decision-making process into curricular issues did not result in the students' electing to learn only what interested them. Cluster teachers maintained their position as experts on both curriculum and methods of instruction while encouraging the students to become involved. In fact, the Cluster students voiced the expectation that their teachers would be knowledgeable in their fields and responsible as educators. Cluster students were concerned that their teachers be aware of their aspirations and their particular needs. The community meeting discussions about the curriculum in the third and fourth years showed the students that the teachers were willing to listen and to make modifications. For their part, the teachers welcomed the students' suggestions because most of the students demonstrated real insight regarding their needs to develop academically and socially and to take their place in higher education and in the working world. In Cluster's history, that insight was not always present; it had to be cultivated and encouraged through frank discussion and confrontation about the obligations of being a student and a member of a community.

ASSESSING PARTICIPATION IN THE
BRONX HIGH SCHOOL PROGRAMS

Recently established just community programs in the Bronx have provided us with a further opportunity to explore the relationship between moral atmosphere and academic participation. The Bronx programs, one with largely disadvantaged and the other with largely advantaged students, have had the advantage of building on what was learned from earlier applications of the just community approach in Cluster School and Scarsdale Alternative High School (Kohlberg & Higgins 1987).

In an analysis of the first six months of two just community high school programs in the Bronx, we asked students to rate a number of school climate-related items on a 5-point scale, ranging from –2 (strongly disagree) to a +2 (strongly agree). As we expected, we found that the students in the just community programs rated items describing their programs as fair, communally oriented, and well-disciplined significantly more positively than did a comparison group from the regular high school. Much to our surprise, however, the students from the just community program in Roosevelt High School rated the item "can get a good education" more positively than did their peers, although the just community program did not include any classes. Although this result may be attributed to a halo effect of the intervention, it may also mean that students feel more motivated to learn in an environment that they feel is fair and caring.

In another questionnaire that focused explicitly on moral culture, we asked students to rate the phase of the attendance norm from three different perspectives: their own, that of other students, and that of the teachers. The results, given in Table 11.1, show that the students in both just community programs gave higher ratings to their teachers than did the students in the comparison schools. This seems to be a reflection of the phenomenon of teacher advocacy that we discussed earlier. The students in both just community programs also gave higher place ratings to themselves and to other students in

TABLE 11.1
Phase of Attendance Norm

Norm	Just Community A	Comparison A	Just Community B	Comparison B
Self-Rating	4.3	2.7[a]	3.7	3.3
Other Rating	17.9	16.6	17.2	14.8[b]
Teacher Rating	19.1	16.4	21.7	17.6

[a] $p = .001$
[b] $p = .05$

their schools than did their counterparts. However, at Roosevelt, only the difference between "self" ratings was significant, while in the Bronx School of Science a significant difference was found only on the "other" rating.

In that same moral culture survey, we asked students to rate the reasons for upholding the norm of attendance for reasons corresponding to the classification scheme developed by Turiel (1983). Turiel distinguishes among the moral, conventional, and personal domains of social judgment. We added the community domain because we do not find that it adequately fits into any one of the other categories (Power, Higgins, & Kohlberg 1989). A goal of the just community approach is to foster a communal perspective on norms. This means that attendance norms, which would be valued normally for personal (instrumental) reasons, should in a just community program be valued as necessary for community solidarity. Note in Table 11.2 that students in both just community schools rate the community justification for "why skipping class is wrong" significantly higher than do their peers. This is an encouraging result particularly because these results were obtained from questionnaires administered within the first six months of each program.

The most recent research to follow the pioneering Cluster School study thus confirms that the just community approach can have a significant effect on the development of a norm of class participation in high schools. Students in the just community programs saw themselves as more committed to uphold the norm of class attendance than did those in the comparison schools. Furthermore, the students in the just community programs judged class cutting not only as a personal issue but as a matter of community concern. From our perspective, this linkage of attendance to community responsibility provides an important source of motivation and support for achievement in the classroom.

TABLE 11.2
Reasons for Not Skipping Class Assessed by Norm Content

Skipping class without an excuse is wrong . . .	Just Community A	Comparison A	Just Community B	Comparison B
1. because the teachers will feel let down. (conventional)	0.6	−0.8[a]	0.7	−0.1[b]
2. because it hurts the spirit of the class. (community)	0.5	−0.4[c]	1.0	0.0[c]
3. because you will not learn as much. (personal)	0.9	1.0	3.6	3.9
4. because it is unfair to those who try to follow the rule. (fairness)	1.2	0.5	0.2	0.2
5. because you might get caught and punished. (personal or low stage moral)	0.6	0.7	0.4	0.5

[a] $p = .05$
[b] $p = .1$
[c] $p = .01$

CONCLUSION

Moral atmosphere influences the educational process in two ways. First, it is a curriculum for moral education in that its norms and values represent a moral point of view that is indirectly communicated to the students. Second, it provides a social context for classroom learning by influencing the way in which students interact with each other and with their teachers. We contend that a school that is consciously communitarian and has an open, democratic governance structure has the necessary components for developing a positive, moral atmosphere. The building of a positive moral atmosphere, we suggest, leads to intellectual as well as moral judgment development. We have described the application of this educational theory in a high school setting, presenting a framework for analyzing moral culture through a focus on norms. Such a framework allows us as researchers to describe the development of collective norms and values and to evaluate the effectiveness of the just community approach.

From the perspective of the educator, this framework helps to clarify which issues will be most stimulating for community development at any particular point. Just as it is important to attend to the developmental level of the individual in deciding which experiences will be most conducive to his or her growth, so too it is important to consider the developmental level of the group in fostering its growth as a just community. In Cluster School, we saw that the staff members were most effective in promoting the democratic establishment of shared expectations about class attendance and participation when they had a theoretical perspective on the limits of the group and on their goals for group development. We hope this portrayal of the Cluster School as a case study of the just community approach and the analysis of its moral atmosphere and that of the new just community programs in the Bronx will offer a direction for practitioners concerned with educating for justice as well as excellence.

REFERENCES

Blatt, M., and L. Kohlberg. (1975). The effects of classroom discussion programs upon children's moral judgment. *Journal of Moral Education* 4: 129–61.

Colby, A., L. Kohlberg, M. Lieberman, and J. Gibbs. (1981). *A longitudinal study of moral judgment*. Society for Research in Child Development Monograph Series. Vol. 48, no. 4.

Dewey, J. (1933). *Democracy and education*. New York: Macmillan.

Durkheim, É. (1925). *Moral education: A study in the theory and application of the sociology of education*. New York: Free Press. Reprinted 1973.

____. (1961). *Moral education*. New York: Free Press.

Enright, R., D. Lapsley, and V. Levy. (1983). Moral education strategies. In *Cognitive strategy research: Educational implications*, edited by M. Pressley and J. Levin. New York: Springer-Verlag.

Hickey, J., and P. Scharf. (1980). *Toward a just correctional system*. San Francisco: Jossey-Bass.

Higgins, A. (1980). Research and measurement issues in moral education interventions. In *Moral education: A first generation of research and development*, edited by R. Mosher. New York: Praeger.

Jackson, P. (1968). *Life in classrooms*. New York: Holt, Rinehart and Winston.

Jennings, W. (1979). *The juvenile delinquent as moral philosopher: The effect of rehabilitation programs on the moral reasoning of male offenders*, Ph.D. diss., Harvard University.

Kohlberg, L. (1970). The moral atmosphere of the school. In *The unstudied curriculum*, edited by N. Overley. Monograph. Washington, D.C. Association for Supervision and Curriculum Development.

____. (1971). Cognitive developmental theory and the practice of collective education. In *Group care: An Israeli approach*, edited by M. Wollins and M. Gottesman. New York and London: Gordon and Breach.

____. (1980). High school democracy and educating for a just society. In *Moral education: A first generation of research and development*, edited by R. Mosher. New York: Praeger.

____. (1984). *Essays on moral development* Vol. 2, *The psychology of moral development*. New York: Harper & Row.

Kohlberg, L., and A. Higgins. (1987). A school democracy and social interaction. In *Moral development through social interaction*, edited by William M. Kurtines and Jacob L. Gewirtz. New York: Wiley.

Kohlberg, L., and R. Mayer. (1972). Development as the aim of education. *Harvard Educational Review* 42 (4): 449–96.

Kohlberg, L., J. Hickey, and P. Scharf. (1972). The justice structure of the prison — a theory and an intervention. *The Prison Journal* 2: 3–14.

Moss, R. H. (1979). *Evaluating educational environments*. San Francisco: Jossey-Bass.

Peters, R. S. (1966). *Ethics and education* London: Allen and Unwin.

Power, C., A. Higgins, and L. Kohlberg. (1989). *Lawrence Kohlberg's approach to moral education*. New York: Columbia University Press.

Reimer, J. (1977). *A study in the moral development of kibbutz adolescents*. Ph.D. diss., Harvard University.

Scharf, P. (1973). *Moral atmosphere and intervention in the prison: The creation of a participatory community in prison*. Ph.D. diss., Harvard University.

Snarey, J. (1987). Promoting moral maturity among adolescents: An ethnographic study of the Israeli kibbutz. *Comparative Educational Review* 31: 241–59.

Taguiri, R. (1968). The concept of organizational climate. In *Organization climate: Exploration of a concept*, edited by R. Taguiri and G. Litwin. Boston: Harvard University.

Turiel, E. (1983). *The development of social knowledge, morality, and convention*. New York: Cambridge University Press.

12

Taking Part: Democracy in the Elementary School

Ethel Sadowsky

Brookline High School was my training ground in school democracy. Prior to becoming principal of the Heath School in Brookline, Massachusetts, I spent 16 years at Brookline High, where I observed and worked with two headmasters of distinctly different leadership styles. The first was an opinionated, competent man who believed in strong central authority. He made the decisions, and they filtered down through formal and informal networks for implementation. He elicited opinions of key people as he deemed necessary to inform the decision-making process; key people were those whom the headmaster trusted and valued. This "office cabinet" was stable in structure, and its members held a most-favored staff status. Other members of the school community — the vast majority of the staff and virtually the entire student body — had no influence upon the decision-making process.

By most criteria defining success, the high school flourished for years under the aegis of this benevolent autocrat. Students attended classes, faculty attended meetings, seniors got into colleges, outstanding candidates applied for teaching positions in the school, and the staff was secure in the knowledge that someone was in charge of the school. The headmaster made it his business to know everything that was going on in this large, complex high school. He seemed to be omnipresent, one moment appearing at a meeting of the math faculty, the next leading a discussion on adolescent development for the guidance counselors. If the staff felt somewhat disgruntled because of their awareness of a small "in" group and a large "out" group, they did not publicly air that feeling. Instead, the headmaster affected a variety of changes in curriculum and organization virtually by fiat. The school hummed along for eight or nine years under his leadership.

Toward the end of the 1970s, cracks began to appear in the veneer of this centralized leadership style. Brookline, surrounded on three sides by the city of Boston, observed and suffered as Boston went through the agonies of school integration. That the community was reading about and watching on television daily confrontations between black and white students could not help but affect the climate at Brookline High School (BHS). Eventually, ugly confrontations between black and white students began to occur at BHS. No sooner was one area under control than a conflagration arose elsewhere. Faculty members were kept busy putting out racial fires. The headmaster's authority was not enough to keep the school running smoothly. Small tensions increased, culminating in a cafeteria fight that involved a large proportion of the students.

As the decade of the 1970s ended, so did this leader's tenure as headmaster. Into the position came a man committed to the precepts of democratic governance for the high school. His vision was for the entire school community — students, staff, and parents — to come together in some sort of governing structure, to develop and implement the rules for running the school, and to vote upon the multitude of issues that arise in the day-to-day processes of the school. Students and faculty went to the polls in the spring of 1981 to vote for the kind of government they wanted for the school. Representative town meeting, similar in design to the government of the town of Brookline, was chosen. The town meeting would act upon issues raised by members, constituents, and even by parties outside the school community. Its mandate was to develop and make known rules — and consequences for violating rules — that would guide the behavior and activities of students in the school. The headmaster could veto an act approved by the town meeting, but the town meeting could override the veto by a two-thirds majority. All parties in the school could bring grievances to the fairness committee, the judicial arm of the school's government.

By the fall of 1981, the town meeting format was in place. Representatives had been elected and seated, a teacher-facilitator was appointed, and a meeting time and place established. From 1981 until 1986, I participated in the school's town meeting, and I was responsible for presenting its decisions in writing to the school committee and thence into the student handbook, the compilation of the school's rules, regulations, and opportunities. From my vantage point as a town meeting member, I saw the strengths in the system.

Empowerment — In theory, students, faculty, civil service personnel, and parents were to share governance responsibility. In practice, parents were not voted membership, and faculty presence from the outset was weak, never filling the allocated number of spots. Civil service representation was virtually nonexistent; the lone delegate was not a person whom the custodial or cafeteria staffs had elected or trusted. Thus, only the student group was empowered. This strength was an important outlet, however. It provided a stark contrast with the sporadic or unfair access to power some students had acquired under the prior leadership. It told students that they had a say in their destinies at school — that they could raise concerns and know they would be heard.

Social Responsibility — Town meetings made participants aware of the school as a society, and it asked them to help strengthen that society. The forum raised students' awareness about the school's — and the society's — needs, and it showed them how members of a society are responsible for the society's well-being and ability to function smoothly.

Classroom in Democracy — Town meeting members had the rare opportunity to learn about democracy by practicing it and applying its principles to real problems. When working at its best, the town meeting is a model of democratic education.

I also found weaknesses in the town meeting, several of which are significant:

Composition — Almost all of the town meeting members were drawn from the same segment of the school: college-bound students with strong academic aspirations. The membership did not reflect the diversity of Brookline High School. Despite efforts to develop strategies to correct this problem, it got worse as the years went on. The youngsters who became town meeting members were already comfortable speaking in public, arguing points, using parliamentary tactics when necessary, and engaging in political action. These students were articulate, self-assured, and entitled. They often had the effect of intimidating students who had been persuaded to join the body to voice the concerns of an underrepresented group in the school. Their elitist attitudes also dissuaded faculty from participating in the forum.

Failure of Communications — The approximately 60 students who were town meeting members represented, in theory, the 2,200 students in the school. The decisions made in town meetings affected the lives of everyone in the school. But the processes for disseminating the information from the town meeting to the population at large was flawed from the outset. Gradually, the established conduits shut down. The result was that few people knew what the town meeting was doing, and not knowing was tantamount to not caring.

Process versus Substance — The procedures of the town meeting often seemed to have a life of their own, separate and distinct from the issues the group was discussing. A kind of half-formed understanding of *Robert's Rules of Order* began to guide the proceedings. Soon, meetings were consumed by such strategies as calling the question, doubting the quorum, and demanding recounts. These complicated delaying tactics frustrated many members who genuinely wanted to address issues of meaning. Those faculty members who were still in attendance were eventually worn down by these procedures.

I began as the principal at the Heath School in September 1986. Despite my criticisms of the high school's town meeting, I was committed to the concept of school democracy. I spent the summer prior to assuming the principalship thinking about how to adapt democratic structures to fit an elementary school and how to provide the children with the training and experience that would enable all of them to think of themselves as competent participants in the democratic process.

To be sure, I was not charting a completely new course. Democratic classrooms were in place at Heath and had been for a number of years. Each of the primary classrooms has a rug, a spot where children gather on the first day of school to formulate the rules that will govern the classroom. Typical rules are, listen when someone else is talking, walk in the hallways, and sign your name on the board to go to the bathroom. All rules are stated positively. "Don'ts" do not exist.

In addition to providing a place for developing rules, the rug is used throughout the year to discuss current problems and concerns. Examples of such issues range from minor behavioral complaints to how best to show concern for a classmate whose mother has died. Moreover, teaching styles in the classrooms emphasize cooperation and collaboration. Not only do children learn to confer with one another in their daily writing process sessions and in science, math, and social studies, but older children regularly work with younger ones. Third graders help kindergarteners with their "frog logs," and seventh graders explain newly learned scientific understandings to second graders.

Clearly, I was entering a setting that was already practicing the principles of democratic education, particularly in the lower grades. My goals were to extend the concept of democratic participation and problem solving to the school as a whole. I hoped thereby to build a feeling for Heath as a community, starting with the youngest students; begin to give children a regular opportunity to express themselves in a group beyond the classroom; teach listening skills systematically, in a forum larger than that of the classroom; give children the chance to bring forward their own issues and interests and to present them to an audience of their peers; and foster self-esteem by providing a place where children could feel comfortable standing and delivering a poem, a reflection on something they had learned, or a song.

This idea evolved into the Heath Family Meeting, a weekly gathering of all children in grades one, two, and three. Now in its third year, Heath Family Meeting is a tradition with an established meeting place and time, a format, and a genuine sense of community.

In September 1987, we began the Heath Community Meeting for grades four and five. The celebration of the bicentennial of the Constitution was the jumping-off point for the formation of the community meeting. The first session of the Heath Community Meeting focused on the reasons our foreparents developed the Constitution. We discussed the need for and the purpose of charters and rules and regulations in general. The children enjoy these kinds of discussions. They have an abundance of information, usually interesting if not always pertinent. So the idea of relating standards established to govern a new nation to the development of a fair and acceptable way of handling conflicts and other issues that arise in a school appealed to these fourth and fifth graders.

The Heath Community Meeting is a direct outgrowth of the Family Meeting. The latter forum is preparatory in terms of developing participation skills. The Heath Community Meeting focuses specifically on the rights and responsibilities of members of our school community. It extends the notion of community by asking what the problems of the community are and how we can go about solving them. It also introduces the children to an understanding that things do not happen simply because we want them to happen. Children — even fourth and fifth graders — have the ability to figure out solutions to problems and the power to implement those solutions. Finally, it emphasizes a process. We can make things better by defining the problem, brainstorming possible solutions, agreeing on the best solution, and putting it into action.

Recognizing the need to apply theoretical assumptions to practical problems, we worked out a means for children to raise issues that they found troublesome in the school. I attached a large manila envelope to my office door, and I encouraged community meeting members to commit their issue to writing and place it in the envelope. The first week the envelope began to fill with problems: saving seats in the lunchroom, cutting into lunch lines, unfair use of playground space, dirty bathrooms, and lack of soap in the bathrooms.

At the next community meeting, I presented the list of topics the children had submitted. The issue the groups decided to work on was the lack of soap in the bathrooms. It was a good choice because it seemed to contain enough interest and conflict to hold the children's interest; its intrinsic importance was evident; and it was solvable. We began by discussing the criteria (we called them guideposts) that would shape our discussions and proposals. They were as follows:

Is it fair? — Does it treat everybody in the same way? If it solves your problem but it makes matters worse for someone else, then it is not fair.

Is it consistent? — Can you apply the solution to a variety of situations and have it work?

Is it safe?

Is it necessary? — Here we talked about the problem of making too many rules and regulations. The children quickly acknowledged that it would be hard to remember a whole lot of rules and that they might find themselves breaking rules they were unaware of. Thus, with adult guidance, they submerged their natural bent to make a rule for everything in favor of having a few well-publicized rules or actions in effect.

The following week we began to discuss the issue of the lack of soap in the bathrooms. We randomly divided the large group (about 82 students) into 8 small discussion groups, each headed by an adult-teacher, a student teacher, and me. I had prepared a sheet to help the adults lead the discussion. Here is the description of the problem:

Students complain that there is no soap in the bathrooms. The custodians resist stocking bathrooms with soap because it disappears immediately. They also are unwilling to install soap dispensers because they are quickly broken.

Still, the principal agrees that children should have soap to wash their hands. How can we, the Heath Community Meeting, help to make sure that if we install soap dispensers, they will be used for washing and not be broken? What problems are likely to arise? What can we do about them? What are you willing to do?

In the small group discussions, the children were intrigued with finding solutions to the problem of protecting soap dispensers. The process required that the adult group leaders record all of the suggested remedies without discussions of their viability. Ten minutes were allotted to generating ideas. After that, groups would examine the proposals in light of the four criteria we had developed. They would then bring an agreed-upon solution to the whole group for a vote.

In this part of the process, the children's imaginations took flight, yielding solutions such as employing a guard to watch the dispensers, installing television monitors, hiring fingerprinters, having the custodians check the dispensers every five minutes, putting alarms on the dispensers, and getting a watchdog to patrol the bathrooms.

These fanciful solutions (or similar ones) emerged in each group. On hearing them, I had a moment of considerable self-doubt. Could these nine- and ten-year-olds possibly believe that placing alarms on soap dispensers was a viable solution to a minor, if troublesome, community problem? Had I badly miscalculated their ability to assess a situation and then formulate a reasonable remedy? Would they merely play with the issues that they had raised as a diversion from the classroom and be unable or unwilling to see them as real concerns requiring their attention?

Fortunately, someone emerged in each group to point out the impracticality or pitfalls of such actions. In the group I led, for example, one student was able to argue persuasively against the fingerprinting idea. She attacked it on both practical and libertarian grounds, saying it would be very expensive to do all that fingerprinting and that someone might be accused of breaking a dispenser whose fingerprints were on it but who had used it appropriately.

Each of the teacher leaders reported that a similar process occurred in the group she led. When the time came to assess the proposals and decide upon the one the group would present to the whole forum, someone was able to point out the flaws in proposed solutions that required electronic installations or the hiring of guards — human or canine. The small size of the discussion groups and the interaction of fourth and fifth graders helped to elicit thoughtful criticism and to yield workable solutions.

In the issue of the soap dispensers, the consensus was this: The dispensers would be installed. Heath Community Meeting members, in pairs, would visit each classroom, explain the problem about the lack of soap, and describe how the Heath Community Meeting had worked out a solution. The children would request cooperation from all the students in using the soap dispensers for the intended purpose and not destroying them. The soap dispensers are for everybody's use and if they get broken, no one will have them, they would say.

There were plenty of volunteers to speak to the lower grades, (kindergarten, one, two, and three), and several children agreed to talk in grade six. Finding speakers for grades seven and eight was more difficult, but ultimately two fifth-grade girls agreed to do it. I rehearsed their presentations with them, and, except for an episode of the giggles in one eighth-grade classroom, the explanations and requests for cooperation went well. (Later in the year I asked eighth-grade students to work with Heath Community Meeting members, helping the students to work out their speeches and, simultaneously, to learn a lesson in political cooperation.)

Working through the problem of soap in the bathrooms enabled us to establish a method for attacking other problems. There was a process to follow: defining the problem, brainstorming, reaching a consensus, and implementing the solution. To the four guideposts we had previously identified, we added one more: Is it workable? Our experience with the soap dispenser problem showed us that although some solutions might generate unbridled enthusiasm — think of the fun it would be to have gentle watchdogs stationed in each boys' and girls' room — they simply would not work.

The process used to deal with the problem of soap in bathrooms worked well. The members of the Heath Community Meeting acquired relevant information about a problem they had brought forth as a serious concern, they designed a remedy that satisfied them, and they used their skills to see that the remedy was implemented.

About a month after the dispensers had been installed and were being used in the intended way, one of them was destroyed. It happened that an eighth-grade boy, angry because he had failed a science test, went into the bathroom and punched the dispenser off the wall. A first grader, who had listened carefully to the presentation Heath Community Meeting partners had made in his classroom, observed the act and said to the older boy, "You're dead meat!" He then came to the office and identified the culprit, who admitted the wrongdoing and agreed to pay for a new dispenser. Although the first grader's mother was concerned about her son's safety after this confrontation, she needn't have been. The dispensers survived the year, although one was emptied of its soap to create a mass of bubbles in the sink.

Other problems have been dealt with in similar fashion. Among the notable issues that were raised and taken through the process were a concern about being rushed at lunch, inequitable access to playground space and equipment, and a lack of a safe place to lock bicycles the children ride to school.

This last issue provided the opportunity to improvise on the established procedure. In Brookline, school buildings are maintained by the school department and school grounds by the parks department. Because bicycle racks would be installed outside the school, they would become the property and responsibility of the parks department. To help the children begin to understand that different agencies in the town must work together and find mutually acceptable solutions — just as we try to do in school — I invited the head of the parks department to join the Heath Community Meeting when the discussion of bicycle racks was on the agenda.

Mr. Paul Willis was delighted to attend the meeting. He asked the children if they could think of some of the considerations he and his department needed to be aware of before they installed any new equipment. He was amazed when the Heath Community Meeting members were able to come up with most of the issues: Where would the bicycle rack be placed? Would it block any accesses to the building? Would it spoil the grounds in any way? Was the equipment safe according to the town's standards? Could it be easily maintained? Could it be vandalized? (The last bike rack had been mysteriously carted away during a summer; the children were intent on having a rack that was fixed to the ground to prevent such an act from recurring.)

Before the meeting ended, eight children volunteered to conduct a survey of the school to determine how many bicycles the rack would have to accommodate. In addition, a decision was made for each class represented at the Heath Community Meeting to elect a delegate to a bicycle rack subcommittee. Once the needs assessment was completed, this group would meet with Mr. Willis, select a piece of equipment from his catalogues that would meet the school's requirements, and present its choice to the Heath Community Meeting for ratification.

This procedure worked very well. The children understood the concept of two agencies of the town cooperating to solve a small but important problem. They loved having a guest come to the meeting who asked them questions about their needs and who listened to their suggestions. And Mr. Willis was pleased to have input from one of his important constituencies — the children who actually use the parks in the town. One result of these meetings was that Mr. Willis decided to make communication with the schools a regular part of his work week. And we in the Heath Community Meeting decided to invite to our meetings other guest speakers who contribute in various ways.

The latter point was influential in helping the children understand that the term *community* has many definitions. We devoted one meeting to discussing what we mean when we use the word *community*. This was a fascinating discussion because, although Heath is in part a neighborhood school, it also has two distinct populations who do not live within walking distance of the school. One group is made up of students in the Metco program, black children from Boston who come by bus to Heath and other schools in cities and towns close to Boston. The other, unique to Heath, is our Hebrew bilingual population, children whose parents have come to the United States from Israel for a specified length of time. The school department provides a special program for these children at Heath (as it provides for Japanese, Spanish, Chinese, and Russian bilingual children at other schools in Brookline). This diverse group of children shared ideas about and experiences in different kinds of communities in ways that were simple, genuine, and affecting. One of the benefits of heterogeneous school populations is that children can learn about one another. The Heath Community Meeting provides an opportune forum in which this kind of learning regularly takes place.

Similarly, the meeting enabled one of the teachers to expand the children's understanding of community in another direction. Faculty members from several schools in Brookline decided that they would provide one meal a month for homeless people at a shelter in greater Boston. This commitment involves purchasing food and then preparing, delivering, and serving it at the shelter. Mrs. Carol Gaskill, a fourth-grade Heath teacher who participates in this effort, thought it would be valuable to let the children at the community meeting know about the project. She spoke to them about the many different ways we define community, sometimes working like concentric circles and sometimes reaching out to areas and groups with which we ordinarily might not have contact.

The children understood this idea with surprising insight. When Mrs. Gaskill asked them if they could say who the homeless people are, one child responded, "They could be any one of us." He then went on to explain how people "like you or like me" could suddenly find themselves without a place to live or other necessities of life. Other children offered their understanding of the problem in a meeting that was especially moving.

At the conclusion of this meeting, the children decided that they would raise funds to purchase food for one meal at the shelter. A subcommittee was formed, and the members decided to ask each student to contribute one dollar that they would ordinarily spend on snacks or other luxury items. Kindergarteners would be asked to donate fifty cents only if they understood what the money was for. Once again, partnership speaking teams were formed (this time helped by eighth-grade mentors), and they took the message to all the children and adults in the school. Although there was not 100 percent participation in the fund-raising effort, the Heath Community Meeting raised enough money to sponsor a meal — a wonderful success.

Each week, I write a column for the parent-teacher organization newsletter. The article on the Heath Community Meeting's fundraiser for the meal at the Long Island Shelter drew warm support from the parent community.

It is clear that the concept of community has become integral to understanding and practicing democracy at the Heath School. The Heath Community Meeting has evolved into a community-building entity as well as a forum in which participatory problem solving occurs. In fact, one aspect of the meeting cannot be separated from the other. Both parts must be present if the children are to acquire a genuine feeling of responsibility for their school and for their behavior and actions in the school.

Although the Heath Community Meeting is a weekly gathering of children in grades four and five, its influence and considerations as described here extend to the whole school — and even to the parents.

Much of this impact is a result of the design of the process by which decisions are disseminated once they have been made. But part of it happens serendipitously. One case of unanticipated "trickle-down democracy" occurred because a third-grade class had to walk through the cafeteria each week when Heath Community Meeting was in session. The children listened to parts of the discussions and decided to raise a concern of their own at class meeting time. The problem was fighting and bickering at recess. The third graders identified the problems and designed solutions. They then presented their thinking to the Heath Family Meeting.

These eight-year-olds began their presentation by saying, "These are problems that affect all of us. They happen fairly regularly. How can we make things get better?" They then gave their best thinking on these subjects:

Are people not letting you play?
  Find someone else to play with.
Are people fighting?
  Start a new game with new friends.
  Be sure to share the fields equally.
Do people say they don't want to be your friends anymore?
  Find new friends.
Are people cheating in games?
  Warn them you won't play with them if they cheat.
  Don't play with cheaters, only with fair players.
  Get a teacher's help if you need it.
Are people hurting your feelings?
  Try to understand that they don't mean it.
  Be kind to them and they'll be kind to you.
Are people "firing" children in football and other games?
  Explain how it makes people feel to be kicked off a team.
  Don't go along with firing. Organize against it.

Without knowledge of negotiation theory, these children — coached by their teachers — arrived at winning solutions for their problems. With great seriousness, they delivered the solutions to their younger friends in grades one and two, a sympathetic and receptive audience. Although this meeting did not end perennial playground problems, it was a small and important step in making the participants themselves aware of their responsibility in changing for the better.

The Heath Family Meeting has been in business for four years, and the Heath Community Meeting for three. Despite the relatively short duration of these experiments, some tentative conclusions can be reached about their impact on the school, their effect in enhancing community feeling, and their potential in helping children begin to regard themselves as responsible and able thinkers and doers:

1. The children like both forums. They attend happily, and they continually offer suggestions for discussion and action. The regular scheduling helps to shape their week.
2. Gathering children together in these forums gives them an opportunity to learn and practice appropriate behavior in groups larger than class size. They listen to the presenters and ask pertinent questions at the right time. One positive by-product is better behavior at school assemblies.
3. Both meetings help build the children's pride in the school. The specialness of the meetings is emphasized. As principal, I have a ready forum to commend a particular child or activity or to speak to the children about expectations for future events. For example, prior to an all-school excursion to the Museum of Science, I talked to them about how each of them would be a diplomat for the Heath School. They responded positively to these high expectations.
4. The children — even the youngest ones — are showing that they understand that they can find solutions to some of their problems and do not always have to ask the teacher for help. One notable example of this understanding occurred when some second graders, unhappy with my decision to have recess indoors because of frigid weather, presented me with a petition requesting resumption of outdoor recess, provided each of them wore appropriate cold weather gear.
5. The forums are an excellent way to capitalize on and share the diversity of the school.
6. Mixed-aged groupings enhance the learning that occurs. The children learn from peers who are thinking in different ways and at different levels.
7. Periodically changing the format of the meetings strengthens them. Heath Community Meeting members would tire of problem solving every week. Bringing in guest speakers and organizing events like the fundraiser for the homeless meal helps to keep interest high and extends the idea of community.
8. My initial fear that we might run out of issues to work on was ill-founded. The children provide an endless supply of ideas and suggestions. Allowing the children to work through some wonderful but infeasible proposals ("Let's have sprinklers on at recess on hot days!") helps them to grow as thinkers.

9. As principal, I find that leading the Heath Community
    Meeting each week gives the children an alternative way to
    get to know me — and vice versa. The results are positive.

On occasion, I have been asked whether the precepts of moral
education are at work in the two meetings we have established for
Heath School children. I call what we are doing educating children
to function well in their particular society so that ultimately they will
function well as citizens. In an article in the February 1988 *Kappan*,
Thomas Lickona writes,

> To do an adequate job of moral education — one that has a
> chance of making a real impact on a child's developing char-
> acter — four processes should be going on in the classroom:
> 1. building self-esteem and a sense of community
> 2. learning to cooperate and help others
> 3. moral reflection
> 4. participatory decision making.

These processes are present in both forums, and they are essential to
the mission of the Heath Community Meeting. I would add one more
goal that is central to our aims: putting ideas into action. An activist
stance completes the loop, showing children that not only can they
think, cooperate, reflect, and decide, but they can also demonstrate
that they have the power to make things happen. From my perspective, effective members of society must be prepared to carry out their
ideas and work hard to implement their dreams. Giving fourth and
fifth graders a regular opportunity to practice activism will, I hope,
strengthen their will to participate as active members of society in the
future. Democracy depends on such participation.

Selected Bibliography

Adelson, J. "The Political Imagination of the Young Adolescent." *Daedalus* 100 (4): 1013–49.

Bardige, B. "Reflective Thinking and Prosocial Awareness: Students Face the Holocaust and Themselves." Ph.D. diss, Harvard Graduate School of Education, 1983.

Belenky, M. F., B. M. Clinchy, N. R. Goldberger, and J. M. Tarule. *Women's Ways of Knowing*. New York: Basic Books, 1986.

Bennett, W. J., and E. J. Delattre. "Moral Education in the Schools." *The Public Interest* 50 (Winter 1978): 81–98.

Berkowitz, M., and F. Oser, eds. *Moral Education: Theory and Practice*. Hillsdale, N.J.: Lawrence Erlbaum Press, 1985.

Blasi, A. "Bridging Moral Cognition and Moral Action: A Critical Review of the Literature." *Psychological Bulletin* 88 (1980): 1–45.

Blatt, M., and L. Kohlberg. "Effects of Classroom Discussion on Children's Level of Moral Judgment." *Journal of Moral Education* 4 (1975): 129–61.

Bloom, B., ed. *Developing Talent in Young People*. New York: Random House, 1985.

Bowles, S., and H. Gintis. *Schooling in Capitalist America: Educational Reform and the Contradictions of Economic Life*. New York: Basic Books, 1976.

Blum, L. *Altruism, Friendship, and Morality*. London: Routledge and Kegan Paul, 1983.

Brown, L., D. Argyris, J. Attanucci, C. Gilligan, D. Johnston, B. Miller, R. Osborne, J. Ward, G. Wiggins, and D. Wilcox. *A Guide to Reading Narratives of Moral Conflict and Choice for Self and Moral Orientation*. Cambridge, Mass.: Harvard Graduate School of Education, 1987.

Chazan, B. *Contemporary Approaches to Moral Education*. New York: Teachers College Press, 1985.

Colby, A., L. Kohlberg, J. Gibbs, and M. Lieberman. "A Longitudinal Study of Moral Judgment." *Monographs of the Society for Research in Child Development* 48 (1983): 1–2.

Coles, R. *The Moral Life of Children*. Boston: Atlantic Monthly Press, 1986.

Damon, W. *The Social World of the Child*. San Francisco: Jossey-Bass, 1977.

Damon, W. *The Moral Child: Nurturing Children's Natural Moral Growth*. New York: The Free Press, 1988.

Dewey, J. *Moral Principles in Education*. Boston: Houghton Mifflin, 1911.
____. *Democracy and Education*. New York: Macmillan, 1933.
____. *Theory of the Moral Life*. New York: Holt, Rinehart and Winston, 1960.
Durkheim, É. *Moral Education: A Study in the Theory and Application of the Sociology of Education*. New York: Free Press, 1925. (Reprinted 1973)
Erikson, E. H. "Growth and Crisis of the Healthy Personality." In *Adolescents' Development and Education: A Janus Knot*, edited by Ralph Mosher. Berkeley, Calif.: McCutchan, 1979.
____. *Identity, Youth and Crisis*. New York: Norton, 1968.
Flavell, J. H., C. Fry, J. Wright, and P. Jarvis. *The Development of Role-Taking and Communication Skills in Children*. New York: Wiley, 1968.
Frankena, W. *Ethics*. Englewood Cliffs, N.J.: Prentice-Hall, 1963.
Gibbs, J., and S. Schnell. "Moral Development 'versus' Socialization: A Critique." *American Psychologist* 40 (1985): 1071–80.
Gilligan, C. "Exit-Voice Dilemmas in Adolescent Development." In *Development, Democracy, and the Art of Trespassing: Essays in Honor of Albert O. Hirschman*, edited by A. Foxley, M. McPherson, and G. O'Donnell, pp. 283–300. South Bend, Ind.: University of Notre Dame Press, 1986.
____. *In a Different Voice*. Cambridge, Mass.: Harvard University Press, 1982.
Gilligan, C., J. V. Ward, and J. Taylor, eds. *Remapping the Moral Domain: A Contribution of Women's Thinking to Psychological Theory and Education*. Cambridge, Mass.: Harvard University Press, 1988.
Gilligan, C., and J. Attanucci. "Two Moral Orientations: Gender Differences and Similarities." *Merrill Palmer Quarterly* 34 (1988): 223–37.
Giroux, H., and P. McLaren. "Teacher Education and the Politics of Engagement: The Case for Democratic Schooling." *Harvard Educational Review* 56 (1986): 213–38.
Giroux, H., and D. Purpel. *The Hidden Curriculum and Moral Education: Deception or Discovery*. Berkeley: McCutchan Publishing, 1983.
Hall, R., and J. Davis. *Moral Education in Theory and Practice*. Buffalo, N.Y.: Prometheus Books, 1975.
Hartshorne, H., and M. A. May. *Studies in the Nature of Character*. 3 vols. New York: Macmillan, 1928–30.
Hersh, R., D. Paolitto, and J. Reimer. *Promoting Moral Growth*. New York: Longman, 1979.
Hersh, R., J. Miller, and G. Fielding. *Models of Moral Education*. New York: Longman, 1980.
Higgins, A. "Research and Measurement Issues in Moral Education Interventions." In *Moral Education: A First Generation of Research and Development*, edited by R. Mosher. New York: Praeger, 1980.
Hirst, P. *Moral Education in a Secular Society*. London: University of London Press, 1974.
Jackson, P. *Life in Classrooms*. New York: Holt, Rinehart and Winston, 1968.
Jennings, W. "The Juvenile Delinquent as Moral Philosopher: The Effect of Rehabilitation Programs on the Moral Reasoning of Male Offenders." Ph.D. diss., Harvard University, 1979.
Johnston, D. K. "Two Moral Orientations — Two Problem Solving Strategies: Adolescents' Solutions to Dilemmas in Fables." Ed.D. diss., Harvard Graduate School of Education, 1985.
Johnson, D. W., and R. T. Johnson. "Instructional Goal Structure: Cooperative, Competitive, or Individualistic? *Review of Educational Research* 44 (1974): 213–40.
Kagan, J. *The Nature of the Child*. New York: Basic Books, 1984.

Kohlberg, L. "The Moral Atmosphere of the School." In *The Unstudied Curriculum*, edited by N. Overley. Washington, D.C.: Association for Supervision and Curriculum Development, 1970. Monograph.

____. *Essays on Moral Development*. Vol. 1, *The Philosophy of Moral Development*. San Francisco: Harper & Row, 1981.

Kohlberg, L. *Essays on Moral Development*. Vol. 2, *The Psychology of Moral Development*. San Francisco: Harper & Row, 1984.

Kohlberg, L., and C. Gilligan. "The Adolescent as a Philosopher: The Discovery of Self in a Post-Conventional World." *Daedalus 100* (1971): 1051–86.

Kohlberg, L., and R. Mayer. "Development as the Aim of Education." *Harvard Educational Review* 42 (1972): 449–96.

Ladenburg, T. "Cognitive Development and Moral Reasoning in the Teaching of History." *History Teacher* (March 1977): 184–98.

Langdale, S. "Moral Orientations and Moral Development: The Analysis of Care and Justice Reasoning across Different Dilemmas in Females and Males from Childhood through Adulthood." Ed.D. diss, Harvard University, 1983.

Lickona, T., ed. *Moral Development and Behavior*. New York: Holt, Rinehart and Winston, 1976.

____. *Raising Good Children*. New York: Bantam Books, 1983.

Loevinger, J. "Stages of Ego Development." In *Adolescents' Development and Education: A Janus Knot*, edited by Ralph Mosher. Berkeley, Calif.: McCutchan, 1979.

Lyons, N. "Two Perspectives on Self, Relationships and Morality." *Harvard Educational Review* 53 (1983): 125–45.

Maccoby, E. *Social Development: Psychological Growth and the Parent-Child Relationship*. New York: Harcourt Brace Jovanovich, 1980.

McPhail, P. *Great Britain Schools Council Moral Education Curriculum Project*. Harlow, England: Longman, 1978.

McPhail, P., J. Ungoed-Thomas, and H. Chapman. *Lifeline*. Niles, Ill.: Argus Communications, 1976.

Mead, G. H. *Mind, Self, and Society*. Chicago: University of Chicago Press, 1934.

Milgrim. S. *Obedience to Authority*. New York: Harper & Row, 1974.

Mosher, R. *Moral Education: A First Generation of Research and Development*. New York: Praeger, 1980

Mosher, R., R. Kenny, and A. Garrod. *Preparing for Citizenship: The Democratic High School*. (Under review)

Musey, B., ed. *Moral Development, Moral Education, and Kohlberg*. Birmingham, England: Religious Education Press, 1980.

Noam, G., S. Powers, B. Kilkenny, and J. Beedy. "The Interpersonal Self: Stage and Phase Coding Manual." Unpublished manuscript, Harvard University, 1986.

Noddings, N. *Caring: A Feminine Approach to Ethics and Moral Education*. Berkeley: University of California Press, 1984.

Orlick, T. *Cooperative Sports and Games Book*. New York: Pantheon Books, 1986.

Paul, R. "Dialogical Thinking: Critical Thought Essential to the Development of Rational Knowledge and Passions." In *Teaching Thinking Skills: Theory and Practice*, edited by J. Baron and R. Steinberg. New York: Freeman, 1978.

Peters, R. S. *Ethics and Education*. London: Allen and Unwin, 1966.

Piaget, J. *The Moral Judgment of the Child*. New York: Free Press, 1932. (Reprinted 1965)

Power, C. "Moral Education Through the Development of the Moral Atmosphere of the School." *Journal of Educational Thought* 15 (1981): 4–19.

Power, C., A. Higgins, and L. Kohlberg. *Lawrence Kohlberg's Approach to Moral Education*. New York: Columbia University Press, 1989.

Rawls, J. *A Theory of Justice*. Cambridge, Mass.: Harvard University Press, 1971.

Reimer, J. "A Study in the Moral Development of Kibbutz Adolescents." Ph.D. diss., Harvard University, 1977.

Reimer, J., D. Paolitto, and R. Hersh. *Promoting Moral Growth: From Piaget to Kohlberg*. New York: Longman, 1983.

Rest, J., and S. Thoma. "Relation of Moral Judgment to Formal Education." *Developmental Psychology* 21 (1985): 709–14.

Ryan, K. "The New Moral Education." *Phi Delta Kappan* (November 1986): 228–33.

Selman, R. L. *The Growth of Interpersonal Understanding: Developmental and Clinical Analyses*. New York: Academic Press, 1980.

Snarey, J. "Promoting Moral Maturity among Adolescents: An Ethnographic Study of the Israeli Kibbutz." *Comparative Educational Review* 3 (1987): 241–59.

Strom, M., and W. Parsons. *Facing History and Ourselves: Holocaust and Human Behavior*. Watertown, Mass.: Intentional Publications, 1982.

Swartz, R. "Structured Teaching for Critical Thinking and Reasoning in Standard Subject Area Instruction." In *Informal Reasoning and Education*, edited by D. Perkins, J. Segal, and J. Yoss. Hillsdale, N.J.: Erlbaum, 1989.

———. "Infusing the Teaching of Critical Thinking into Context Instruction." In *Developing Minds: A Resource Book for Teaching Thinking*, edited by A. Costa. Rev. ed. Vol. 1. Alexandria, Va.: Association for Supervision and Curriculum Development, 1991.

Tom, A. *Teaching as a Moral Craft*. New York: Longman, 1984.

Turiel, E. *The Development of Social Knowledge: Morality and Convention*. Cambridge: Cambridge University Press, 1983.

Walker, L. "The Sequentiality of Kohlberg's Stages of Moral Development." *Child Development* 55 (1982): 677–91.

Wilson, J. *Moral Education and the Curriculum*. London: Pergamon Press, 1969.

———. *Practical Methods of Moral Education*. London: Heinemann Educational Books, 1972.

Wilson, J., N. Williams, and B. Sugarman. *Introduction to Moral Education*. Harmondsworth, England: Penguin, 1967.

Wynne, E. "The Great Tradition in Education: Transmitting Moral Values." *Educational Leadership* (January 1986): 4–9.

Index

List of Contributors

Jeffrey Pratt Beedy, executive director, Sports P.L.U.S. Foundation, Milton Academy, Milton, Massachusetts

Barry Chazan, professor, Center for Jewish Education in the Diaspora, Hebrew University, Jerusalem

Andrew Garrod, associate professor, Department of Education, Dartmouth College, Hanover, New Hampshire

Ann Higgins, assistant professor, Department of Psychology, Fordham University, Fordham, New York

Robert Howard, director of values education, Sacramento City Unified School District, Sacramento, California

Robert Kenny, founding partner of Kenny and Howard Associates, Concord, Massachusetts

Mary Johnson, executive director, Facing History and Ourselves National Foundation, Brookline, Massachusetts

Kay Johnston, associate professor, Department of Education, Colgate University, Troy, New York

Thomas Lickona, professor, Faculty of Education, State University of New York, Cortland, New York

Ralph Mosher, professor emeritus, School of Education, Boston University, Boston, Massachusetts

Nel Noddings, professor, School of Education, Stanford University, Stanford, California

Thomas Pavkov, research assistant, Center for Urban Affairs and Policy Research, Northwestern University, Chicago, Illinois

F. Clark Power, associate professor, Program of Liberal Studies, University of Notre Dame, South Bend, Indiana

James R. Rest, professor, College of Education, University of Minnesota, Minneapolis, Minnesota

Ethel Sadowsky, principal, Heath School, Brookline, Massachusetts

Martin Sleeper, associate director, Facing History and Ourselves National Foundation, Brookline, Massachusetts

John Snarey, associate professor, Candler School of Theology, Emory University, Atlanta, Georgia

Margot Stern Strom, executive director, Facing History and Ourselves National Foundation, Brookline, Massachusetts

Robert Swartz, professor, Department of Philosophy, University of Massachusetts at Boston, Boston, Massachusetts